LOST AND FOUND

The Story of a Family after Divorce

LOST AND FOUND

The Story of a Family after Divorce

by

ANN LOVELL

LONDON
VICTOR GOLLANCZ LTD
1984

First published in Great Britain 1984
by Victor Gollancz Ltd,
14 Henrietta Street, London WC2E 8QJ

Copyright © Ann Lovell 1984

British Library Cataloguing in Publication Data
Lovell, Ann
Lost and Found.
1. Divorce   2. Family
I. Title
306.8'9   HQ814
ISBN 0–575–03405–X

Typeset at The Spartan Press Limited, Lymington, Hants.
Printed in Great Britain by
St Edmundsbury Press, Bury St Edmunds, Suffolk

To Ray and Vera

"That's how it goes my friend. The problem is not falling captive, it's how to avoid surrender. . . . "

NAZIM HIKMET

Contents

Preface   11

1   The End of Many Things   13

2   After the Storm   26

3   First Year: Struggles   39

4   Second Year: The Priest and the Judge   61

5   Third Year: Rebuilding   83

6   Fourth Year: Moving On   101

7   Fifth Year: Time Present and Time Past   117

8   Sixth Year: Cracks in the Ground   134

9   Seventh Year: Landslide   151

10   Seventh Year: Continued   171

11   Eighth Year: Building Again   188

12   Ninth Year: Tom   207

13   Ten Years On   226

14   The River Goes on Leaping   249

Preface

This is not a book of helpful hints on how to survive as a one-parent family — though I hope that some of our experiences may help others to avoid some unnecessary difficulties. I do not feel qualified to write anything so academic. Our situation is as individual as the combination of personalities involved in it, and, since these range from the gifted to the mentally handicapped, it is not really possible to generalize.

On the other hand, the fact that I have had to face alone a wider range of child-rearing problems than occurs in many two-parent families, and that, thanks to the help I have received, the job is almost completed, may give heart to others.

I do not think that I could have succeeded if I had not finally found this help — and that, perhaps, is one of the main points of this book. Children do not thrive on marriage breakdown. I believe that in every case, however thoughtfully and amicably arranged, it harms them to some extent in the development of their emotional life. The hurt may be healed with constant, sensitive, loving care, but the scar remains, and scar tissue is fragile. Yet divorce is still on the increase. It is the simplest, most obvious answer to the problem of an unhappy marriage, which does not necessarily make it the right one — not, that is, in terms of the children.

Today, in the United Kingdom, over a million of them live in one-parent families, often in conditions of severe financial and emotional deprivation. Some become delinquent, others grow up unable to form satisfactory adult relationships. They will be the inadequate parents of tomorrow — and the cycle will be perpetuated. Unless, that is, we take some realistic steps to help them.

"We cannot protect children from divorce," I read in an article by a lawyer trying to prove that deserting fathers should not have to pay maintenance.

I think that we can. Our failure to see the urgency of the problem, to provide extensive and realistic back-up facilities and conciliation services for families in distress is not due to lack of means, but to a lack of judgement which is likely to cost us, in the potential threat to the stability of society, far more than is realized. Even in areas such as Bristol, where such services have come into being, and are showing signs of success, they are being starved of funds to a point where their continuation is being jeopardized. Which is pure folly. Problems, as I learned, do not just go away if we don't look. They have a bad habit of growing bigger.

Our story is an example of the effects of marriage breakdown on the family, and of our own desperate need for help — which we only found when we were on the brink of disintegration. I have written it with the close cooperation of the children, especially, of course, of Joanna, who has subjected every word of my account of her illness to careful scrutiny. The process has not been without pain, but at the same time it has helped us, in that we have discovered that there is a positive side to the story.

We all hope that the telling of it may awaken those in a position to help to the need for realistic and far-reaching action to ease the plight of one-parent families. By those in a position to help, I do not just mean the government, though they must, in their neglect of the recommendations of the Finer Report, carry the greatest responsibility, but also those who function at grass-roots level: churches, schools, family doctors, youth organizations, and the social services.

The first step towards helping has to be a full understanding of the needs of these deprived children. It may not be possible to meet them fully, but far more could be done than is being done at present.

If this book contributes even a little to that understanding, then we shall all feel that it more than justifies its existence.

Ann Lovell
November, 1983

CHAPTER ONE

The End of Many Things

It all finally fell apart on a dark November morning in 1973. Paul, the four children and myself were in the process of getting dressed. He had come in very late the night before, and was sleepily humming to himself. I drew a deep breath. I was about to do the hardest thing I had ever had to do in my life.

"I've been to see a solicitor," I told him. "On his advice, I'm asking you to move out of the house. I can't go on living with you any longer."

I had the strange sensation of being three separate people: one was actually speaking these unbelievable words, another was an efficient automaton who was directing the operation, while the last was the real, sentient self who was locked, screaming, deep inside me. They seemed such trite words with which to end nearly fourteen years of marriage — the more so as I still loved the man to whom I was addressing them.

Only absolute necessity had driven me to speak them. I had, for the children's sake as well as my own, to end the bitter pain in which I had been living daily for the last three years. Since the sudden, tragic death of his father in 1969, Paul had treated me with a slowly increasing coldness and detachment, until I had come to feel as if I were one of his less appealing business clients being politely, if reluctantly, entertained in his house. Sex, indeed even the slightest emotional contact, had long since ceased. I did not know why. The only answer he could make in reply to my frantic questions was that he was sorry, he simply did not love me any more. There are few more destructive answers than that — particularly in my position, with four young children to care for.

I had not found out about his affairs for certain until a few months previously. I had ascribed his changed behaviour to shock and grief at the loss of his father. Paul was an only child, and the responsibility of administering an unexpectedly small and complicated estate had fallen entirely on him — his frail mother could not cope. Shock and grief made useful pegs to hang his withdrawal on. There is such a condition as functional blindness, and, all unconsciously, I had availed myself of it. Shaken, and deeply saddened by the death of my father-in-law, who had replaced in my life my own long-dead father, with two babies and two small children to look after, I could not afford the luxury of seeing clearly. I could not have managed alone at that stage. It was better to cling, in the face of all the evidence, to the belief that we were merely passing through a very bad patch in our marriage, and that patience and understanding would pull us through.

As matters grew worse, I tried to get help. Paul would not contemplate marriage guidance. Having taken a brilliant degree in psychology, he viewed such types of counselling as amateur and inadequate. A local minister listened to me and advised patience. The doctor prescribed tranquillizers. Paul remained silent. It was the silence, the icy barrier of reserve, which defeated me. I had come from a home where words were valued, and used, violently or gently, to express every shade of feeling. My parents' rows were multicoloured affairs — and the reconciliations warmed us all. I did not know how to deal with silence.

I was in no real shape during those last years to rekindle any last flicker of affection, let alone desire. Depressive people are not very attractive. I cried easily and often. Constantly tired, I lost weight rapidly. If I had been unfaithful to Paul, if there had been any concrete reason for his ceasing to love me, it would have been less destructive to my personality. As it was, I had given all I had to give to our marriage. I could only conclude that everything I had done was wrong. If I had not wanted children so badly, to the point of adopting our fourth, Paul might never have changed. Yet he had appeared to want them too — and the children's officers had probed hard enough into our separate motivations at the time of the adoption. I could not understand what had happened.

Building our family had not been easy for either of us. Frequent miscarriages, a minor operation, the diagnosis of Simon, even a false pregnancy, had only strengthened my compulsive desire for four children. Such a succession of setbacks, and such a rock-like determination to overcome them, probably do not enhance a wife's attractions. Only a deeply perceptive and mature man could have helped her to preserve them.

This compulsion to have a large family had sprung from many sources. The main ones were, I think, social and, in a sense, historical. My early childhood had been a disturbed one, disrupted by repeated wartime evacuations. When I later reached university, although I learned to question accepted beliefs in many areas, it never occurred to me to subject the social structure itself to any kind of objective scrutiny. Feminist ideas had not penetrated the French Honours class at Leeds in 1951, despite the large majority of women students in it. With war so recently behind us, its wounds still raw, most of us wanted and needed all the emotional security we could find. Marriage was a safe haven, into which one contracted for life — a contract which entailed, if possible, the bearing and rearing of children. Few thought otherwise, or, if they did, voiced their thoughts.

By the time I married, in 1959, I had still not become conscious of the feminist movement. I merely knew that I wanted to gain all the qualifications and professional experience that I could before I 'settled down'. Even this was considered 'hard' and 'modern' by many of the young men of my acquaintance. My view of marriage was, I thought, a very realistic one: it was a partnership which could be successful provided that both partners were prepared intelligently to work to make it so. Rearing a loving and harmonious family seemed to me an eminently desirable occupation, into which I could happily plough back all that I had gained from my education. I was deeply in love with Paul, as well as lost in admiration for his brilliant mind. I knew nothing whatsoever about emotional maturity, either in myself or in others. So that I signed the marriage register joyful in the belief that my days of wandering were over. I had not been left on the shelf, despite my brains. We had been engaged for over eighteen months — ample time to think things over very carefully. I believed I knew exactly what I was doing.

The trouble was that seven years of university, followed by three and a half years as an advertising copywriter, had left me ill-equipped for the role of full-time wife, mother and house-wife in a small provincial town where I knew no-one, and where there was not even the solace of a first-class library. Simon's birth in 1962 had been normal, but had left me very tired. He was an intensely wanted baby. We had been obliged to wait for his advent, first for financial reasons, and then because I did not conceive immediately. By the time I finally held him in my arms, he seemed like a miracle. I was as overjoyed at being admitted to the great sisterhood of mothers as if I had just become a member of the best gang at school. Even at twenty-five I needed desperately to be like everyone else.

My loneliness and depression, therefore, as I dragged myself despondently round the pretty new house we had moved into a few weeks before Simon's birth, were both unexpected and confusing. Whilst I had still been at work, I had dreamed constantly of being what I saw as a real wife, devoted to nest building. Now that the dream had become reality, my boredom, isolation and unhappiness frightened me. I felt I no longer existed as a person in my own right. I had lost my identity along with my interesting job and my salary, and could see no way of recovering it.

My long academic career had yielded me no knowledge of child psychology. I was as ignorant of the development of the little creature I spent so much time feeding, cleaning and playing with as any teenager leaving school without O-levels. The fact that Simon, with the disabilities which were only to become clear at a later stage, could not respond to me as much as other babies, no doubt made matters worse, but at the time I had not the slightest suspicion that there was anything wrong with him. On top of all this, I found it terribly hard to be financially dependent on Paul after years of managing on my own. I hated asking him for money. I seemed to have given up all my freedom. When he came home in the evenings it was as if he were coming from a different, brighter world — one which I had once shared with him, and from which I was now excluded. The one for which I had exchanged it seemed a dreary, monotonous place in contrast.

There were, as I could see it, only two possible solutions to my situation: either I could engage a nanny, and return to the very job I had yearned to leave only six months previously, or I could go ahead and have several children, and so play the maternal role to the full.

All my upbringing, as well as all the strength of my newly awakened maternal instinct, forbade more than a momentary hesitation over the first option. Simon needed me, his mother, and I wanted to be with him. So I settled resolutely for the second, with Paul's apparent support. Joanna was born in 1963, after one miscarriage, and Tom in 1967, after another. I countered loneliness by having au pair girls to help me after Joanna's birth. I had been an au pair myself and found it a system which could be of real benefit to both sides, provided it was carried out with due respect for the needs of all concerned.

I also threw myself into the work of the National Childbirth Trust, which had recently started a branch in our area. This not only made my job of caring for the children far more interesting by giving me a chance to learn more about them through lectures and discussions, but it also increased my desire for a large family by giving me intensely satisfying experiences of childbirth — experiences I still regard as some of the most marvellous of my life. Any gaps in my day I filled by keeping up a small but constant output of creative writing — mostly children's stories at that time, which I sold to the BBC. Gradually, I became much happier. Working for the Trust, I built up a wide network of friends and acquaintances, and loneliness and boredom dropped back into the past.

This period of readjustment must have been every bit as difficult for Paul as it was for me. He must have found this earth mother a very different person from the girl he had married, who had been interested in advertising techniques, music and French literature, not children. The importance I was learning to attach to the upbringing of young children, as I grew more experienced, must have made him in his turn feel very excluded, since office hours and an arduous commuting journey precluded him from sharing in any great part of it. He played his role well enough to convince me that he entirely shared my new interests. He was a kind and fun-loving father to the children, who adored him, and an affectionate husband. He never spoke of his boredom and dissatisfaction with the way we were living our life, but it was there, as he eventually revealed. The diagnosis of Simon's autism, with all the extra patience and compassion it called for, must have seemed like the last straw. I had made him, willy nilly, the corner-stone of the whole elaborate structure, without first checking to see if he could stand the strain. He, for his part, seemed to accept the position allotted to him, leaving the decisions to me. We were already, at that early stage, heading for marriage breakdown, only I was blissfully unaware of the fact. I had not the faintest suspicion that he was beginning to look elsewhere for the girl he had lost at home. Even while he was looking, he remained kind and considerate towards me — until his father's death. Everything changed then.

The final decision to break, the visit to the solicitor, made only after agonizing hesitations, represented to me an act akin to vandalism. I had been driven to destroy by my own act the beautiful dream around which I had built my life over the last fourteen years. It went against the grain of my whole nature. I was forced to it by a desperate need to survive in order to protect the children. I had come to believe that children needed whole-hearted commitment, a continuity of loving, perceptive care on the part of their parents. Paul, I felt, could not give it to them — he had proved it in my eyes by refusing to look for help in solving our problems. I had no other option but to speak the hateful words.

We agreed, that dark November morning, that he should be the one to break the news to the children — I could not bear to do it. He was to leave home two days later, after attending a big Bonfire Night party to which we had all been invited. Ironically, it was the best such event I had ever attended, with extravagant fireworks, a huge bonfire, and hot soup for all. It could hardly have been watched by six more miserable people.

The next day, I could not face going round our home with him to divide up our property. I told him to take whatever he wanted, and fled to the shelter of a friend's house while he made his selection. Making the decision, and implementing it, had taken all my strength. I could not see ahead, much less plan. I still seemed to be functioning as three separate people, one of whom did not believe in what was happening. Paul would not really go. Once he was faced with the reality of leaving behind the love and warmth that had surrounded him in our house, he would change his mind. I was unable and unwilling to see that Paul could not stay. His need to escape was every bit as compulsive as mine to have children. We cancelled out perfectly.

Half an hour before the children returned from school — fortunately it was not my turn to collect them — I returned to the empty house; to find that it was I, not Paul, who had at last to face up to reality — not the attractive one of escape, but the terrifying one of being left. He had, in fact, taken very little, but each empty space on wall or bookshelf hammered the fact home: he had left us. He had gone. We were on our own.

I began, symbolically enough, by hurrying round the place to hide the evidence of his departure: the house, I felt obscurely, must still present a solid, undisturbed appearance to the children when they came through the door. I laid tea in the kitchen, closing the door on the dining room with its larger table. The last of our au pairs had left us in the summer, after completing her year — our numbers were decreasing rapidly. Yet there were still five of us. I looked round at the children when they had finally gathered at the tea table. There were still enough of us to be a family, and a united, caring one at that.

Three years of coldness and tension between their parents, however, had not helped them. There was much work in front of me if I was to repair that past damage, let alone what was happening now.

Simon, now ten, had recently moved to a special school for autistic children in Ealing. He went there daily by taxi. Obtaining admission to this school had been the culmination of many years of struggle. I had wept for joy when we heard that our application had been accepted.

Autistic children, although they see and hear normally, cannot form a coherent picture from their impressions. Their language development is impaired — some never speak at all — and they cannot form relationships with others. They look normal, even intelligent, and are often outstandingly good-looking. Most, during childhood, present considerable behaviour problems, ranging from hours of screaming to hyperactivity and self-destructiveness. The cause of autism is unknown, and so, perforce, is the cure. The handicap is therefore lifelong. We had been lucky in that the National Autistic Society was formed in the year Simon was born, so that by the time he was diagnosed, nearly four years later, at least some information about this strange condition was available to us. From this we learned that it was likely that Simon could and would improve considerably provided that he received an education appropriate to his very specialized needs. As there was at that time only one school providing this in the entire country, his eventual admission to it, five years later, seemed little short of a miracle.

Although Simon had never unleashed upon us the worst excesses of autistic behaviour, his early years had been difficult enough, and he was still not always easy to deal with. Like all autistic children, he intensely disliked change, and was not yet completely settled in. Slow and apathetic by temperament, he was having some difficulty adjusting to Mrs Elgar, his firm, dynamic new teacher. He was being required to make an effort for the first time in his life, and was expressing his disgust at home in a series of go-slows, of which the most disruptive was at breakfast time. He had reached the point of refusing entirely to eat breakfast — a heroic act for him, since he dearly loved his food. I had been advised to ignore such protest, but it was easier said than done. Inevitably, I was anxious about him. He was tall for his age, calm faced, and with a very sweet, gentle smile. He looked very like his father, whom he worshipped. Paul had always been patient and affectionate with him. It was going to be, I knew, excruciatingly painful to explain to Simon that his father had gone to live somewhere else, and was not coming back. I knew he would never ever be able to understand, much less come to terms, with a change as drastic as this.

Joanna had been giving cause for concern for some time, too. She had been growing increasingly sad and solitary at school to the point where we had taken her to see an educational psychologist in search of advice and guidance. She was outstandingly musical. I had realized this during the music therapy sessions which I used to hold with Simon when he was first diagnosed. Her fury at being left out and her persevering attempts to insinuate herself into our playing had finally goaded me into letting her have piano lessons when she was only four, which were a resounding success. At seven, she had started on the cello, thanks to a chance remark from her headmistress, and her progress on this instrument, leaping ahead in a series of high distinctions in her grade exams, had been such that it was making the matter of her general education something of a problem. We had consulted the National Association for Gifted Children on this subject only the previous month, and had taken Joanna along to play for their music consultant. The verdict was that, with the right tuition and nurture, she would one day make a very fine cellist.

The words had both delighted and appalled me, especially in the circumstances. They made our responsibility as parents even greater than usual. After some discussion, we had decided to try to solve the educational problem by encouraging her to try for a music scholarship to a large boarding school in the Midlands, where music was something of a speciality. She had been interviewed at the school only ten days previously, and had, as a result, been awarded the scholarship. She was to start there the following September. Now, as I watched her pale face, and drooping shoulders, I wondered if this move was indeed wise. She would need in the future all the support and love I could give her. I did not know what to do. Although there was a strong

bond between us, she had always been very close to Paul. I had
no idea how she would react as she realized that his absence was,
indeed, permanent. I only knew that my heart ached with pity
and love for her. Her tenth birthday was only a few weeks
away.

Tom, too, had been going through a difficult patch. Of
extremely high intelligence, he had been in turn an easy-going
baby, a truly awful toddler as he gradually turned away from
me to meet the full impact of the outside world, and a
hypersensitive schoolboy. He was highly imaginative, capable
of intense concentration, and as musical, it seemed, as his sister.
At six, he was already showing signs of promise on the piano,
and we had been wondering recently which should be his
second instrument.

The reverse side of all this was that he was quiveringly
vulnerable to the slightest hint of criticism, and demanded of
himself that he should always perform perfectly any task he
attempted — a somewhat painful code of behaviour for all
concerned, only partially offset by a wry, quirky sense of
humour which was a perpetual delight to me. He attended the
kindergarten section of Joanna's school, but he was reacting
badly to the disciplined atmosphere there, and, again, I was not
sure what to do. We had opted out of the state system in his case
because with a birthday so soon after the beginning of the
academic year he would have been unable to start school despite
his growing boredom at nursery school.

I sometimes thought that this second son of mine, this
longed-for normal one, had been born without a skin. I had, at
his birth, delivered his head myself, and I vividly remember the
pained expression he wore as he entered the world. He had
recently developed a slight stammer, which boded no good, I
felt, for the months that lay ahead. It was unbearable to think
what losing his father would mean to a child of this type. I was
afraid for him. I was also afraid of forging too strong a bond
between him and me, the mother.

David, fourteen months younger, was completely different
but, in his own way, just as vulnerable. He had started at Tom's
school in September, and was still settling down. He, too, was
tall for his age — as tall as his older brother — with glossy, dark
curls and a sunny, open disposition. I always felt that I knew
where I was with him. David was one of life's survivors. Born a

puny four-and-a-half-pound baby, he had more than made up for his perilous start, and now cheered the rest of us with his wide grin, his sense of fun, and his effervescent energy.

He and Tom fought as much as any brothers, but they were deeply attached to each other, for all their widely differing personalities. We had never hidden from him the fact that he was adopted — he would have realized it soon enough anyway, being of mixed race. The first months of his life, which he had spent in a short-term foster family, had left him very insecure, and he needed a great deal of understanding support, from both his siblings and ourselves. He always rushed to be first when it came to helping the grown-ups, as if to prove his right to a place in the family, and this could upset the others. He was physically very clinging towards Paul and me — sometimes I felt as if he regarded us as climbing frames. In future, I reflected grimly, he would have only the smaller, weaker climbing frame to cling to.

Again, as with the others, I was sickened that a deep additional hurt should now be added to those he had already endured. In adopting David, I had wanted to give him security, affection and happiness — not grief, anxiety, and further rejection. I felt acutely that I had failed him, as if by failing to foresee the disintegration of my marriage I had committed a crime against him. He, too, was musical, though in a less intense way than the others, and had recently started learning the piano.

My spirit quailed as I sat looking at these four very different, very demanding young creatures. The task of caring for the potential of each one, guiding and protecting it until it blossomed, represented a far from ordinary challenge for two parents. Now it had devolved upon me alone. Even if they saw Paul regularly, as I hoped they would, it was to me they would come with the constant small daily troubles and trials that are the stuff of parenthood. I was sorely afraid I would not have the strength to see the job through. A chill touched me as I wondered what would happen to them if anything befell me — if I became seriously ill, or was hurt in an accident. There was no-one to help out. This was a fear which was to become very familiar as time went on. It had suddenly become essential that I should stay alive and well. I did not know then how extraordinarily attuned the female body can be to such a directive from the brain.

Children from one-parent families, I had read, often became delinquent. I did not really know how to meet that possibility either, and it, too, frightened me. Delinquency to me signified a wastage of precious human material. I could only grope for the answers. Blindly, I felt that if I could only continue to give them the love, the stability, the interest and encouragement they needed, if I could soften gradually the anger and hurt they must be experiencing, channel the violent feelings into safe forms of expression, the catastrophe might be averted. The danger, however, was real.

We moved through the evening routine in a state of shock. Music practice had to be supervised, and Joanna's homework, though I avoided all pressure. While I was bathing Tom and David, I tried to reassure them. It was vital that they should not associate Paul's departure with any naughtiness of their own. I told them, emphasizing the words, that he had left them because he did not love me any more, and wanted now to live with someone else, that it was no fault of theirs, and that he still loved them. I had a very naive belief in the power of words. Children are far too egocentric to believe that an action such as Paul's could have been provoked by anyone but themselves. Rejection cannot be explained away to a child, however cogent the reasons. It can only be felt — and the feelings hurt. Words can do little at so deep a level as this. On the other hand, they are all that we have.

Deliberately, I allowed bedtime to take an age that night — for their sakes and my own. I repeated the same futile reassurances to Joanna in her turn. After baths, I read to each one, curled up beside him or her on the bed, choosing books I knew would grip them. I was to keep this practice up for several years, in fact, for we all found comfort in it. Books have always been one of my own chief means of escape from pain — first discovered as a homesick evacuee. We worked hard at escaping that night. Simon, fortunately accustomed to Paul coming home in recent months long after he was asleep, did not miss him now and upset anyone else with anxious, obsessive questions. They would come later, and I would have to find the extra strength to deal with them. Finally, as I kissed them goodnight, one after the other, I gave them my solemn promise that I would never leave them, ever, until they were ready to leave me. I knew they could not accept these words in their present dazed state — the trust in parents that all children are born with had just been shattered

— but they needed to be said, often, however many long years it was going to be before they could believe me.

When at last I went wearily back down the stairs I knew I had just made a sacred commitment. It had in fact already been made when each was born or adopted — now I had put it into words and solemnized it, so to speak. No other way had truly been open to me from the moment I first held Simon in my arms, only now I was fully conscious of what I was doing. I could see clearly and totally, and raise my banner, the better to encourage my little band.

But it was time now, at last, to weep. I closed the sitting-room door behind me, and let the tears come. I was weeping for us all, for the children's helplessness and my own. The great gift I had wanted to give them — a childhood free from the pain and fear of separation which had marred mine — was no longer in my power to give. The tears rose in a flood tide and spread over everything that had ever gone wrong in my life. They were necessary and normal, but the violence of them frightened me. I was afraid I was losing my sanity — yet another danger to threaten my family.

There was, however, a wintry ray of light falling on all this desolation, and from time to time it penetrated my grief. Tonight, at least, no-one was going to come in very late and give me fresh pain. I could bolt the doors, and know that, whatever lay ahead, I had at last escaped from a three year long session of mental torture. Recovery might be long and painful, but I had taken the first step. That agonizing, freezing politeness was gone now. I had survived my exposure to it, but only just. Escape had cost me so much, and had left my strength so diminished, that I knew I was going to need help and support if I was not only to survive personally, but to go on holding the family together. The trouble was that, though I knew this instinctively, I had not the least idea how to set about finding it. There simply was no-one, no-one at all, to whom I could turn.

That night I was more alone than I had ever been in my life. When at last I switched off the smiling, happy couples on the television, laid the breakfast table, cleaned the shoes, and dragged myself exhausted off to bed, I did not see how I could possibly cope. Sure, the torture was over, but it was too late. It had destroyed me, and I had no more will to live.

On my way to bed, I looked in on the children. Three were asleep, for it was very late, but Tom was still awake. He was very hot, and I could see from the state of his bed that he had been turning restlessly. I sat beside him for a while, to soothe him, and held his hand. We did not say much, for there was little more that words could do, but that small, burning hand clutching mine stiffened my resolve. I would find the strength, by myself if necessary. I did not know how, but I knew I would find it.

CHAPTER TWO

After the Storm

The feeling of having no-one to turn to arose from the fact that Paul, the children and I had been very much a nuclear family. My father had died while I was still in my teens. My two brothers had both emigrated shortly after the war, one to Canada and one to Brazil, and both had married in their new countries. I had thus been left to carry the responsibility of my mother's welfare as effectively as if I, too, had been an only child. A couple of years before Paul's departure, at the age of seventy-seven, she had started to have bad falls, and had broken bones on more than one occasion. It had become clear that she could not continue to live alone. Fortunately for us all, the Benevolent Fund of the large corporation for which my father had worked for over thirty years took her under its wing, allowing her to enter the large, comfortable home which it ran for the convalescent and the aged among its staff and their dependants. She had settled there very happily the previous year. All of which now seemed a miraculous piece of luck, as I could not possibly have cared for her as well as for the children. I longed to turn to her for comfort, but that time was now long past. These days she, too, depended on me for all practical decisions as well as for affection and support. The problem was to find sufficient time to visit her during my hectic days, for the home was nearly forty miles away.

My mother-in-law had moved into a flat in a nearby town after my father-in-law's death. She was younger than my mother, and did not have her physical disabilities, but her sudden bereavement had laid her very low. Of deep religious convictions, she had been overcome by the breakdown of our marriage, to the point where there was little comfort or practical help she could offer me or the children.

Although my two brothers had not become total strangers, having done their best over the years to maintain the contact with home, the children inevitably only knew them very slightly, from the occasional, rare visit. Ian, the eldest of the family, had in fact been to stay with us that very October. I had confided some of my distress to him, but he was unable, with the difficulties of distance and some severe family worries of his own, to do more than sympathize and assure me of his concern. He must, in fact, have felt very helpless when the time came for him to leave. Bob, the younger brother, came to England more often on business trips, but as he only rarely came to see us, and at that for a flying visit, the children hardly knew him. This was very sad, for uncles could have been of very considerable help to them at this time when they were first beginning to feel the loss of their father. I was not close enough to any of my own cousins, uncles or aunts for them to be of any support. I had never before longed so ardently for a sister.

I was nervous about approaching friends for help. Most of my friends were Paul's as well, and they would be in a delicate position. Besides, even the best of friends can take only a limited amount of the outpourings of grief, and I was not sure I wanted to admit anyone to what I saw as the poisonous, murky depths of my feelings, from which they might well recoil in distaste. Since I could not have brothers or sisters, I longed for someone impersonal, uninvolved but caring, someone who could listen without judging or condemning, yet who would help me to find a path through this morass of emotion, and out the other side. Unfortunately, I had not the faintest idea where to look for such a person, if indeed they existed.

As the news of what had happened spread, however, we discovered that we were not, after all, entirely alone in this desert place. An outer, protective ring of support appeared which, while it could not help on a day-to-day basis, at least took away the feeling of total isolation. Although Paul had been an only child, his father had been one of a large and very united family. Time, distance and marriages had strengthened rather than loosened it. Its members met often. Its unity was symbolized every Christmas in a large gathering to which fiancés, wives and new babies were brought as soon as each duly appeared, and where everyone caught up with the news and exchanged gifts. Deprived of family myself, I had found great pleasure in being admitted to this kindly clan, and had always enjoyed attending the parties.

Now, with Paul gone, I was unsure of my position, except with Joan, his cousin, who had been my bridesmaid, and who, over the years, had become one of my close friends. She alone in the family had been privy to my growing unhappiness, and had done all she could to help. But, as the days passed, one member of the group after another phoned to offer support and sympathy. We received our invitation to the Christmas party as usual, and, not without trepidation, and chiefly for the sake of the children, I decided that we would go. I valued these gestures deeply. We had not been rejected here, too, but could continue as part of a caring extended family which was able still to give the children some sense of belonging. They helped me too in that they made me feel accepted in my strange new role of a single parent — a role for which I felt I needed every ounce of strength. At this stage the feeling was crucial to survival, for it helped to keep alive the last, faint flickers of an all-but-quenched self-confidence.

Unfortunately, no-one lived very near, so that contact was mostly limited to the phone, but even this was far better than nothing.

As we moved further into winter, however, it was becoming increasingly clear to me that I needed support on a much deeper level than this if I was to face all the problems heaped in front of me. I was moving through the days automatically, in a state of shock. I could make no plans for the future. It was as if I had dived from the comfort and security of an ocean liner into freezing, angry seas. I was without compass or life belt, half drowned, and with no idea of where I was going. Only the will to protect the children kept me afloat — I had no other energy. Paul, while not crushed by rejection as I was, was not behaving any more rationally. Although when he came at the weekends to take the children out, or spoke to me on the phone (the sudden presence of his voice causing my heart to lurch sickeningly), there were no overt quarrels, no fights over the children, the pressure of unspoken feelings was so great that it was impossible to communicate intelligently, or to make plans. Neither of us could think long term. It was hard enough to contend with the multitude of small decisions which arose immediately from our sudden change of circumstances. Even those we dealt with superficially and in haste.

I could not in fact accept the reality that Paul, my husband, was gone for good. I believed that he would return when he saw the children's distress, ready at last for their sake to work at improving our marriage. I fantasized for hours about the nature of this return, about the long talks we would have, talks which would reveal the reasons for his unhappiness and give me a chance to set it right. All the time I knew, deep inside me, that this could never be, but I did not want to heed this secret knowledge. I still could not understand what had happened to us, why my happy dream, which to me had been real and solid, had disintegrated like the most fragile of bubbles. All I could do was to blame myself — and I was an old hand at doing that — for not having been the perfect wife. I remembered my early morning tetchiness, my frequent anxieties, my constant fatigue — all of which must have been very boring. I could not be angry with him, for I still loved him too much. I could only be angry with the woman who had taken him from us, and myself for not having known how to keep him. I had nightmares about her. I hated her — quite unable to see that our marriage was already dead when she came along.

These violently conflicting feelings, this mess of anger, guilt and self-blame, hampered my relations with the children. I was determined they should not think ill of their father, for I felt this would harm them, so that for a long time I tried to hide my pain. In any case I felt it was too primitive, too ugly, for such young creatures to witness. I strove with all my might to act reasonably, to appear calm, and to speak collectedly. It was just as well that I was not totally successful, or their confusion would have been complete. They had to live with their own profound hurt; and to see me accept so painful a situation with utter serenity would have applied intolerable pressure to them. Children, even young ones, are very clear-sighted, even if they do not always understand what they see. My frequent apologies to them for irritability, or sudden outbursts, must at least have had the virtue of conveying to them something of my unhappiness, which in turn allowed them to express a little of their own. It would have been better if we could all have wept openly together, but we had to learn to do that.

We muddled on. When Paul came to take them all out, he had to take the car since we live in a rural area, far from all sources of amusement. I could hardly protest, in any case, since the car was a company one. It was being left with me because without it I could not get the children to their school, which was five miles away. When they drove off together, however, I was left confined to barracks, unless I chose to go for a cold, solitary walk. I stayed indoors, where it was warm. Each time he came, Paul would leave his briefcase just inside the front door. It had been my

father's and I wondered what he would have thought of my
situation.

As the weeks passed, I became more and more desperate for
someone to talk to, someone impartial, in whose judgement I
could have absolute trust, someone who could help me to
understand what was happening to us. It was the same acute
longing I had experienced after the diagnosis of Simon seven
years before. There had never been any support in coming to
terms with that loss either — the loss of the perfect child I had
believed him to be — and I had had to work my way through it
alone. That had been hard, but this was far, far harder — in fact
I began to doubt that I could survive without this help. The
trouble was that I did not know where to look, nor whom to
ask, and I was in far too chaotic a state to think clearly. In the
end, I decided to ask my doctor to see if he had any suggestions.
He had been very patient and caring when I was worried about
Simon. Unfortunately, the façade of cheerful efficiency with
which I had seen fit to present him and everyone else over the
years now became a very real obstacle to communication,
obscuring the desperate nature of my need. When I insisted that,
"I must have someone to talk to — a psychiatrist — anyone . . .",
instead of putting me in touch with a local social worker who
might have acted as the anchor I longed for, he arranged for me
to see a psychiatrist at a local hospital. He also gave me a repeat
prescription for Librium, which I accepted gladly. It helped me
to sleep, and it at least dulled some of the symptoms of my
distress.

I went off to keep the resultant appointment with the
psychiatrist, happy in the belief that I might now at last find
some help, help that would also encompass the children. Had I
been luckier, this might in fact have been the case, but my luck
just then was flowing out on an ebb tide. An hour and a half
later I drove home again, choked with angry sobs. After an
hour's wait, a brief interview with a patronizing young man
who clearly thought I was wasting his time had yielded not a
single word of comfort, not the smallest scrap of constructive
advice, nothing but the reinforcement of my conviction that
was totally responsible for the breakdown of my marriage. I
had obviously not occurred to him that the wellbeing of four
children depended on the woman who was so vainly asking for
his help, and that, in supporting her, he would be supporting

them too. It was only the certainty of their great need of me which kept the car on the road and the other drivers safe during that grim journey.

This experience greatly accentuated my feeling of being completely alone. No-one, it seemed, cared — at least, not enough to do anything. This was, of course, untrue, but no friend, however willing to listen, could supply the huge emotional needs of that time. I felt more and more sick and ill. The hundreds of small daily jobs which hitherto had been shared between the two of us — three when there had been an au pair — were now a crushing load.

We lived in a very beautiful, rambling old house in a somewhat isolated position, surrounded by a large, leafy garden which itself could have kept a gardener in employment. I loved gardening, and found even now much pleasure in it, but there was no way I could keep this one as beautiful as it once had been. It had been laid out in the 1930s, with sunken paths and elaborate herbaceous beds, by the family of my present next-door neighbour, Joy. I had not known her very well while Paul was with us; but when she learned that he had left us our acquaintance quickly grew into strong friendship, for she did all she could to help, and took a lively interest in the children. We had much in common, for she was a writer, too — a very successful free-lance gardening correspondent. Her independence, and matter-of-fact attitude to hard work was an inspiration to me, and she also gave me many tips to help with the problem of the garden.

Even she, however, could not come to my rescue by harbouring the children for me occasionally to allow me the odd respite, which was fast becoming another main area of need. Her health was not of the most robust, and they were too many and too much for her. I was growing more and more frightened that physically I could not stand the demands being made upon me, to the point where one Sunday I broke down, and begged Paul to return — on any terms. The old torture now seemed preferable to this overwhelming feeling of inadequacy and isolation. Gently, he refused, and went away leaving me in despair.

I felt as if I were walking through a devastated landscape, where everything was broken. My days became grey and mindless. Everything hurt. Nothing could give lasting comfort. When friends tried to cheer me by inviting me to dinner, I could not bear the fact that the other guests were in couples. All such occasions were a battle against tears — yet I was grateful for being invited. I wanted to go. Some flicker of pride in me wanted to show others that I was down but not out. I both wanted sympathy and could not bear it, which made things difficult for those who tried to help. Joan, whose work as a personnel manager had given her much experience of problems, was the one who seemed best to understand these confused reactions, and to be least thrown by them — she took care to invite me out for a meal on my birthday, which fell shortly before Christmas, for instance — but even she, with a full-time job and an elderly mother to care for, could not give me the regular, skilled support I so desperately needed.

Its absence was heightened by the fact that I could not find any in other, practical areas, either. Although I had visited a local solicitor, recommended to me by a friend, to ascertain my legal rights before daring to ask Paul to leave, it had not occurred to me that the law has its specialities, of which divorce litigation is one. In fact I knew absolutely nothing about the law. Those two visits to a solicitor's office were the first of my life. I had not at that time even leafed through a book on divorce or separation, so alien had the whole matter been to my outlook, and so little did I want either. The vital information, therefore, that in my utterly vulnerable circumstances I needed an expert divorce specialist, simply did not come my way. In my ignorance and chaotic state of mind, I could not even reason my way to a reliable source of advice, such as a Citizens Advice Bureau. Lawyers are not allowed to advertise, a state of affairs which tends to make ignorance widespread, but the CABs have long experience behind them, and can usually guide their clients in the right direction for their individual requirements.

A skilled, experienced divorce lawyer knows how to support a client as he or she leads the way through the mazes of the law towards a settlement. He knows every short cut, and is conversant with every gambit. He has probably seen more pain and anger than almost any other practitioner of the law, for few people are more exposed than husbands and wives when once they turn on each other. He knows, too, how much extra pain can be caused by the cold phraseology of the legal world, and is able to soften it by explaining it in human terms. For a woman left alone with young children this skill and humanity are essential.

Suffice it to say, that in those early weeks and months, when it was so vital, I did not find it. Not that I was making much sense in stating my needs. The notion of divorce appalled me. Against all the evidence to the contrary, I clung blindly to the idea that Paul might return. A legal separation, I thought vaguely, might still leave a door open. It seemed preferable to be a separated wife, with a faint hope of reconciliation, than to be nobody's wife at all. It was extraordinary how much I longed for the return of the man who had been, and who still was, hurting me so deeply. But I could not conceive of life on my own, permanently without a partner.

One thing, and one thing only, I was clear about. Friends had warned me that it was necessary, indeed vital, to obtain a proper and adequate financial settlement, for the children's sake. This shocked me, for I was certain that Paul cared at least enough to provide for them, but fortunately I saw the sense of it. Paul had told me to continue to draw on our joint account for housekeeping money, and to send on any major bills to him. This could obviously only be a very temporary state of affairs, and its very temporariness served to heighten my anxiety. I had only a few hundred pounds of my own — barely enough to keep us for even a short time should he decide to cut himself off entirely. The house, which we had bought with the help of a mortgage, was in our joint names. I blessed my mother for urging me to insist on that when we had bought our first house, never dreaming that it would ever actually help me. Such a settlement was, indeed, an urgent necessity, the first practical step towards lessening tension, and worry, and protecting the children. It was to be, however, over a year before it materialized — and by then I had found my way to the expert lawyer I had needed from the start. In the meantime, all I could do was worry increasingly at the delays.

I did my best to shield the children from these financial anxieties, which were, I felt, adult affairs. My efforts were none too successful, however. Inevitably our expenditure had to be severely pruned, and it was difficult to explain this without betraying my feelings. It was even more difficult in that we were all used to a fairly comfortable style of living, whilst the neighbourhood was one of the most affluent in the Home Counties. Outwardly, nothing about us appeared to have changed — we lived in a pretty house, I drove a large car, and the children went to an independent school. Only I knew that all this was completely hollow, and could fall to bits any day.

Usually the post arrived after the children had left for school, and for this I was devoutly grateful. At least they seldom, if ever, saw me as I opened the thick white letters which now began to arrive from the lawyer. They destroyed what equilibrium I had managed to regain during a Librium-softened night, and reduced me unfailingly to a shivering, sobbing wreck, frightened yet again at losing my sanity. Extremities of sorrow are very frightening, even when they are entirely normal. I was, in fact, going through all the emotions of bereavement. They were a sign, not of sickness, but of ordinary, healthy human reaction to pain and loss. Yet I was afraid and ashamed of them.

However dazed my state of mind, there was one problem which I knew I had to face and deal with immediately, and this was a decision about Joanna's school. We had received the news of the scholarship award only a week before Paul's departure. It only covered one-third of the total fees — for the rest we had been negotiating a bank loan. While I had told the teachers at the children's schools what had happened, and asked them to be particularly gentle towards all four of them, I had not yet informed Joanna's headmistress of the proposed transfer — there had been no need, since it was not to be until the following autumn. Now, however, I was not at all sure that it would be wise to move her when all her security had been so rudely shattered. Great as was the honour of winning the scholarship, I felt that it might be better for Joanna to forego it, and remain at home. I was desperately uncertain, and equally desperately anxious not to make a mistake that might jeopardize my daughter's whole future. In the end I phoned the advisers who had put us in touch with the school in the first place, and told them what had happened. I could not trust my own feelings. I wanted guidance.

All the same, I was taken aback by the form it took: I was urged to transfer Joanna at once, the following term, even though this would mean that, at ten, she would be the youngest child in the school. Free of the anxiety-laden atmosphere of our home, I was told, she would be able to flourish and grow, finding comfort in the bonds she formed with other children. She was very bright, and she would easily catch up in academic subjects. Despite my doubts, I was in no condition to argue. I agreed, and it was arranged for me: the new head was persuaded, Joanna was accepted for the January term, and all I had to do was explain to her present headmistress, who fortunately was both kind and sympathetic.

Joanna herself then had to be prepared for the coming change. I told her calmly all about it and gave her the reasons which had led to the decision. She seemed quite pleased and excited. Neither of us said a word to the other of the panic that lay behind our smiling faces. Now that the decision was made, my instincts had woken up and were shouting that we were wrong, that Joanna needed to be at home whatever the anxiety we were living through. She would share it, inevitably, but so would she share the love and support which we gave each other, and which she needed as a fish needs water. Only here at home could she be certain that I, too, was not about to leave. But I felt that I could not possibly know best, not now, not when I was so full of hysterical emotion. It was easier, and surely better, to rely on an outsider's judgement — or so I told myself, turning a deaf ear to the voice of my own maternal knowledge. Thus came about one of my worst mistakes.

We were approaching Christmas, with all that this implied in terms of the children's activities. Schools were already deep in preparations for nativity plays and carol services, and I had not even started on ours at home. It was the first time that I had ever faced the whole task entirely without help, either in the house or with the children, and, perhaps fortunately, I found myself living continuously at a running pace.

Amid all the commotion, there was just one small but significant area of my life where I could find a measure of peace and personal enjoyment. I have written elsewhere of how I came to learn, thanks to Simon, to play the recorder. The group of teachers with whom I played had been taken in hand that autumn by a serious and expert musician, the head of music at a local school. Not only did she improve the quality of our playing, she also taught us to listen more acutely, and to take a far more lively interest in the possibilities of the instrument and in the music written for it. Some members of the group dropped out as a result of this new approach, but those who remained became very committed, including myself.

It was not easy to get to the sessions, for they were held some miles away, and the timing was awkward, since what suits teachers inevitably does not suit parents; but the fact that I somehow found my way to them each week despite all obstacles shows how much they meant to me. It was my own music therapy. Somehow, playing these gentle instruments in harmony with others, learning to control lungs, fingers, eyes and ears to a pitch of sensitivity undreamed of before gave me both a quiet challenge and a pleasure which refreshed and sustained my parched spirit. Gradually, the members of the group became friends, though we did not talk much. We supported each other as our leader encouraged us to enter local music festivals and to play at concerts. This Christmas we found ourselves playing, to our terror, at a large carol concert in a big local town hall, in front of hundreds of school children. Somehow, surviving that ordeal together cemented the bond between us, and at the same time did something for the morale of each of us. For me it was the first timid shoot of new growth.

It was as well that there was this small area of light. All else seemed very, very dark. Christmas is the most difficult time of year for the sick, the lonely, the old and the bereaved. The accent is heavily on group enjoyment. To be alone at Christmas is to invite pity. Social pressure in the form of a general expectation of pleasure is at its height. Excitement rises as the wave of spending gathers momentum — spending is an essential part of the pattern. Children are the symbolic focal point, not, I suspect, just because of Christianity, but because at Christmas the child in all of us is apt to take over. We don our paper hats and forget that we ever grew up. It is the annual, very necessary, 'Great Escape'. But for those in pain and grief, out of tune with the chiming carols, it seems like farce, farce turned to nightmare.

Throughout my marriage, in my driving desire to build a happy and harmonious family, I had inevitably seized upon Christmas as the perfect symbol of all I was trying to achieve. No tinned chestnuts found their way into *our* turkey. Fresh ones, laboriously peeled, were alone acceptable. Work went on for weeks beforehand, preparing it all. When the great day finally came, we basked in the atmosphere, warm and turkey-scented, of the ideal home, decorated with real holly and ivy, and the large Christmas tree that I had always longed for as a child and never had, for my North-country mother, bred up to poverty, regarded them as an extravagance. Grandparents would come, and we would proudly introduce the current au pair to the rituals of an English Yuletide.

There was no way it could be like that this year. I could hardly bear to think of it, let alone plan it. Which was no doubt why I fell in with my mother-in-law's suggestion that she and Paul should spend the day with us — for the children's sake. As nothing seemed real any more, one more unreality, I thought mistakenly, could not make any difference. Paul, for his part, agreed. Above all, we wanted to avoid tugs of war over the children.

So I went ahead after all, and worked away to prepare a day as similar as I could make it to those they had always known. The evergreens were brought in and festooned our old beams. The cards were hung. The tree was decorated. And when Paul and his mother arrived, we all played our parts religiously — opening presents around the tree, manifesting surprise and pleasure, drinking toasts, setting fire to the home-made pudding. Only we were enacting a black comedy, and I felt as though an iron band was squeezing my heart. The contrast between our behaviour and our feelings was risible. Presumably, the whole miserable charade had been suggested in the forlorn hope that the warm, memory-charged atmosphere of the day might weaken Paul's resolve and tug him back once more to the family from which he was wholly bent on escaping. His mother understood Paul no better than I did. Needless to say, it achieved nothing and after tea they both departed, leaving the children and me to reality once more.

Unhappy though all this had been, it had one extraordinarily salutary effect, though not the one desired by my mother-in-law. We all of us realized that their departure was a relief — a relief in that now, at least, we could stop pretending. I felt this so strongly that it stopped me in my tracks. The truth was appallingly bleak, but at least it was the truth. It reminded me of the time, seven years before, when we had discovered that Simon was autistic, after years of anxiety about him. The truth, terrible though it was, had come as a relief then, too. Reality, however harsh, is less devastating than anxiety. Once reality is fully faced, it is possible to attempt to deal with it.

We began to learn, that Christmas day. Christmas might never again be completely joyful for us, but at least I would make sure it was never again like this one. Future Christmases, however difficult, would be built on our real situation, and our real feelings, not on a wistful fantasy. They might still be painful, but at least, in facing the pain squarely, we might stand a chance of one day coming to terms with it, however remote that day might seem just now.

CHAPTER THREE

First Year: Struggles

New Year's Eve 1973 was spent watching television on my own in a state of profound self-pity. For years, the baby-sitting problem had been neatly eliminated by the presence of au pairs. Now it hit me doubly hard. I could not join a group, since I could not take my turn without leaving the children. If I was successful in finding a sitter, the pleasure of going out was considerably diminished when, on my return, I still had to drive her home, with the house unguarded during my absence. It was far easier to stay at home. In any case, I did not like going out too often, for Joanna and Tom seldom went to sleep until after my return, showing the extent of their anxiety lest anything should happen to me. It was only the knowledge that for all our sakes it was necessary for me sometimes to get out and be with other adults that spurred me into making what felt like a huge effort and accepting invitations.

Once out, I felt so unprotected, so vulnerable, that the whole experience was a distinct strain. I had been dependent for over thirteen years. I was, I felt, no longer a whole person. It was as if I had given my whole identity into the safekeeping of my husband. Now he had discarded it, what was left did not seem worth owning.

Late that night, just before the arrival of the new year, I wrote a purple passage in my diary to relieve my feelings, and finally greeted 1974, like the news announcer, with a weary curiosity. It certainly did not seem to hold much promise.

All too soon after its beginning, the day for Joanna's departure to her new school was upon us. It had dawned on me rather late that, instead of being one of an efficient rota to deal with ten-mile local school runs, I was on my own to cope with a two-hundred-mile round trip. Fortunately, the journey had at least the merit of being cross country. I had only learned to drive when I was in my thirties, and was still very nervous of city centres and dense traffic. Nor had I realized that modern boarding school life involves a great number of such trips for parents owing to exeats and half term holidays — the short spell of boarding I had experienced during the war meant going at the beginning of term and staying till the end. Joanna's transfer thus brought upon me a complicated problem of organization, since each time I travelled up or down to the school, I had to arrange for someone to cover for me at the home end for unpredictable periods of time.

One of my friends accompanied us on the first day of term. She had offered to come so that I would not have to make the long journey home alone. It was a kindly, thoughtful gesture, which lessened the hazards of the drive in that her presence obliged me to control my feelings.

Joanna looked very small and vulnerable in her smart new uniform as I kissed her goodbye and turned away, leaving her in the charge of a couple of younger teachers. As I went, I felt as if I had torn off a living part of myself, and handed it over to strangers. I was repeating to myself the advice that I had been given — that it was for her good, that it was the best possible thing I could do for her in our present circumstances, for her and for her musical talent — and trying not to hear the voice that was screaming inside me that what I was doing was wrong, wrong, wrong. I wanted to turn and rush back, and grab her to me in a passion of love and protectiveness, but I didn't. I walked away with my friend, got into the car, and drove off down the southward road. We stopped for tea on the way and chatted brightly, making the most of the unusualness of an uninterrupted spell of each other's company — but all the time, deep inside me, I was weeping. I had just said goodbye to yet another person that I loved.

The rest of the family was very subdued that evening after my return. Simon, whose inquiries about his father had been increasing in volume and frequency, now wanted to know where Joanna was as well. He had always adored his younger sister, who was close to him in age, and who had always exerted what amounted to a benevolent dictatorship over him. Being bossed by Joanna had worked marvels for Simon's learning potential as he struggled to obey or to emulate her. Now he had lost her, and his puzzlement was painful to see. "Joanna's gone away to school," he would echo after me as I moved around the house, only to ask again, a few minutes later, "Where's Joanna?"

We all missed her badly, though I tried not to let this show too much in my weekly letters — there was a balance to be struck between making it plain that we cared and would have liked her back, and making her worried that we might not be able to cope without her. She wrote home very seldom. Those letters she did write leaked a deep, bitter homesickness, painful to read. I wept for her. Many friends in the neighbourhood had children in boarding schools, and these, when I mentioned my worries, all reassured me that it was always like this in the first term, and that she would gradually settle down. Which did not really comfort me, for I could not help thinking that most children do not start boarding school so soon after the break-up of their parents' marriage. I felt completely helpless. All I could do was to maintain, to the best of my ability, a steady façade of cheerfulness and reassurance, and avoid giving too much sympathy. I really worked on that façade.

When the first exeat weekend came along, I decided to take Joanna away for the two days — with Paul's agreement — rather than risk increasing the homesickness by taking her home. I made arrangements for the other children, and took her to Cambridge, where I was reasonably certain I could keep her entertained for thirty-six hours. It proved a good idea, for it gave Joanna something fresh to think about, and it gave me the pleasure of introducing her to the old haunts of my student days. We wandered happily round the Backs and through the colleges, and dawdled round the busy market. She sampled her first Indian meal in a small restaurant off Trinity Street, and picked her way through curries and birianis with great self-possession. They were enchanted hours for us both, stolen out of time.

The drive back to the school was very silent. Joanna was battling to keep back the tears, and I was praying she would win, or my own would start. She lost, and the pent-up misery was released in a great flood. I had to stop the car for I was soon in no better a state.

The talk we had then helped us both. I did my best to encourage her. She was finding the academic work extremely difficult. It did not seem as if her teachers were taking into account that she was a year younger than her classmates. Joanna, like Tom, needed to succeed (I was not to discover for many years that one of the reasons for this was having a mentally handicapped brother, for whom she felt she needed to compensate her parents), and had always done so with comparative ease. Now, persistent failure in a new school where she knew no-one, and had no-one to confide in, was terrifying her. The one and only area of happiness was her cello. She liked and admired her new teacher. The interest he took in her and the encouragement he gave her seemed to be all that sustained her. I felt that this at least was a small, positive sign. Not everything was entirely black.

Not very long after this weekend, however, the school phoned me to say that Joanna had been caught stealing. I knew enough about child development to be aware that stealing at this age tends to be either an experiment or the expression of a desperate need for affection. In this case, the reason seemed to be pitifully obvious — at least to me, who had stolen from Woolworths at the same age and for exactly the same reason. It was nothing very terrible — she had taken a bar of chocolate from a shop in the town — but the voice on the phone sounded shocked and judgemental. Joanna, I was assured, would be made to pay for the chocolate and apologize to the shopkeeper for her misdeed. I agreed, there was little else I could do, but I did not think that the punishment would help anybody except the shopkeeper. They were treating the symptom, but it did not seem as if anyone was particularly concerned about the cause. I began to worry in earnest now — about the choice of school.

I heard no more, however, and resigned myself to sitting back and hoping that things would gradually improve for Joanna. She came home at half term and seemed her normal self, until it came to going back, when her grief upset us all. Paul was to collect her for her next exeat and give her a day out before bringing her home. I had hoped that seeing him might help her, but he fared no better than I had. None of us seemed to be able to comfort this distress. Years later, she was able to tell me how appallingly alone and friendless she had felt at this time, and, worse, how cut off and excluded from all the important and worrying things that were happening at home.

It was as well that the boys, at least, seemed less disturbed, apart from the days when Paul came to take them out. These were growing more, not less, difficult. They were a great strain on all of us. Tom and David felt guilty because they thought they were being disloyal to me and did not want to hurt me, though at the same time they did, badly, want to go out with their father. David, in particular, was by now showing definite signs of deprivation — throwing himself at any adult male who came into our house, and climbing all over him, in a way that brought a lump into my throat. I, for my part, while I did my best to reassure them that I wanted them to go, and did not mind, was quite unable to conceal my pain as they skipped away at Paul's side. I blamed myself severely for these feelings. I had watched discussions on television in which divorced couples spoke of their 'civilized' methods of making access arrangements, putting the children's welfare before their own feelings. I was trying to do the same, but my feelings were making it impossibly difficult, for there was nothing civilized about them. They were primitive, and raw, and bleeding, and somehow I had to go on living with them.

It was just when I was beginning to feel that I could not, in fact, do so much longer that something happened which was to affect our whole future, and, in time, change the picture entirely, though I had no inkling of its importance then. When the very thing for which I had been craving for months fell into my lap, I was too far gone in misery to recognize it.

A fellow writer, whose daughter had been a classmate of Joanna's at her old school, phoned me one day for a chat. During it, she mentioned that another friend of hers, who had also been left alone to care for a mentally handicapped son, had been given great help and support by an NSPCC social worker. If I felt I needed help myself, she would willingly give me the necessary phone numbers. I thanked her gratefully, and duly made a note of them, but, surprisingly, I did not follow them up at once. The interview with the psychiatrist had hurt me badly. I did not think I could face any more such censure. Also, the NSPCC was an organization I associated with violence towards children, not with help for parents. It was not long, however, before yet another accumulation of pressures took me to the phone, and in a distinctly shaky voice I asked for Ray Jenkins; so making my first contact with the deep Scots voice I was to come to know so well. He listened to my story, and asked a few questions. He wanted to know if I had received any help at all. When I told him about the interview with the psychiatrist, the explosion of wrath at the other end of the phone made my ears tingle, and set me smiling for the first time that week. Ray, it seemed, did not think much of the interview either.

Unfortunately, as we did not live in his area of work, he could not take me on as a regular client, but he told me I could phone him whenever I needed to, and that he would see me from time to time outside office hours if things became really bad. By the time I put the receiver down, I knew that I had found at least some of the help I needed — someone to turn to when despair threatened and the ability to cope seemed to have disappeared — and this knowledge buoyed me up.

Something else happened then to increase this feeling that the world was not completely hostile and happiness for ever at an end. One of my oldest friends is my original French pen friend to whom I began to write when I was a schoolgirl of thirteen, and with whom I had exchanged visits. Anne Marie was married now, with one little daughter. A hastily scribbled note on my Christmas card to her had given her our news. A reply to this suddenly came, inviting me to take the children to visit her at her home in Metz during the Easter holidays — a generous offer in view of the size of my family, and the fact that she worked full time as a teacher of English. Her husband, Yvon, she wrote, would meet us at Calais, and drive us across Northern France.

I was thrilled. It was the first really exciting thing to happen in so many months of unremitting sadness that it was hard to believe in it. In the eighteen months I had lived in France during my degree course, I had come to love it, and I had missed my visits there during the years of my marriage. It would be a deep pleasure for me to introduce the children to a real French household, so that their first impressions of the country would be from the inside, as it were, rather than as tourists.

Simon, however, represented a problem. Although on the whole he was very placid and easy-going, change upset him, and he was liable to become very disturbed when his routine was disrupted. Taking him with us would have imposed a heavy burden on him, on me, and not least on Anne Marie, who had no experience of autistic children. In the end, discussing it with Mrs Elgar, his teacher, I was able to arrange for him to board at school for the week of our absence. I hated the idea that he was missing out on a family treat, but I had everyone's wellbeing to consider.

The excitement transformed us all: the train journey, the hovercraft, the first steps on French soil. Our troubles melted away as we filed through Customs and caught sight of Yvon filming our arrival. He was a first-class photographer, and we were to be given many an amusing and poignant souvenir of our holiday, taken by him. It was dark and very late by the time we reached Metz, but even David was still awake and grinning broadly when we greeted Anne Marie.

The next few days were pure delight. Isabelle, Anne Marie's daughter, took charge of the boys and Joanna, and whisked them off outside to become honorary members of her gang. We only saw them at meal times or on visits to places of interest, such as the cathedral, where Joanna, to her incredulous happiness, was allowed to play on the old organ, thanks to the good offices of Yvon, who was more than a little proud of the talent of his small visitor. The language barrier did not appear to exist. Only Tom, from time to time, found it hard going, and sneaked back inside to read one of his Narnia books — a personal escape hatch. David openly enjoyed himself. His bubbly personality and infectious grin endeared him to everyone. As for me, I luxuriated in the rest and the change of environment. For a few precious days, I could leave the organizing to others and simply enjoy being back in France. The mirabelle plum trees were in flower, and it was Easter week. For the first time, the idea of rebuilding our lives seemed a possibility.

All too soon, it was time to go back to England and pick up the strands of ordinary life again. We were never to forget our French holiday, however — it was the first happy time we had spent together since the family had assumed its new form, and it gave us hope that there might yet be others. Simon was obviously glad to see us, but seemed to be none the worse for his week as a boarder.

The break had done more for me than just giving me a rest. Anne Marie was my own, personal friend — she had barely met Paul. She had invited us out of affection and sympathy, and this was extraordinarily comforting and reassuring at a time when my self-esteem was almost non-existent. Long talks with her had re-established continuity between the person I was as a girl, before I met Paul, and the woman I had become. It was as if she had placed in my hands the thread which one day might lead me to find myself again. For the very first time I began to think consciously about the independence I had given up when I was married. It was another very faint flicker of new life.

It was fanned by my admiration for the way Anne Marie ran her life. Besides caring for a large house, and providing gourmet meals for an appreciative husband, she earned a good salary in an interesting job. I was envious of her financial independence. The only income of my own I had enjoyed in the latter years of my marriage had come from writing stories and articles for women's magazines or newspapers — and even this I had faithfully put into the joint account until the last year, when at last I saw sense and began to put it into a newly opened account of my own. I was finding it all but impossible to write now, for I had the administrative affairs of the family to attend to as well as its practical needs, and in any case I had not the slightest inspiration for writing romantic short stories. Every plot I did manage to dream up ended invariably in marriage breakdown. Needless to say, few sold, and the long periods of silence from my agent did little to raise my morale. I began to toy with the idea of finding an outside job. It would have been hard to come up with anything more unrealistic, but I had to find that out for myself — the hard way.

Reinvigorated by the holiday, I decided to explore possibilities. I had never wanted to teach, and had indeed gone to some lengths to avoid doing so, but now it seemed to be the most obvious job for someone in my position, since it fitted in best with the children's timetable. Although I had a degree, I had never done a diploma in education, and, since I had no actual teaching experience, it seemed a sensible idea to try to learn something about the craft by doing one. I wrote off to a nearby training college to see if they would accept me for a course. I was given an interview with gratifying speed, but it soon emerged, during the course of it, that, unsupported by other adults as I was, I was never going to stand up to the rigours of a timetable that made absolutely no concessions to the difficulties of mothers with small children. The course, it was emphasized, was very stressful. That finished me — there was no way, I knew, that I could take more pressure. With a great deal of reluctance, I abandoned the idea of imitating Anne Marie. All of which renewed my feelings of being trapped, and, far worse, of inadequacy. There were women, I knew, who were able to blast their way through all obstacles to reach their chosen profession. Many of my friends, some with several children, were teachers. Here was another rich source of guilt, and I made the most of it.

As if to ensure that morale dropped once more to zero, a phone flasher started up at this time. It seemed the cruellest irony that someone should choose to make obscene phone calls only months after Paul's departure, but so it happened. I felt that if I were showing signs of becoming paranoid, it was not without reason. In the end, he was so persistent that I had to have the phone monitored, for fear that Joanna might be the one who lifted the receiver. Fortunately, this worked, and we were left in peace.

The summer term opened peacefully enough. Joanna returned to school in tears as usual, but her letters sounded a little less desperate. It began to appear possible that she might, as all had predicted, settle. The boys were still attending the independent school, but, as I thought about it, it became clear that this did not make sense. Paul's salary, by no means enormous, was now being stretched over two households. The additional burden of an educational loan could hardly continue to be shouldered for much longer. With his agreement, I made arrangements for Tom and David to start at a good state junior and mixed infants school the following September, and, more than a little sadly, once more informed the headmistress of their current school of the impending move. I worried about giving two such young boys a change of school to cope with on top of everything else, but she was very reassuring, and, again, very kind.

An educational psychologist who lived nearby, and who was a friend of ours, was less comforting when he called in to see us one day. David, as was his wont, had climbed onto his lap, and generally twined himself round his neck. He saw this excessive display of affection to a total stranger as a sign of extreme deprivation, and made no bones about telling me so, forecasting that David might well be delinquent by the time he was thirteen.

I have never been too sure what he hoped to achieve by this remark, which might well have had disastrous effects. If, as I now prefer to think, it was thrown out as a challenge, then it was an excellent, shrewd move. After he had gone, I went to my room and wept, totally demoralized; but before long a great anger kindled within me, and an equally great resolve. It was only normal, I told myself, that David, after what had happened, should be showing signs of disturbance and deprivation — but if it were possible that a single, remaining parent could bring back security and stability to his life, then, if it meant I never went to work again, I would do it. If constant care, affection and support could make his future development healthy and straightforward, then I would supply them. If his superabundance of energy represented a threat, then we would find safe channels for it, though just where I was not too sure.

The answers to David's problems, in fact, seemed relatively clear cut. Tom, if anything, worried me more, for I could see that his hurt went very, very deep. We had been to see a speech therapist, who had been reassuring about his stammer, and it had, indeed, improved a little. He was still, however, a thin, pale, nervous child, who ate little and spoke less, unless he was playing with his brother, when he relaxed. I sometimes thought, watching them, that the coming of David was the best thing that could have happened to Tom. He slept poorly. No matter how late I went to bed, I always found him awake. Ray explained that he saw himself as the responsible male of the family, and felt he must be sure that I was safe and, above all, still there, before he could allow himself to sleep. I hoped that the more permissive atmosphere of the state school might reduce his condition of high tension when he started there the following term. He, too, I felt, needed plenty of athletic activity through which to express himself — but I was uncertain how to go about procuring it.

As if in answer to my need, a friend of mine, a qualified swimming teacher who gives private swimming instruction in her own pool, phoned me up to offer free lessons to both boys. The offer was kindness itself, for she worked very hard, and I accepted gratefully. Tom and David loved their lessons, which they attended regularly, and soon both learned to swim. As time passed, this offer became more, not less, valuable, for it opened up to them much inexpensive enjoyment, and Margaret saw to it that they both developed a good style, of which they were proud. As very little swimming tuition ever came their way at school, they might otherwise never have learned, for the local baths are a long way from our home. Learning to swim well was to be, in fact, an important part of the various solutions I gradually found to help with the boys' problems.

The difficulties with Simon were of course far more complex. I could not foresee any of his future development, nor guess how best to help him now that he had come, at twelve, to the verge of puberty. Although there was hope that he still might improve considerably, the psychiatrist at the Maudsley Hospital, whom I consulted when any difficulties concerning the care of Simon came up, warned me that he would probably always need a sheltered environment. He was just twelve, and school-leaving age, irrelevant though it is to a mentally handicapped person, was not so very far ahead. Certainly, at that time, caring for him was proving far more difficult than it had ever seemed. He was very confused, and his obsessive repetition of questions about his father was incredibly painful, despite the advice the psychiatrist had given me over answering them. He would, I felt, never be able to understand what had happened. Divorce or separation are far too abstract for the literal minds of autistic people to make any sense of.

I was increasingly worried in case I should not be able to cope with all his needs as he grew older and bigger. Towards the end of the winter, a possible solution had appeared in the form of a project among the other parents at Simon's school, a project which included Mrs Elgar herself, which was to meet the future needs of the pupils by opening the first ever community for autistic adolescents and adults, where they could stay for the rest of their lives if need be. The more I heard about it, the more interested I became. A property had been found not far from Burnham-on-Sea in Somerset, with some twenty acres of grounds, where the residents would be able to keep livestock, grow some of their own food, and generally lead meaningful lives in a beautiful rural environment. They were to be in the care of Mrs Elgar, and others who understood and had long experience of their special problems. Now I came to a decision, and phoned Mrs Elgar to ask whether Simon might be included in the number of her pupils who were to go to Somerset with her to be the founder members of the community when it opened in August. To my intense relief she agreed.

It was the third hard decision I had been faced with in the last six months. It was as well, perhaps, that in this one I did not have too many options. I could not afford to turn down a chance like this, which I well knew might never come again. Once Simon reached school-leaving age matters might well have become desperate. Very few other facilities existed for him and others like him, and those that did were not geared to the specialized needs of the autistic. It was essential to try and think long-term, impossible though that seemed. I did not want Simon to be reduced to living alone at home with an ageing mother, isolated from his peers, and able to enjoy only the barest snatches of community life. That, to me, was real poverty for him. So at least in this I had the consolation of being reasonably certain that I was acting rightly — there was no inner voice that I was trying to stifle, shouting that I was making a mistake — though I did have to combat a great deal of painful guilt at the whole idea of sending him away. He would, I knew, come home for four main holidays a year, with long weekends in between, and there would be Sundays when the community would be open for parents to visit and take out their children. I was not rejecting him. I found I had to repeat this to myself many times.

Settling Simon's future seemed to take the last of my energy. These days, I was always tired, to the point of retreating to bed in the afternoons and falling into a heavy, unrefreshing sleep. Each weekend encounter with Paul left me more exhausted than ever. I felt as if I were being subjected to constant punishment. I dreaded the weekends by now, when all the stability and harmony I had built up during the week was roughly broken up, and the boys, strained and overexcited, drove off with their father to be returned a few hours later fractious and sticky with sweets. The struggle to hide my feelings from them was growing harder and harder, as each sight of Paul, spruce and breezy and clearly enjoying his freedom, added to my sensation of nightmare. Whilst in theory I thought that access was necessary, I felt obscurely now that it was being wrongly used — that these trips did nothing whatsoever to help the children, but confused them, and also made my job far harder.

In the end I phoned Ray — I had to talk it through with someone. Above all I was worried that my feelings were not 'civilized', and I told him about the magnificently reasonable couples I had seen in discussion panels on television. He blew their reasonableness apart with the effectiveness of a hand grenade in a nineteenth-century salon. Once again, I put the receiver down laughing, reassured that my own feelings were normal, and that there were many others who felt as I did. This constant reassurance of my normality at a time when I was always being frightened by the violence of my feelings was perhaps one of the most valuable pieces of help that Ray could give me just then. Violent though they were, these stormy emotions had to be lived through if there was to be any hope of my ever again finding peace, and I had to try to learn to live with them. Denying them only brought on worse depression, as I had already found. I felt as though I could gladly sleep for ever.

It only needed an emergency to bring my energy back, however. At the end of the summer term, it suddenly became necessary for Joanna to go into hospital for a small operation. Increasingly bad catarrh had begun to affect her hearing, and she needed to have her adenoids removed and her eardrums checked. A local hospital was extremely helpful in fixing the date for the beginning of the school holidays — though that turned out to be the sum of their helpfulness. The children's ward turned out to be a dark, gloomy place where most of the light came from the TV set, and mothers were told peremptorily, "No visiting on operation day". I remembered the welcome I had been given at the hospital where Simon was diagnosed years before, and the cubicle I had shared with him, and my hackles rose. Joanna should not, on top of all her recent unhappiness, go through the trauma of coming round from the unpleasant little operation without me there if I could prevent it. I turned on the staff nurse, who caved in at once the moment she saw the light of battle in my eye. I stayed. It was just as well, for Joanna the musician was very frightened that her ears might have been damaged. All was well, however, apart from having to stay an extra twenty-four hours in hospital to be on the safe side.

It was the sort of ward where the nurses watch the television all day and leave the children to their own devices. Only the rationed visitors took the slightest interest in their emotional wellbeing. I took in books and games, and did my best to keep Joanna distracted, but the forty-eight-hour stay seemed interminable to both of us. As we were leaving, the staff nurse commented on what she regarded as my excessive concern for my daughter. I told her something of Joanna's story — about Simon, and her father's recent departure — and she had the grace to apologize. "You should have told us," she muttered. She had not asked me if there were any special problems — nor any other parent, for that matter. It was the first time that I had come across nursing that dissociates parts of the body such as ears, noses and throats from the rest of the child, and it was not a heart-warming experience.

The long summer holidays now stretched uninvitingly ahead. Hitherto, the family had gone every summer to spend a fortnight in a cottage on the Pembrokeshire coast. It belonged to a farm, and stood beside a small cove with shallow, safe bathing, ideal for Simon. It was very remote, but over the years we had come to know several other families who holidayed there, as well as the farmer and his wife, and it had become very much a home from home, beloved of the children. This year I had not renewed the booking. I felt that I could not cope with the long drive alone with all the children, especially as the last lap of it was over twisty mountain roads which demanded maximum concentration. I regretted this decision now, but it was too late to change my mind. In any case, I doubted whether enough money was available.

Some friends came to the rescue by offering us the use of a large caravan, tethered in an orchard which was part of the grounds of their house near Maidenhead. I accepted with relief. My imagination was refusing to function, and I could come up with nothing more exciting. I was apprehensive at the prospect of keeping four children of differing ages and abilities happy and occupied should the weather prove bad; but in the event the sun shone benevolently, and we were able to live entirely out of doors.

The week was a definite success for the children. They loved the novelty of fold-away beds, a galley kitchen and the camp fire where we baked potatoes in the evenings and sang all the songs I could remember from my Ranger days. My feelings were mixed. Whilst I was happy to see Simon, Joanna, Tom and David enjoying themselves, I myself was feeling acutely isolated, and appallingly lonely. The lack of privacy inevitable in caravan living deprived me of all my resources: I could not read once the children had gone to bed, for the light kept them awake, I could not listen to music for the same reason, and there was, of course, no TV. It was my introduction to what was to prove a virtually insoluble problem of single-parent holidays.

All too soon after our return home came the day when I had to take Simon to the meeting place at Ealing, where the coach was to collect the new residents of Somerset Court, and take them off down the motorway to begin their new life together. I had done my best to prepare him for the separation, but I knew I could not spare him the distress he was about to live through, any more than I could avoid it myself. I was, all the same, greatly comforted that he was to be in the care of Mrs Elgar, among familiar faces. At least I was not sending him away to strangers. I was reasonably certain that he would be happy once he accepted the new pattern of his life, for he had a gentle, easy-going disposition. He would be treated with respect, and have the dignity that was his due as a member of the human race.

Nonetheless, I cried all the way home. I felt that I had betrayed his trust in me. I could not bear to think that the bond of affection which I had worked so hard to create might weaken and disappear. Autistic people have unpredictable reactions, and this seemed quite possible.

The other three children were still on holiday. The summer seemed to be going on for ever. All my friends were away, and the village was quiet and sleepy when I went to do my shopping. I grew more and more depressed. Parting with Simon had, I thought, brought to an end yet another phase in my life. Ever since his handicap had been diagnosed, just before his fourth birthday, helping and teaching him had shaped my days. Now I had handed that responsibility across to someone else and the emptiness at the centre of my life seemed greater than ever.

Perhaps this was what spurred me into action on behalf of Tom and David. Seeing an advertisement for a judo club on a notice board, I wrote off to the secretary and arranged that they should join. It was, I felt, exactly the right sport for them in our present circumstances. I was rather surprised when Joanna insisted on being included, even though she would only be able to attend during her school holidays, but soon realized that it could help her too, just as much as the boys. They all, even the gentle Tom, took to it at once. The two instructors, a husband and wife team, were excellent with young children, and I made sure that they were aware of the background of the family, so that tears should be treated gently — though in fact they always were, no matter whose. Judo, with its mat-slapping breakfalls and controlled aggression, where putting up a good fight is just as important as winning, is a highly therapeutic sport for children with problems, as well as for their parents as they watch. I never quite learned to relax when someone put a strangle on one of my children, and grew as tense during a contest as if I were watching Harvey Smith doing a clear round; but I never grew bored at judo, and was far too absorbed to feel aware of my single-parent state. It had for us the great advantage of being a very cheap sport, requiring little equipment — kits can be bought second-hand, and the mat fee is minimal. Joanna, Tom and David all became dedicated judokai, and we rarely missed a week.

I also arranged at this time, shutting my eyes to future problems, for Tom to start his second musical instrument. In our precarious financial position this was, from a common-sense point of view, total foolishness, but I was determined. Somehow, I would find the means. I knew Tom to be intensely musical, like his sister, and I knew the healing powers of music — the memory of Simon quietening, when at his most disturbed, into an entranced statue the moment I put on a classical record, was still vivid. I believed that music could help my family more than perhaps any other activity, for it gave them a way to express their feelings, to acquire a sense of beauty and order, and to communicate with others in harmony and understanding. I think that there is music in everyone, however tone-deaf they may believe themselves. Certainly my children responded to it, and I felt that if I encouraged and supported it, it would help them to survive. I had no clear idea to what it might lead — I only knew, blindly, that it was something I had to do for them.

One of the biggest difficulties in doing it was the cost of good instruments. I had been negotiating for some time already for a full-size cello for Joanna, to replace the three-quarter size she was playing when she grew out of it. Prices, I realized, would be going up, and it behoved me to buy while I still could. I was handicapped by my own ignorance, for when Joanna started to learn I knew nothing at all about stringed instruments. Luckily, I had already picked up some facts. I knew that with very musical children there was no point in buying poor instruments, for the sound they produce gives no pleasure — I already knew better than to buy a factory-produced cello, for instance. Since we were not in the running for really good instruments, with their Monopoly-money prices, either, I had to find a middle road, which meant enlisting the help of a reputable dealer, and telling him what we could afford.

The trouble with starting Tom off at this point in time was that we could not afford anything at all. I did not dare to withdraw anything from our scanty savings. It was this, in fact, which brought about a big error of judgement. I calculated that if we began by hiring a small cello for Tom, which cost very little, he could gradually succeed to Joanna's instruments as she left them behind. It seemed worth the risk of intensifying sibling rivalry if they could both eventually have good instruments, and at the same time allow me to spread the cost. In fact, it was a far greater risk than I knew, but I was unaware of that at the time.

We went ahead. Tom was enrolled for cello classes at the local school of music, and lessons started. He loved his teacher and the feeling seemed to be reciprocated. He looked forward to his cello lessons throughout the week, though he continued to enjoy his piano.

This was less true for David. For a child who found sitting still a trial and a torment, the piano had not been perhaps the wisest choice of instrument. He tried hard, however, as did his patient, gentle teacher, Sue, and I did not think the effort he put in was doing him any harm. I could not face any more decisions just then.

Both boys now started at their new school, and I heaved a sigh of relief, for both of them enjoyed it from the very first day. It was a school which encouraged all creative activities, and where great pains were taken to mount and display beautifully the children's work. I had been to see the headmaster, to put him in the picture concerning the family situation. This was a step I felt to be essential, for they would need all the support they could get. They could now go to school by coach, and, as this passed our gate, I suddenly found myself let off all the local school runs. I could hardly credit my luck — and nor could Tom and David, who found it far more fun to go to school in a bus.

A week or so later, and Joanna went off in her turn. The new academic year was at last under way. She was repeating her first year, which seemed to me very sensible after the difficulties of her first two terms. She would now be in her own age group, and would also have all the advantages of being an old lag, who knew all the ropes. Surely, I thought, she would at last settle down and begin to be happy.

Now that I had a little free time at last, I signed myself up for a bookbinding class once a week at a local technical college. This was hopefully intended as an antidote to the depression which still hung around like an early morning fog. Collecting second-hand books is a hobby of mine, and I thought I might find a great deal of pleasure in learning how to refurbish them. There were many other classes which interested me, but I could not afford the fees. I envied the senior citizens, who could go for nothing.

Thus, even with Simon and Joanna away from home, life was extremely full and busy. Unfortunately, I was still very tired and run down, for there had been no real break for me throughout the entire summer. Encouraged by both Ray and Joan, I decided to try to take a weekend away, just to draw breath. I succeeded in arranging for the boys to stay with friends, found a cheap break offer at a hotel in Worcester, and set off by myself, for once little caring that I was on my own.

It was my first visit to Elgar country. There, exploring the great, dim cathedral, and pacing beside the quiet river, I could stand back a little from my breathless daily life, and take stock. Moved by the reflections in the water, the autumn colours already touching the trees, and the sad words of a woman who passed me by, I started to write a story — one of the few of that period which sold — and found I had paid for my weekend. For that brief space of forty-eight hours, I managed not to dwell on my anxieties, not to wonder what was to become of us all, and to make the most of every moment of peace.

Which was wise, for there was no more of it to be had when I reached home. Only a few days later, the phone rang one morning just after the boys had left for school. It was one of my friends. Excitedly, she asked me if we had seen Paul on television the evening before displaying photos of Simon and Joanna. Aghast, I answered in the negative, for, although we had been watching at the time she mentioned, it had fortunately been on a different channel. Pleased to be the first with the news, she went on to tell me all about it.

I had known that a book of Paul's on certain aspects of child behaviour was to be published that autumn, but I had not been expecting any such publicity. He had not warned me about it, nor had he consulted me as to the advisability of involving the children, which I thought totally wrong so soon after the marriage break-up.

I was still trying to digest this when, a couple of days later, I received a phone call from my aunt in Carlisle asking me if Paul had come back to us. It turned out that she had seen an article in her daily paper about Paul and his book, in which he spoke of his stable marriage and happy family life. I disillusioned her. By the time I put the phone down, however, I was seeing the world, and Paul, through very different eyes. For the first time since he left us I was totally, blazingly angry as I had rarely been in my life before. Only chance had prevented the children from seeing any of the publicity, and from being hurt and still more confused by it. There was nothing I could effectively do about it, but I could at least prevent it ever happening again — by divorcing Paul, and applying for sole custody of the children. I phoned my solicitor, and went to see him the next day.

In my anger at the time, I could not see the tight spot that Paul was in. If a book is to sell there must be publicity surrounding its launch. If he had admitted his recent marriage breakdown to the media, we all might well have been far more colourfully, and far more painfully involved. He had chosen, in fact, the lesser of two evils, and, though it certainly hurt me, it also did me the great service of kindling an anger great enough to give me the strength finally to end our ill-starred marriage.

The moment the petition was filed, everything between us seemed suddenly to harden. A terse note from Paul announced that he was closing the joint account, and that from then on he would simply send me a cheque whenever he could. I had, in fact, recently drawn heavily on it, for there had, as usual, been heavy expenses at the start of the academic year. At least those bills were paid. There was no chance now of even the most remotely amicable discussion of our financial needs. We were both panicking. From then until such time as the lawyers achieved a proper financial settlement, and this looked as far off as ever, the children and I were to be entirely dependent on Paul's whim. I never knew when a cheque was coming, nor for how much it would be, so that it was impossible either to plan or to budget.

My anxiety round this time was so great that it affected every physical function. I did not see how I could hold things together for long on such a financial basis.

I had never known security. My father had been slowly dying of TB throughout my teens, and, whilst his firm had paid his medical expenses, they had not given my mother a pension — though they had recently more than made up for this. My state scholarship had consequently seemed like a fortune, and my twelve pounds a week in my first job pure luxury until I tried to pay the bills with it. It had been a precarious existence, but I had always coped. I had only myself to worry about, and I could live very frugally indeed if need be. It was different now. Four children depended on my good management, four children whom I loved passionately. I had visions of being turned out of the house or, worse, of the children being taken from me and put into care — an updated version of "Cathy Come Home". If that happened, I vowed, I would kill myself.

Only the financial settlement could do anything to curtail this nightmare. I could not understand all the delays as the lawyers haggled over details. Ray urged me to change solicitor, as did Joan, and, indeed, all my close friends who, by now, seeing our situation, had rallied round. I shrank from this. I felt I had not the strength to face the scene that would surely ensue when I indicated that I wanted to transfer the case — I could not bear to face yet more anger. I had been told to apply for legal aid, and the subsequent interview cost whatever pride I had left. I had not believed it was possible to sink so low in the social scale in so short a time. I, who had earned more than Paul when we first married, whose money had paid most of the down payment on our first house, had now become little more than a piece of social flotsam — all because I had married and had children. Feelings such as these made the weekly meeting with Paul when he came to take out the boys quite unbearable. I could hardly endure the sight of his politely smiling face. The contrast between the act of taking them out for an afternoon and giving them treats, and the reluctance to come quickly to a sensible and realistic financial agreement stuck in my throat and all but choked me. Each successive departure left me a weeping wreck. In the end it was my solicitor who came up with a solution to this.

I had mentioned to him some of the problems that were accumulating around access, and he now proposed that we try to find some neutral ground — a family or retired couple not involved in our situation — where I could safely leave the children to be collected and returned by Paul, so that I myself need no longer meet him.

It seemed a very sensible idea. It meant that the children need not lose touch with their father, whilst I could step back, out of the relationship, and have a chance to pull myself together, instead of having my wounds reopened week after painful week with deadly regularity.

The trouble with it was that I had not the faintest idea how to begin to put it into action. There were many difficulties. Because Paul and I had only one car between us, our future hosts had to live within walking distance both of the station and of our house. This, in a rural area, reduced our options considerably. After some fruitless cogitation, I decided to phone the vicar of our local church to ask for suggestions — his network of acquaintances would be far wider than mine. I had met his wife, Marilyn, a couple of times, but I had never spoken to him. I had never entered his church either, for I was an agnostic, but my need was too great to let such considerations stand in my way. I simply needed help, and he seemed a good person to ask. Equally simply, he gave it to me. He listened to my story, and then at once offered to have the children at the vicarage, just across the common from our house — despite the fact that he already had four children of his own.

I demurred at first — it seemed too great a burden to place upon an extremely busy pair of people — but he briskly overrode my feeble arguments. Sunday, he assured me, was the day when his family was almost always at home, and a few more children around for part of it would make little or no difference. It was the understatement of the year, but in the end, with enormous relief, I accepted. A heavy weight had just been lifted from my shoulders. Henceforth I need never again set eyes on the husband who had hurt me so profoundly.

I was immeasurably grateful to Peter and Marilyn. This was solid, practical help which actually lessened the load I was carrying. It was also the beginning of a very intense experience, though I was not to know that at the time. I only knew that when, in desperate need, I had asked for aid, it had been given me without hesitation or condition, in a way I was never to forget.

Christmas was approaching again — our second Christmas since Paul's departure. There was to be no question of pretence this year. We had travelled a long way in twelve months, despite the wrong turnings we had occasionally taken. Although it was still quite impossible to see ahead, I felt I had gained a rough idea of the direction we needed to take, and had set our course accordingly. My priorities at least were quite clear.

The children were to spend Christmas with me at home, where they had always spent it, and in the way they had always spent it. Then, at the end of the month, the three boys would spend a week with Paul and his girlfriend. Joanna had pulled out of this arrangement — she wanted to attend the holiday orchestral course she always went to in the Christmas holidays, and the dates clashed. She was so much away from home that she was also loth to give up any of the precious days she spent there. I let her do as she wished, and Paul, for his part, put no pressure on her.

We all duly attended the family party, and this year I managed to enjoy it. The uncles and aunts made us warmly welcome, and I found much comfort in being with them, along with the children.

I even managed to host a small party of my own — for my friends in the recorder consort. Each member brought a dish, one brought wine, and it no longer mattered that money was tight. Afterwards, as the sweet voices of the recorders joined in carols — not for nothing do the French call them '*les flutes douces*' — and the children listened or joined in, our home did not seem such a bad place to be, despite the storms that howled around it. Everyone in it that evening, I observed, looking round, was enjoying him or herself, and the realization warmed me, and renewed my courage. It was worth every moment of the struggle to hold it together.

CHAPTER FOUR

Second Year: The Priest and the Judge

We had survived, even enjoyed Christmas, but the accumulation of financial worries which gathered in its wake threatened once again to overwhelm me. I was absolutely desperate for a regular income. There was still no sign of anyone reaching an agreement, and the situation looked like going on for ever. All my feelings of anger against Paul were being exacerbated by this frightening, constant penury. Prices in the shops were rising fast, and the children were all growing. The contrast between appearances and the real state of our bank balance as we moved around our affluent neighbourhood struck me daily more forcibly. Half the house was my only asset, and it was virtually useless to me, for we had to live somewhere.

The house itself, strange to say, gave me a kind of comfort. It was so old that it stood, in my eyes at least, outside the rat race and the material values of the day. It could afford to be eccentric. People had lived in it who had been far poorer even than I had become. They had had no central heating to warm them in winter, nor even hot water to wash themselves, their clothes and their utensils. Countless children had been reared in it over the centuries. Its uneven floors and exposed beams tolerated their untidiness and mess in a way no modern house would ever do. Roy's father had converted and modernized it in the nineteen thirties. It was she who had told me how nine boys had been reared in only half of it, not so very long ago. All of which gave me a sense of perspective.

So did the days when I went next door to her cottage, one of the original three which had been joined together, to be warmed out of my low spirits by the huge coal and log fire she always kept glowing in winter, and by her down-to-earth sympathy. The firelight in her sitting room, the red coals in the grate were, I think, a symbol for both of us in the damp and darkness of that long winter. The human spirit is not so easily quenched.

The week they had spent with their father had left the boys very disturbed. I was particularly worried about Simon. The upheaval seemed too soon after his recent removal to Somerset

Court. He had seemed to be settling down there very well indeed, and was making good progress, but now he started once again wandering anxiously round the house, asking questions about his father until I thought I would go mad. Once I misguidedly tried to stop him by suggesting, "Let's not talk about that" — whereupon he merely stuck "let's not talk about that" onto the end of every obsessive question. I was glad, though full of guilt at feeling glad, when the time came for him to return to Mrs Elgar. At Somerset Court there was a chance that he might interest himself in other things.

Tom and David came home tense and defensive. The fact that Joanna had refused to go made them feel guilty, and there was a great deal more friction between the three of them than was usual.

Joanna herself had not enjoyed her orchestral course very much, either. As she was usually brimming over with enthusiasm, the coaches commented on her apathy to me, wondering what was the matter with her. When I arrived near the end of a rehearsal to ferry her home one day, I saw what they meant, for she was sitting slumped listlessly over her cello, paying little attention to what was going on around her. At home she had become silent and withdrawn. When I tried to find out what was wrong, she turned away from me. I felt instinctively that it was better not to probe too hard — she would tell me when she was ready. Nor did I want to make matters worse just before the beginning of term. When this came, she went off in tears once again, but the mother who had done the run (I had by now providently found others with whom to share it) phoned me to say that by the time they reached the school she was perfectly bright again. I sighed with relief.

Tom and David were by now both flourishing in their new school. The more relaxed atmosphere had been exactly what they needed at this time. Tom's stammer disappeared completely as he told me long, detailed stories about class projects and new friends he had made. Drawings and paintings of great vividness were brought home by both boys, and I pinned them up with pride. The school was small, and the children received plenty of individual attention. It did not seem to worry Tom that he was the eldest in his year, and he certainly was not bored. It looked very much as though this change, too, was to prove a good one, and as if I myself might also begin to relax a little on the score of the children. I could not know that this was only the calm before the storm.

In the hope of finding some more support for myself, I had recently joined a newly-formed, local one-parent family group, and had begun to attend meetings. My hopes of enjoyment were soon dashed, however. I found myself reacting to the group in exactly the same way that I had reacted to the Autistic Society when Simon was first diagnosed — I did not want to become one of an organization when the only thing I had, or felt I had, in common with the other members was misfortune. Whilst over the years I had come to enjoy working for the Autistic Society, there had been constant, strong motivation in the shape of Simon, but no such motivation was present as I tried to come to terms with the new group. In fact, I bitterly resented being labelled as a single parent — it was to me an insignia of failure. I found the atmosphere of bitterness, the compulsion to talk over injustices, intensely depressing. Finally, after a meeting which seemed even more negative than usual, I decided to opt out. I needed to belong to a group very badly, but I wanted one that was less angry.

Before I left it, however, I had received one invaluable piece of help from a fellow-member — the kind of help which is perhaps the real *raison d'être* of the organization — in the form of the name, address and phone number of a London solicitor, who was a divorce expert, and who had greatly helped her.

It came at exactly the right moment. The impasse which my legal affairs had reached was now daily increasing my depression and despair. All my letters and phone calls urging speed had no effect. Polite replies held me at a distance, until one day an assistant solicitor, goaded no doubt from both sides, lost his temper with me down the phone. It was the last straw, and at last made me angry enough to dare to make the much-needed move.

Next day, I rang the number I had been given. A cheerful, friendly voice greeted me. Its owner listened to the outline of my story, and suggested that we meet two days later. This meant, of course, going into London, which in turn meant increased costs, but by now I knew it was worth it.

When at last I found myself in the new solicitor's office, I was so nervous that my hands were shaking, and my voice was tight with incipient tears. I had no idea how to effect the transfer correctly, and I was terrified of incurring extra costs when I had so little money. I was met, however, with such breezy kindness that I soon began to relax. He reminded me of Ray. As with him, I sensed a very deep and genuine compassion. I felt I could talk openly, even of my feelings, and trust this man. I began by confiding my fears concerning the transfer. In that one interview, John lifted a great load from me. He showed me how to write the letter, and promised to be as speedy as possible in taking over my affairs. He had children of his own, and I felt that he understood.

It would have been better, no doubt, if I myself had had the strength to act with the grace, tact and diplomacy which would have avoided offence, but I had been driven to my knees, and panic measures such as this were all that I could manage.

Two days later, I received a letter from the Law Society informing me that my legal aid had been rescinded. I could not understand this. My financial circumstances had only changed for the worse since it was granted. No reason for the decision was given. Once again, John told me what to do and where to write. It was several weeks before I heard that the grant had been reinstated, again without reasons being given, and no hint of an apology for the extra anxiety I had been caused. I had, apparently, lost my status as a human being, as well as my husband. The mistake, for such it must have been, had cost me many sleepless nights.

It was during those anxious weeks that I took what was to be a very important step. Sunday after Sunday, I had been leaving the boys at the vicarage for Paul to collect. For many weeks, I simply left them there and hurried straight home, fearful of meeting him. Then, one Sunday, Marilyn asked me to stay on and have a cup of coffee. She promised me I would not see Paul, for he did not come into the house, and I would be safely hidden away in the sitting room. Such was my need — for the afternoons spent by myself without the children were of unspeakable loneliness — that I was ready to risk the hurt of hearing his voice and accepted gratefully.

Sitting in that warm, comfortable sitting room, with the vicarage children and their friends running in and out, I felt like a child myself, a child who had just found some loving arms offering safety and protection. Marilyn, with her sure instinct for perceiving need, would not let me go off by myself straight after coffee. "Do stay," she would say. "We'll be having tea later on, and, besides, I'd like you to meet . . ." and she would name others who, sure enough, dropped in during the course of the afternoon. As often as not, these others would be in some kind of need too, and were as much searching for a haven as I was. Later, a big table would be spread with an assortment of home-made cakes, scones and sandwiches, such as must have taken hours of preparation, and Marilyn would preside over it all with a smile and a laugh, as if having a weekly open house was the most natural thing in the world. Somewhere — she never told me where — she had learned the comfort value of good food and company for the sick at heart. No-one preached at me, as I had been afraid they might do — I was left to form my own conclusions about what was happening. There was no bitterness in this room to sadden me, just this feeling of being protected and accepted for what I was, a feeling I needed then more than anything in the world.

It was this feeling which set me thinking. I had never before encountered Christians like these. All those I had met, especially during my student days, sought to pressurize me into thinking as they did, thereby giving up that freedom of judgement which I valued as my most precious right. The pressure had the effect of kindling a stubborn resistance. Here in this room, my defences went down. This living out of Christ's teachings about loving and caring spoke to me far more eloquently in my profound emotional hunger than any words could have done. Affection, protection, comfort — I craved these as only the emotionally deprived can. Here they were being offered me with unstinted generosity. If this, I reasoned, was Christianity, then for years I had been misjudging it. The time had come, it seemed, to learn more about it, and this time it would be of my own free will.

So it was, that, swallowing years of agnosticism in one gulp, I started to go to church, and the children, who had also felt the warmth of that sitting room, went with me. There, we found a welcome as smiling as the one we had found in the vicarage. I recited the half-forgotten prayers of my childhood with the feeling that we had come at last to a safe anchorage. The boys, attracted by the prospect of wearing bright red cassocks with snowy surplices, asked if they might sing in the choir, and there, too, they were made welcome. We had, I felt, at last found somewhere where we might safely feel we belonged.

An unusually beautiful Victorian church building, of harmonious proportions, enhanced by the rich colours of old wood and brass, stained glass and an abundance of flowers, added to the solace I found there. Peter was a preacher such as I had never heard before. An unassuming, bespectacled man with big blue eyes of extraordinary mildness, he seemed charged with electricity when he stood in the pulpit. When he spoke to his packed, rapt congregation, he did not rant or rave — he simply seemed to speak privately and exclusively to each individual there, as if he knew his or her heart. I sat spell-bound, amazed at his insight, and at the vibrancy of his faith. I drank in every word he uttered.

It was as well that he uttered them, for a storm now broke about my ears which, in its unexpected violence, might have broken me apart if I had had nowhere to turn. It was the middle of March. The phone call came out of the blue. The headmaster of Joanna's school was on the line. He told me that Joanna's behaviour had become so disturbed that he had come to the conclusion that he could not keep her at the school any longer. He was phoning to ask me to take her away as soon as I could.

I was flabbergasted. For over a year there had not been the faintest murmur from the school that all was not as it should be. Believing Joanna to be gradually settling down, I had even begun to relax a little on her account. She had not confided in me — and that hurt. I pressed the headmaster for details. To my relief, she did not appear to have committed any serious offence — the list he recited was one of petty misdemeanours. It seemed to me that most of them could have been dealt with by a teacher with any insight into what was causing them, but no such teacher seemed to have come my daughter's way.

The term ended some ten days later, and I asked the head if he would keep her till then to give me a chance to make some new plans at our end. He agreed, and I put the phone down in a state of shock and rising indignation. It was not so much the decision which angered me — for it was now more than obvious that all along this had been the wrong school for Joanna — as the failure to keep me informed of the difficulties they were having. I would have brought her home much earlier if I had been aware of them, and spared her much unhappiness. I felt sick when I thought of the misery she must have known. Worse still, the suddenness of the decision dropped us headlong into a major crisis.

Joanna was now eleven and a quarter. She would, therefore,

since she would now have to attend local day schools, need not one new school, but two — one for the remaining term of the academic year, and then a senior school for the following September, when she transferred to secondary education. It was not a very promising outlook for a disturbed child. Nor was that all. I would have to sign her up with a new piano teacher, and a new cello teacher, as well as find the money to pay for the lessons which in the last year had been covered by the music scholarship. My knees knocked at the size of the task that now lay ahead. If she was indeed in the state suggested by the headmaster, nobody was going to have an easy time of it. The balance of attention at home, always a delicate matter, would become weighted by her need, and this would be very hard on the boys.

Behind my fear and my anger, however, lay a growing determination: somehow I would nurse Joanna back to emotional health. I would use every means in my power to help her. "Mother her, but don't smother her," advised Ray, and I smiled. I would do my best to get it right.

I set to work. I contacted the boys' school to see if the headmaster could take her for the one term, but regretfully he told me that the top class that year was overlarge, and it would not be fair to the teacher to add an extra child who needed special care. Which set me back, for I did not really know where to try next. Then I thought of the church school, which had the added advantage of being nearer to our home. I flew to see Peter, who was on the point of leaving his house. He turned back at once when he saw my face. He listened to my breathless story, and went off at once to phone through to the headmaster of the little school, which stood beside the church. He came back smiling. "No problem," he told me. I hugged him. The church school, with its family atmosphere, set on the edge of the common, was, I felt, the ideal place for Joanna to recover a little peace of mind. I knew she would be treated with loving care and sensitivity, and she would be so close to home she could almost see our house from her classroom window.

With the summer term settled, I had a slight space in which to consider the choice of a secondary school. I decided in fact to turn my attention first to finding the music teachers, for I felt that they were essential to her wellbeing. Music might well prove to be Joanna's lifeline, though I had little idea then just how right I was to prove. It was, of course, completely the wrong time of the year to be looking for a teacher. All the timetables would be full but this, I knew, could not wait. I phoned Sue, who had taught her piano so well during the years before she went to boarding school. Despite a crowded timetable, and a waiting list, she agreed to have her back at once when I told her the story.

Which left the most important problem of all: I had to find a cello teacher. I had to find exactly the right person, and I was not at all sure that the right person so much as existed. For, in her present troubled state of mind, Joanna needed not just a teacher who was an excellent musician, but also someone who could use the teaching of an instrument as a form of therapy, as a means of healing. I felt certain that it was through her cello that my daughter would eventually come to terms with herself, and find her niche in the world. Hundreds of small impressions had contributed to this certainty, from the way she seemed to come alive when she handled her instrument to the quality of her absorption when she listened to music.

I had not the slightest idea where to find such a teacher, nor even where to begin to look. I did not want to go too far afield, for a long journey would add pressure to Joanna, but all the odds were against finding so unusual a person in our own provincial locality.

What happened shows that one should never allow oneself to be discouraged by odds. It suddenly occurred to me that it might be worth asking around at my bookbinding class, where I had noticed one or two people binding music. Having exhausted my own circle of acquaintance it was a way of extending my range a little. It was a shot fired completely in the dark, for I did not know any of them at all but, as things turned out, it might have been fired by William Tell. At the next class, I accosted the only one of the music binders with whom I had ever exchanged words and put the problem to her. She surprised me, for I was not really expecting any response at all, by hesitating and looking very doubtful before shaking her head. She explained that she did in fact know an excellent teacher — a friend of hers — but she felt that this teacher was already overworked and under too much pressure. She was very apologetic. I thanked her and turned away — but she must have seen the anxiety in my eyes, for a little while later she came over to the bench where I was working, and suggested that I write a letter to the teacher in question, which she would deliver.

I did no more bookbinding that morning. I sat down and put my heart into a long letter, telling the unknown cellist all about the family and Joanna's troubles, and assuring her that I would be looking for psychological help for my daughter to back up her work. I gave the finished letter to my new friend, who was somewhat taken aback at my promptness of action, and went back to my sewing with a sigh. Now I could only wait and hope.

It never fails to amaze me, when I look back on it — the apparently random way in which that vital connection came about. I did not know, when I wrote that letter, that Christa herself had a mentally handicapped sister, as well as three children of her own, so that of all possible teachers she was perhaps the one best equipped to help my unhappy daughter. Not only was she a fine cellist, performing regularly, but she had a special gift for teaching, especially children. Her response to my letter was immediate, and typically warm-hearted: she would take Joanna as a pupil, provided that I could negotiate with her school, so that she could have lessons during the day, for her evening timetable was full to capacity. I agreed at once, for I knew the school would recognize the importance of this to Joanna. I also agreed to take my daughter across to meet her during the Easter holidays, so that they might become acquainted with each other before the first teaching session.

I could not believe my luck. Out of four major problems three were already solved, before even the start of the holidays. I would be able to give Joanna, who had still not been told that she was to leave her boarding school, a working idea of her new pattern of life, so that she would not come home only to feel lost.

It occurred to me that it would be wise to prepare Tom and David for the change that was about to happen, since it was going to affect them deeply. It was highly unlikely that their sister was going to be very easy to live with after what she had been through, and I wanted to enlist their sympathy, and explain to them the need for tolerance. Such a request was, after all, in a family which contained an autistic member, no new thing, and they listened to me gravely. The story of Joanna's unhappiness dismayed them, and they promised to do all they could to help make things easier for her. I was afraid that they were going to have rather a thin time of it — they, too, were going to need all the reassurance I could give.

As if to encourage me, good news now came from John, my new solicitor. A financial agreement had been reached, only a month after first going to see him, and, to cheer me still more, he had appointed a counsel for the divorce hearing, which he thought was likely to be in late June or July. The sum agreed on was by no means princely, but it was enough to live on if I was careful — which was all I wanted.

The picture was beginning to look altogether brighter and more definite. I felt far less hopeless now that I had facts and dates to work on, though I dreaded the divorce hearing. I now needed all my courage for a forthcoming interview with Joanna's headmaster. I had written to him, expressing my indignation at the summary way in which we had been treated, and he had replied by giving me an appointment to see him. Despite the distance, and the traffic, I managed to arrive precisely at the stated time, which helped my morale. It needed all the help it could get, for when I entered his study, it was to find him flanked by half a dozen or so of his staff, whom he had invited along to help him put his case. I was, of course, alone. It felt exactly as if I were being put on trial for Joanna, only there was no counsel for the defence to support me. The whole room seemed hostile. Only the cello teacher appeared embarrassed and averted his eyes.

I had to listen once more to a recital of Joanna's misdeeds or, rather, suspected misdeeds, for not very many of them were proven. Once again it was obvious to me that this was the behaviour of a child beside herself with loneliness and unhappiness. She had made no close friends and could confide in no adult. It had not occurred to anyone that her distress, if they were aware of it, might be alleviated by counselling help. They simply wanted to be rid of the problem.

Probably no boarding school would have been able to help Joanna at that time. Whilst many children may benefit from being removed from an unhappy home atmosphere, this cannot be made into a general rule. It must depend on the individual personality of the child in question, as well as on the nature and causes of the unhappiness in the family. In ours, while great stress had certainly come upon us, the remaining relationships were strong. If we faced our difficulties together, the chances were that we would come through them together, each supporting the other. Sending Joanna away at such a time had caused her acute anxiety and confusion. All her security had been destroyed. It remained to be seen whether we could give it back to her again.

Outnumbered and outargued, I ended the interview, of course, in tears. Gathering up what was left of my dignity, I finally got myself out of the room, to savour the glorious relief of knowing that I need never ever meet any of them again. I wondered how happy the more sensitive ones must have felt about the scene that had just been enacted.

It remained to collect Joanna and her belongings, including the new pet hamster she had lied about in order to buy — appalling crime — and beat a swift retreat for the safety of home. A little way outside the town, I stopped the car, and broke the news to her that she was not going back. Incredulous joy lit up her face. Then, as we drove on, I began to tell her about all the arrangements I had been making. It was a happy drive.

Over the next few weeks, the details of her experience gradually began to emerge. It was deeply painful for me to hear them, as I realized how much emotional suffering she had undergone. It was even more painful for me to acknowledge that she had suffered because I had made a mistake. I tried hard to make her understand that it had been just that — a bad mistake, made when I was under great stress — but I was never sure that she quite accepted this. She needed to be angry with someone, and I was there. I, too, needed to be angry with someone, and, again, I was there.

Delighted to be living at home once more, she settled at once into the top class of the church school, amazed at the relaxed, informal atmosphere. The perceptive teacher mothered her gently. It was a fine spring and early summer that year, and I used to walk across the common to meet her in the afternoons outside the school, with the other mothers. She would come rushing out — no more depressive slouch — her face breaking into a great smile as she saw me, and we would walk companionably home together through the trees. No behaviour problems appeared at all. She adored the teacher, and the school, and quickly made many friends.

At home, things were less happy. Small signs of tension and repressed anger were visible every day, and worried me a good deal, for I was not at all sure how to deal with them. Fortunately, I had to take Simon to keep a routine appointment at the Maudsley Hospital. His psychiatrist, as was his wont, inquired after the other children, and I was able to voice my anxieties about Joanna. He at once offered to see her for me, but, worried as I was, I baulked at the idea of making the long and tiring journey by train and bus on the regular basis I felt Joanna would need. I explained the difficulties to him, whereupon he helpfully suggested that I take her to see a colleague of his at another hospital, closer to the centre of London, and I agreed.

This, in fact, was to be my next big mistake. I forgot how supremely important it had always been for me to feel that I had found the best possible place to which to turn when problems arose with Simon. In the general tiredness which beset me whenever there was not an actual crisis afoot, I allowed myself to be put off by purely practical difficulties from an offer of help I knew to be the best of its kind. My values had slipped. I made an appointment at the other hospital.

In the meantime, Joanna had started lessons with Christa. They were an immediate success. I had been asked to provide a strong exercise book to take to lessons. This was to be Joanna's 'cello book', in which Christa wrote the important points she wanted her pupil to remember usually illustrated by vivid thumb-nail sketches, many of them distinctly comical. Joanna loved this and responded warmly. She began to work hard to please this kind, vivacious new teacher.

We were definitely, I thought, making progress, and this feeling was now reinforced by another of our random strokes of good fortune. I discovered that a new state senior school was to open in our area the following September. New buildings were already under construction on a site only ten minutes from our house, though for its first year the school was to be housed in a disused primary school until they were ready. Since the school, being new, would remain very small for some years to come, it looked as if it might well be the ideal environment for Joanna. My only doubt was whether or not it would prove flexible on the subject of cello lessons — I wanted no more battles — so I wrote to the future headmaster, and put the whole matter of Joanna to him. He suggested that I go to see him and meet the future head of music. He could not suspect how nervous I was at the interview, for the boarding school had left scars on me, too, but I soon relaxed, as he treated me with the utmost kindness, as did the head of music. I left them, filled with hope. The fourth and last problem was, I felt, solved.

Despite the court order, money was still proving a great anxiety. Although a sum was now being paid regularly into my bank account, it was still not the full amount that had been agreed. This made me bitter and angry. I did not know until months later that Paul had been made redundant. We no longer saw each other at all, though he still took the children out regularly. It would have been better if he had told me — unnecessary anger could hardly improve our situation. The cost of Joanna's music lessons was a heavy extra load, which I could only meet by pruning everything else back still further. Treats had become very few and far between. Yet the fanatical determination to keep the music going also kept *me* going. It gave me a purpose for which to work, and a direction in all that I was trying to do for the children.

Somehow, the meeting with the new psychiatrist was out of tune with it all. The whole family went together to see him at his request. We felt tense, vulnerable, and totally unable to communicate, for he was a very silent man. Despite my own continuing concern, he did not appear particularly alarmed by Joanna's recent history. We arranged further appointments — he wanted me to see a social worker once a month — but I returned home feeling that I had not really been given any help at all. Ray gave me more at the end of the phone. I did not feel so defensive with him.

The divorce hearing was now upon me. John had warned me that I would have to appear in court, and I was acutely apprehensive. I did not want to describe my unhappiness, my most private feelings, to strangers. I felt, as I stood in the box before the judge, exactly as if I were on trial — for the second time that year. I remembered standing with Paul before the priest. He had been an old man, too, and I wondered irrelevantly if priests and judges ever met and, if so, what they talked about together.

I had split into three again, to play this strange role. My voice did not belong to me at all. Joy had accompanied me to the court, and so had Lionel, my other neighbour, a First World War veteran who had begged "the honour of escorting me" in such a way that I could not refuse. He, in fact, saved the day, not only by recounting scenes from his Flanders campaigns in gory detail to a fascinated John and our counsel as we waited in the heat to go into court, but also by insisting on taking Joy and me to lunch in Simpsons when the hearing was adjourned until the afternoon.

It was over at last. I was given my decree nisi, and we could leave. My kind friends returned home, and I made my way to Hampstead, to Joan's flat. To add to the unreality of the day, she and her mother were taking me out that evening. We dined in an elegant restaurant in Holland Park, and somehow, inexplicably, the mood became one of celebration as I ordered strawberries for dessert for the second time in a day. Hot sunshine, the extraordinary texture of Counsel's wig, the lined face of the judge, barbed-wire entanglements in Flanders, and the taste of strawberries — those are the vivid memories of that strange experience. I do not remember feeling pain at all. It was as if the whole thing had absolutely nothing to do with me or my real life with the children.

Even in the days that followed I could not believe it had actually happened, or that it had any meaning. I still, even then, clung to the belief that Paul might come back to us, that he might change back into the man I had once known. The last few years were a nightmare interlude, nothing more. I did not want to face reality — the terrifying emptiness at the centre of my life that even the vicar's pulsing words could not reach. I rushed around attending to the multitude of jobs that required my attention, and refused to think more deeply.

Simon was causing some concern. I received a letter from Mrs Elgar telling me that he had had a couple of small fits. She did not think that they were anything to worry about unduly, but suggested that I inform the hospital so as to have him checked over when he next came home. He was now thirteen, and it was more than likely that the onset of puberty was causing some disturbance. He had settled down very well at Somerset Court, and appeared very happy, though he had become considerably more withdrawn in his behaviour at home. He could, of course, tell me nothing about his life in the community, and I depended on the quarterly newsletter that had been started up for all details of his activities. He was growing very fast, and seemed himself very surprised at the sheer length of his arms and legs. I phoned the Maudsley, explained what had happened, and arranged to take him in during his next holiday for a couple of ECGs, just as a check.

The music runs were enough to keep any mind distracted — they were now of a complexity which really called for a computer to keep me heading in the correct direction at the right time. Five miles was the minimum distance from any teacher, and I was fast acquiring an intimate knowledge of all the local short cuts. Christa wanted Joanna to have the enjoyment of playing regularly in an orchestra, and suggested that I take her to one where she knew the conductor, in a town some eight miles away. Unfortunately for me, they met on the same evening as Tom's cello lesson, which was in a different town, and which could not be changed. Somehow I managed to deliver them and collect them up again, but it was like a military operation, particularly as I had to work my way through late shopping night. It all seemed more than justified to me, however, when I saw the delight in Joanna's face at being appointed leader of the cellos, and being promised the chance to play a concerto the following winter.

The previous autumn, I had renewed the booking of our Welsh cottage. Mrs Elgar assured me that Simon could have time off from Somerset Court — since it ran on a four-term year only two of its holidays coincided with those of state schools — so that we could all go together. It meant something of a detour to add to an already long journey but I did not mind that — I simply wanted the holiday to be for everyone. I knew that past memories would not be easy to live with, but we all loved the place, and, most important, I knew my way round there. Finding anywhere else called for far too much effort.

It was a remote, beautiful spot between the mountains and the sea. I was very proud at accomplishing the long drive safely on my own, and this made the arrival a very happy affair. Soon, however, inevitably, loneliness beset me. Although we had become friendly in the past with several people there, no-one seemed to be aware of my desperate need of adult company. The children were invited out for boat trips and excursions, and for this I was grateful, but this left me more solitary than ever with my books and my self-pity. There were, it seemed, no other single people around. All the couples seemed to be long and happily married — as they always do to the newly divorced. I hid my growing depression from the children as best I could, and encouraged them in all their doings, but the days seemed endless. Simon, too, was much more difficult than usual, easily bored, and no longer enjoying the sea as much as he once had.

Hard though it was, I still felt it was an improvement on the previous summer. At least I had given the children what I regarded as a 'proper' holiday. They all looked brown and well, especially Joanna, who never seemed to feel the coldness of the Irish Sea, and whose chief pleasure in life seemed to be diving in and out of the breakers on days when the rest of us stood around shivering on the beach. What is more, Paul had, of his own free will, sent us a contribution to the cost, which comforted my aching feelings, for it seemed to me to show that he still cared a little about us. He had also started to send the full amount stipulated in the court order, so that my financial worries were easing up a little. I could now work out a budget, and even save a little.

The return home was followed almost at once by the start of the new school year. I watched Joanna set off for her third new school in eighteen months with some trepidation. She looked very cheerful, however, especially when she met up with several of her friends from the church school who were also 'going up'. Within days, she was quite at home, and chattering enthusiastically of all that she was doing. In a school of just over a hundred pupils, she soon knew all the teachers, and thrived in the family atmosphere. I collected her one afternoon a week for her cello lesson, and the new routine was soon established. It looked indeed as if the crisis was over. After a couple of visits to the hospital it had been decided that these were no longer really necessary, though I continued to take Tom, as well as to see the social worker myself.

A letter from Paul informed me that he had bought the company car, and was giving it to me. This was the most enormous relief, as he had given me no inkling of his intentions. I could not possibly have afforded to buy a car, and the loss of it would have left me helpless to do anything at all for the children, as public transport was non-existent on the routes I used. I could, however, afford neither to run, maintain nor insure so large a vehicle — the fact that it had been a company car left me without a no-claims bonus. I decided therefore to trade it in, and bought a Ford Escort in its place — an unexciting but reliable workhorse, which could transport cellos and children, and, if I was lucky, not cost me too much in parts, servicing and petrol. Buying a new car for the first time in my life gave a great boost to my morale. The new one was mine, and there were no memories attached to it. I drove it home feeling very grand.

This feeling was totally deflated by the arrival of the decree absolute. My heart contracted as I read it. The knot, it seemed, was finally untied. I could not know then that the dry, legal phraseology could not in itself wipe out a marriage which had produced children. When I looked at mine, all but David looked back at me with their father's eyes. They resembled him closely, especially Simon. In caring for them, I was, in a sense, still caring for part of him — and there was no way I could stop doing that. Loving them tied me to him with bonds stronger and subtler than any religion or legal system could devise. I was to discover this very slowly and painfully in my long struggle to free myself of the past. Just then, however, the decree absolute seemed absolute indeed.

It left me feeling more lost than ever before. All the work of the past year seemed suddenly meaningless. I was now an ex-wife, and it seemed a very negative thing indeed to be. Nothing could comfort me. I hardly knew anyone among my friends who had been through a similar experience. In church, everyone seemed to be solidly married, and I felt that no-one could really understand my feelings. Despite Peter and Marilyn's extraordinary kindness to me, I had begun to feel that the Church of England as an institution does not really care to acknowledge the existence of divorced people, perhaps because they represent a proof that beliefs and ideals can fail, and so constitute a threat. Most of the time I pushed this thought away to the back of my mind, but it kept returning.

Not surprisingly, I became ill. An attack of 'flu felled me. It was a brief but nasty variety and, not being entirely sure what was wrong, and fearing as always the onset of something really incapacitating, I phoned the doctor and asked for a visit. He had encouraged me to do this when I felt I needed him, because he knew how totally the children depended on me. As he put it himself, in me he was treating not one but five people. While I lay aching and sweating in bed, awaiting his arrival, the phone rang. It was one of our old university friends. He sounded nervous. Apprehensively, he asked me if I knew that Paul had got married again at the weekend. He had worried in case I did not, and had felt that someone ought to tell me . . . he hoped that it was not too much of a shock. . . .

I did not hear the rest of what he had to say. Mechanically I answered that I had not known. We chatted for a few minutes, though I had not the least idea what I was saying, and the call ended amicably. I lay there shivering and crying — crying as if there was nothing in me but tears. This, now, was reality. I could not hide from it any more, or escape it. Paul had taken another wife. It was not, therefore, marriage that he was rejecting. It was me.

Into the middle of this emotional earthquake walked the doctor. Only he was not my doctor — the one who had delivered my babies — but a new partner, recently arrived in the practice, and a complete stranger to me. He was annoyed at being called out to a simple case of 'flu, and had no time to listen when I tried to explain the state I was in. He advised me to stay in bed, keep warm, and, as I seemed somewhat depressed, to call at the surgery as soon as I was well enough for some antidepressants. Then he went.

I hit bottom then. No-one cared. I did not want to give my 'flu to anyone else, so I did not like to phone Joy or the vicarage. I tried to reach Ray, only to find that he had been taken seriously ill and was in hospital. The NSPCC officer on duty, hearing the distress in my voice, gave me the name of another worker in another area, who would come to see me if I asked, but I could not ask, not then. I needed a friend, not another stranger. I plunged into black despair.

All the grief and pain came rushing out. There were, in fact, no friends who could help at these dark depths. No ministry could give any comfort. If anything, it was poetry that alone could speak to me. The poets of despair must have saved many lives. Their words came to me like the hands of fellow prisoners in the dark, and, in my need, I held them fast. I copied and recopied the words of the tortured Gerard Manley Hopkins and the sad, mad John Clare, and made them part of me. They understood. I even wrote poetry of my own. There was a relief to be had from the intensity of the struggle with words.

Another member of the family had, unbeknownst to me, been finding an identical outlet for his feelings. It had not been possible, this time, to hide my grief from the children. It was too violent. Paul had not prepared them, either, for his remarriage, so that the task of telling them that he had a new wife fell on me. I tried my hardest to be objective about it, to tell the story from Paul's point of view as well as my own, but there was no disguising my pain. It was better so, for this enabled them to admit their own. For the first time, we all wept together.

A week or so later, tidying Tom's bedroom — a task of some complexity for he was an inveterate collector of odds and ends, including some two thousand burnt matchsticks — I noticed a rough piece of paper with writing on it, lying on the floor. I picked it up, intending to throw it in the bin, and glanced at it casually . . . then I sat down on the bed and read it carefully. Tom, I realized, had been living in darkness every bit as black as mine, and his poem, like my own attempts, revealed his struggle to come to terms with feelings too frighteningly strong for him. Only it seemed to me, as I read and re-read it, that Tom's seven-year-old voice struck a note of infinitely greater purity and poignancy as he sang of his loss than that of any adult — a note which, once heard, is enough to stop the thoughtful in their tracks.

THE RIVER

The river was flowing
And with it shapes glowing,
Rippling, turning,
Jumping and swirling,
Twisting and leaping
From stone to stone.

The sun rose,
The wind there blows,
But the river never stops chanting
Its beautiful song.
The frogs come out,
Ducks start preening,
But the river keeps on flowing.
The graceful swan
With heaven along
Comes gliding down the river.

Her neck is bent, her feathers are white,
And her beak is beautifully carved.
Then boys come along,
And try skimming stones,
And the swan glides away.

Noon is near,
I shed a tear,
For the swan is nowhere to be seen.
Then suddenly, oh joy!
For there among the reeds
There is the swan.

The boys come back,
and feed the swans.
But are they boys?
No, they are girls,
Dressed in white with
Wings on their backs, they
Have come to take the swan away.
I then saw the blood trickling down her wing.
A boy had thrown a stone
And hit the swan by its wing.

The swan lies dead.
I feel as if I am dead, and
The river is not the river.
Bubbling, turning,
Tossing and quivering, it
Goes on leaping from stone to stone.

Twilight is near,
In pubs men drink beer.
And still the river is going.
Suddenly, down
It rushes leaping,
Jumping and swirling. It
Pours down the waterfall
With crashing and booming.

There is a flood,
Within seems like blood
Filling the whole of the world.
A dam is needed, for which
Rich men are pleaded
By the men who live near, but
Still the water keeps leaping
From stone to stone.

The dam is built
Supported by stilts.
The river is quieter
And the flood
Is now mud.
And the river still keeps leaping
From stone to stone.

Once again, it was Tom who was holding out his hand to me in my distress. Whatever happened, I knew I must find the strength to go on, to support and protect a child like this. I could not let him down.

I typed out his poem, and sent a copy to his headmaster, who I knew collected children's work and would treasure this. Tom might never write anything comparable again, but in "The River" I felt that he had spoken for all hurt children.

December approached, and the pace of life quickened as it always did. There were several school functions to be attended. I still found them very difficult occasions as I sat alone among the throngs of married couples. I had expected this to grow easier with the passage of time, but this was far from the case. I longed to have a partner with whom to share my pride in the children, and I felt for them as they watched their more fortunate friends who had both mums and dads. Obsessive pain makes us very egocentric — it never crossed my mind that there might be other unhappy people there, unhappiness hidden behind a smiling mask as mine had once been.

The replacement social worker from the NSPCC came in the end to see me, but, in a well-meant attempt to make me look ahead and plan realistically, only succeeded in depressing me more. Ray had perceived the paralysing nature of my anxiety, and had encouraged me to take life a day at a time, so that each successful day could be, as it were, a stepping stone to the next until the ground underfoot felt firmer, and my sense of security consequently stronger. That way I could cope, and, when a bad day came, it was not too damaging. Telling me to look clearly into the future was to awaken every hobgoblin and werewolf in the neurotic bestiary.

Just before Christmas, the same friend who had told me of Paul's marriage phoned again to tell me this time that Paul and his wife were to emigrate to Canada at the beginning of January. He had apparently secured a very good job. It was another shock, but not, as I came to think about it, an altogether unpleasant one. On consulting my solicitor, I discovered that my court order was still enforceable out there, though I preferred not to dwell on the possibility of ever having to try to force money out of my ex-husband — it was too unpleasant, as well as frightening.

In practical terms, Paul's emigration meant that I was now completely alone to deal with any emergency that might arise — I would not be able to summon him to come to the bedside of a sick child, or to rush to hospital in the event of an accident. But I was able now to tell myself firmly that, in reality, I had already been alone with such possibilities for over two years. I would cope. I was now supported by good friends and a wide church fellowship, and that made all the difference.

The real relief was that henceforth the weekly or fortnightly access visits would become a thing of the past. They had caused so much tension and anxiety, with one child refusing to go and another feeling guilty about going, and everyone trying to hide their real feelings, that they had made my job much harder — it often took as long as two days for the discord aroused by a single visit to die down. If we, and Paul, had received counselling help so as to make these hours with their father a time of real communication and discussion, they might have been very beneficial. As it was, they did little but harm.

Paul's departure would mean for us a long period of uninterrupted peace, which would give us a chance, I felt, to reconstitute ourselves as a family, to lick our wounds, and to support each other. I showed the children where Canada was on the map. There was, after all, a certain status in having a father living in such a distant part of the globe. It looked very far away indeed.

Christmas this year was becoming a distinctly breathless affair. Everyone, it seemed, wanted to help — to the point where the short time spent alone together became distinctly precious. As we put our hearts into the church carol service, I reflected that we had, in fact, good cause to rejoice. We had many friends. Our especial luck was that we lived in a village, where everyone knew everyone else, so that a family such as ours was part of a caring community. The caring showed in hundreds of small ways, from the greengrocer who let me have bargain price apples for the children, to the old age pensioner who buttonholed me on the common, and forced a pound into my reluctant hand, "to buy sweets for the children". Life would have been much bleaker without them. They could not in themselves heal the great central hurt, but they certainly soothed the bruising around it, and helped to give me the strength to go on.

CHAPTER FIVE

Third Year: Rebuilding

The previous two years had been so full of stress and conflict, culminating in Paul's remarriage, that it was hard to believe, with his departure, that we had come to the end of them. It was rather like finding myself on a wide plain after a period of high adventure in the mountains. The plain, too, held its own dangers and challenges, as well as beauties, but, to begin with, I could only see its utter loneliness.

Distance had now made us definitively a single-parent family. Paul was thousands of miles away. Ray was still ill in hospital. There was still absolutely no-one to whom I could pour out my troubles for as long as I needed to. Even now, I did not dare turn too often to my friends, however close — I was afraid of losing their friendship if I wearied them overmuch. I did not even dare to confide much in Marilyn and Peter, for I was forever ashamed of my feelings, and profoundly guilty at what I saw as their un-Christian nature — a guilt which I could well have done without.

We were living, in fact, on two levels. On the surface we were supporting each other, as I had hoped, and receiving support from others which we accepted gratefully, with smiling faces. But underneath this lay depths of anger and misery which we hid from each other and from the rest of the world, just as I hid the Librium bottle, to which I still had regular recourse, in the depths of the medicine cabinet. The children and I were all too afraid of hurting and losing each other to reveal the truth. So we buried it far out of sight, and rebuilt our lives over the top of it.

The London hospital, unfortunately, had done nothing to halt this dangerous process. I saw the social worker once a month, but somehow I always managed to avoid approaching the areas of real pain. She did, however, make one or two practical suggestions that were of real help.

The fact had emerged, for instance, during talks, that the children all lived in perpetual fear that something terrible might happen to me, that I might die. No amount of new-found Christian faith could allay this anxiety — their immediate concern was not whether I went to heaven or not, but what would happen to them here on earth without me. The social worker assured me that if I wanted to give them real comfort, I must make practical arrangements for such an eventuality. I looked at her despairingly. This was one of my own major anxieties, too, and I simply did not know how to find an acceptable solution. Every road accident I passed, every stumble on the stairs, reminded me of the fragility of human life. If such a calamity *had* come about, they would no doubt have gone to live with Paul; but this was not a solution they could accept at the time, when their trust in him had been shattered. I approached my two brothers, to ask them if they would agree to be legal guardians to the children in the event of my demise, but both refused — for reasons which were valid enough, but which could only intensify my feelings of isolation and rejection.

In the end, it was Joan who agreed to accept this responsibility. The social worker had been right, it seemed, for the moment she communicated her acceptance, we all experienced a great feeling of comfort — far greater than I had foreseen. She had known the children since their birth. To her they were already 'family'. We held the same values, and I knew that her loyalty was unshakeable. Once she had been named as my executor, and guardian of the children, in the will which I now duly drew up, our disproportionate anxiety diminished to a far more manageable size.

The London social worker could not give me the in-depth support I needed, however, despite help such as this. Our talks lacked continuity, for there were too many pressures on me to be dealt with in monthly meetings. I often left her office feeling that all the important things had been left unsaid, and would reach home in a state of frustration and irritation. I missed Ray grievously. It seemed as if he, and only he, had the gift of going straight to the core of a problem — where it hurt — and doing something about it. The substitute NSPCC worker called a few more times, but with no greater success. I felt as if I presented to him an image of suburban, middle-class prosperity. The fact that I did not own my house, that I worked the garden myself, and ran the car mainly to transport the children did not seem to come into it. I was, to him, I thought, a parasite. He left me feeling that I had no right to anything at all since I was not earning our keep. Caring properly for my four demanding children, doing the job of two adults, could not, it seemed, be regarded as being of any value — though if those children had gone into care, doing my job would have cost the state a not insignificant sum.

Inland Revenue, I discovered that long January, subscribed to the same ideas. My far-from-princely maintenance payments fell just inside the income tax bracket, and were classed as 'unearned income'. My bile rose when I read the phrase, which smacked of lazy afternoons on a lounger by a swimming pool, languidly accepting my revenues from a band of trembling serfs. If ever any human being earned her income, I reflected sourly, as I shopped, cleaned, gardened, cleaned, cooked, exhorted, soothed and nursed, I did. I longed to invite the man — it had to be a man — responsible for the phrase to take over my job for a month, on his own, naturally. Later, the solicitors found that by rewording the court order, so that, on paper at least, the money was directly payable to the children, I could be spared this reluctant and inequitable contribution to the state.

Income tax forms filled me with panic. It was over fourteen years since I had last completed one, and then, as a single woman, the task had been relatively simple. Now it was far from that, owing to the complications of my small irregular earnings as a free-lance writer on top of maintenance payments of varying amounts. Paul had always employed an accountant, and now, as I stared hopelessly at the form, I began to think it might be sensible for me, too, to find some expert help. Uninformed as I was, I naturally went to the wrong place first. It had seemed sensible to ask my bank manager for advice. I should have foreseen, perhaps, that this would lead me straight to the bank's own large accounting department, impersonal, and exceedingly formal. This was no doubt excellent for large companies, but for a penny-watching, vulnerable individual like myself, it was completely useless, and very expensive. Like solicitors, accountants are not allowed to advertise, so that a year went by, a year of great worry and difficulty, before a friend's recommendation finally took me to the small firm which now deals with my financial details in an entirely personal and kindly manner.

The same lesson had to be learned in the area of car insurance. At first, I blindly paid far too much, and only gradually discovered, from talking to friends, that it behoved me to shop around, and find a broker who would advise me in a friendly way of the most advantageous way of paying this heavy bill.

My experiences with the law, and with the financial experts, have led me to the conclusion that for the newly divorced or bereaved woman the essential ingredients in these professional relationships are expertise and humanity, and that the one is useless without the other. Without friendliness and sympathy from the people to whom she turns for help, she cannot function properly, for she must be able to feel that they understand the nature of her difficulties and anxieties. My whole family would have benefited if at that time I could have avoided the mistakes I made, and turned to an easily accessible pool of advice and information. But no such pool existed.

I was at least fortunate in that my contact with the Department of Health and Social Security during that first period was minimal. Since he was of school age, Simon's fees at his community were paid by the Department of Education and Science, and this was all very straightforward. It was not to be for another couple of years, when he reached the age of sixteen, that I was to experience the rigours of being in any way dependent on the Welfare State. I am, still, deeply grateful to Paul for sparing me those humiliations — which I doubt I would have survived.

As it was, contact was limited to the drawing of the extra child benefit payable to one-parent families, a minute sum which only served to convince me the more firmly that no-one had ever troubled realistically to cost the expenses of clothing and feeding growing children, and, immediately after my decree absolute, of establishing my payments, as a single woman, of National Insurance stamps. I was advised to pay, being self-employed, Class One contributions, which were a significant drain on our income and a constant, niggling worry, for I kept my own card — something I had never had to do when I worked in a large firm. As what writing I did was squeezed in between myriad other tasks, I never really looked upon it as a job, and, though I was sometimes unwell, it never occurred to me to claim sickness benefit, though my high rate of contributions entitled me to it. I felt as though I did not really fit in anywhere.

Although I was very promptly informed that I was now required to pay insurance stamps, no-one troubled to tell me of a benefit to which I was entitled, and which, not knowing of its existence, I had never claimed. This was attendance allowance. I heard about it from a woman in the butcher's queue. I had, it seemed, a right to it for the periods when Simon was at home, for he could not be left alone without danger to himself. Although he had been diagnosed when he was four, and was now nearly fourteen, no-one had ever told me about it, and had it not been for that chance conversation in the queue I would have remained in ignorance, and lost still more money. Families of mentally handicapped children are always under stress, and are not always in a position to make inquiries at the right place, or of the right person. It seems very wrong to me that no trouble is taken to ensure that they are aware of all the help to which they are entitled. I have met many others who have not been aware of the existence of this benefit, and so have never claimed it.

I promptly wrote off to apply for it, and the payments, once established, were a considerable help. Our financial position had now, in fact, begun to steady, though the rate of inflation was worrying, as no provision had been made for it in the court order. Nothing, in fact, really succeeded in reducing this anxiety about money. It arose from the fact that we were completely dependent on Paul, and my trust in him had now vanished. Every month, I put a portion of our income into a Building Society as a cushion against disaster, and also as a reserve into which I might dip when it became necessary to buy a musical instrument. It would have proved a sadly thin cushion had disaster actually occurred, but I was obeying a blind instinct which had no logic about it, trying to ensure the safety of the nest, rather than look to its comfort. To me, it seemed always to be perched precariously on a cliff top from which it might any moment be swept by the least gust of wind.

The constant state of high anxiety in which I lived in those days, focusing first on one problem, now on another, created tensions within my new religious faith — tensions I could not resolve. I clung to it very hard, for it gave me a great deal of comfort. I loved and needed to feel part of a fellowship, one of a group. Going to church had become the highlight of the week-end which, before we started to attend, had been long and empty, the time when the "real", ie two-parent, families kept them-selves to themselves and when we felt the most acutely our sense of loss. Yet I could not find the peace of mind I was promised. Nor could I, committed as I was to the care of my family, give any time to the various activities of the church, for I was already at full stretch. I really needed a great deal of reassurance, but unfortunately I did not know how to ask for it.

Belonging to the tiny minority group of single parents within a far
larger one of two-parent families increased this unconscious
feeling of not really belonging. It was very hard, with my self-
inflated sense of failure, to sit with the children at a Family Service,
for instance, which opened with the words, "What did your
fathers say to you at breakfast time this morning?", and not feel
abnormal, maimed, as we looked first at each other, then round at
all the other children, safely tucked between the protective wings
of both mothers and fathers. It would have taken far more self-
confidence than I had in those convalescent days to feel proud of
the job I was doing, and to rejoice in the fact that the family was still
united and caring.

Again, the affluent nature of the parish was not without its
effect. No-one else that I knew was threatened continuously by
financial catastrophe, or, if this should occur, by the subsequent
loss of their children. Only someone as experienced and perceptive
as Ray could have understood these fears, and known how to calm
the hysteria in them to enable me to live with them, for in a way the
anxieties about money had come to symbolize all my insecurities.

There was, unfortunately, no Ray in our fellowship, so that the
tensions quietly grew beneath the smiling surface of my faith. It
was easier to try to ignore them, and infinitely preferable.

I was still keen to lessen our dependence on Paul by part-time
work if I could only find some. A friend suggested to me one day
that I try for an opening in the field of adult education, since I had
sufficient qualifications and some experience in employment.
This seemed a very good idea, for it would have met some of my
craving for adult company as well as easing our finances a little
more. I wrote off to the local centre, and obtained an interview.
Once again, this proved futile: there were no vacancies at all for the
daytime classes when I was free, although there were several for
the evening ones, when I was not. I knew there was no way I could
meet the weekly evening demands of piano lessons, Tom's cello
lessons, and judo, as well as give an adequately prepared class and
have even a minimal social life. There seemed to be no way of
reconciling the demands of congenial employment with the needs
of my children, especially with those of Simon, whose irregular
holidays cut across all our routines. Every time I tried for a job, I
only felt more trapped than ever.

If I could only have met another partner at this time — however
temporary — the pressures and the sense of isolation might have

felt less acute. Even a small amount of emotional input would have made a great difference, but I had been hurt too badly to allow even the most superficial contact. The rejection had been so crushing, so complete, that I no longer felt like a woman. There was too little money around to make buying clothes a pleasure, or so I told myself, and contrived to feel guilty at even the most modest and utilitarian acquisition in this direction. And even now, over two years after Paul's departure, I could not face up to brusqueness from any male.

Slowly, inevitably, since there was absolutely no outlet for them, these tensions built up. It seems incredible, as I look back, that nothing major went wrong with my health, although a number of minor ailments — constant digestive disorders, headaches, almost unbearable premenstrual tension — indicated the intensity of the strain. Then, at last, a frantic phone call to Ray's office brought the unbelievable good news that not only was he fully recovered, but back at work. Never had any voice sounded as welcome, and as comforting. His down-to-earth, common-sense approach, couched in the now-familiar broad Scots accent, had an instant calming effect. As he disentangled the various problems, and showed me ways of assessing them, life became possible once again — though I had started by telling him that I could not take any more. Realizing how much pressure had accumulated during his illness, he made an appointment to see me after office hours, and we talked at length. He tried to show me how much I perpetuated my own hurt, how constantly I punished myself, but I could not, then, understand what he was telling me. I was only really conscious of the fact that he was there once more, that he did not criticize or judge me, and that he cared. His absence had taught me how vital his support had become to me.

Joanna, unlike me, appeared to have made an excellent recovery, and to be on an even keel once more. At the London hospital, everyone had been satisfied that the disturbance had died down. There were no more signs of anger and inner tension — she seemed secure and happy. At twelve, she seemed a different creature from the unhappy child who had wept so many tears at boarding school. She was bouncy, extrovert, and interested in everything that was going on. She loved her new school, and worked with a will, obtaining excellent marks and getting on well both with the staff and with her fellow pupils.

The family atmosphere suited her completely — she received all
the individual attention she could desire. She was by no means the
only musical pupil. Even in this, the school's first year, the
standard of music was extraordinarily high. Her musical education was, in fact, being greatly enriched.

One completely unexpected thrill, both for her and for me, was
when she and her friends were given the chance to sing at Covent
Garden in the chorus of *La Bohème*. The dedicated and gifted head
of music had over the years nourished a link with the Royal Opera
House, and now his care had borne fruit in this marvellous
opportunity for his new pupils. Joanna found herself, to her
ecstatic delight, singing cheek by jowl with Pavarotti and Kiri Te
Kanawa. It seemed like a fairy tale. Some kind fellow-parents
invited me to see one of the performances from their box, and I felt
as if I were in a magic world. It was one of the most uplifting
experiences I had had in the past few years. I have a passionate love
of opera, and used to go frequently with Paul. The sudden loss of
this great pleasure had been yet another much-felt deprivation —
Covent Garden seats, even the cheapest, were out of my orbit as a
single parent. Now, thanks to Joanna, I was there once more —
though it did not seem quite real, as I watched my child, my own
flesh and blood, skipping round the make-believe world of an
opera set.

After appearing in *La Bohème* the children who, I gathered, had
been very well behaved and disciplined were again in demand,
this time for Verdi's *Otello*. For this, we parents were given
dress rehearsal tickets — a completely new experience for me. I
loved the whole business of going to the opera during the day,
amongst an audience composed of music lovers rather than
businessmen and their clients. The workshop atmosphere fascinated me, and it was pleasant to go in comfortable clothes,
armed with a thermos and sandwiches.

For Joanna, it was a fantastic experience which she absorbed
through every pore. It was as if she were being compensated now
for all she had suffered. At home we soon became blasé about
references to backstage, to famous international singers and conductors, and to her "stage Mum" — a lady of the chorus whose job
it was to keep an eye on the wellbeing of her "child". She partook of
the atmosphere of professional performance of the highest standards, and observed the sheer hard work and the perfectionism of
the great artists. I knew she would never forget it.

Every Tuesday afternoon I drove to the school to pick her up and take her to her cello lesson. By now this weekly lesson with Christa had become the high spot of her week. The cost of petrol precluded too much driving around for me, so I remained during the lesson, as did the other parents of Christa's pupils. I learned a great deal myself from listening to the teaching, and never ever regretted the loss of my afternoons. I was anxious in case Joanna resented my presence at her lesson, but when I asked her, I found that both she and Christa preferred me to stay, so that I could be of help during practice at home, when I might remember crucial points that Joanna had forgotten. In fact, the atmosphere was again very much that of a workshop, for we sat in on the end of the previous lesson, and our comments were requested — tactfully, of course — whilst the incoming parent and pupil would do the same at the end of Joanna's lesson. In this way, everyone became used to playing in front of others, and so learned to relax. Every pupil, I noticed, did his or her best for Christa, who expected no less.

One of the drawbacks to being a 'music parent' is that one is usually treated as a set of wheels for transporting pupils and their instruments, rather than as a human being who can feel heat, cold, or fatigue. By making me feel welcome, and of use, Christa helped me, and through me the family, as well as Joanna. Sue, our piano teacher, did much the same, and it helped me to keep going with the never ending music runs.

Early in the year, Christa encouraged Joanna to audition for a County Junior Music Exhibition. This would have paid for all music lessons as she grew up, so that it was, in fact, an extremely valuable award. Unfortunately for us, it was given on the strength of a single, short performance, with no account taken whatsoever of the child's background, history, or the financial situation of the family. After the audition, Christa, who had acted as accompanist, told me that although Joanna had not played her best, her talent and potential were clearly perceptible. We were both sad when she was not given an award. It would have been of enormous help in many ways, not the least the feeling of being encouraged and supported.

It was not to be, however, and I just had to grit my teeth and go on juggling with the money. It was even harder when I learned that awards had gone to families who could well afford to pay for lessons, and who had never experienced insecurity such as ours.

It is extremely difficult, if you have only a small income, and many responsibilities, to obtain a thorough musical education for a talented child, especially one like Joanna, who could not fit into the life of a music boarding school. It is perhaps one of the most expensive forms of education, for it involves far more than simply paying for lessons. Instruments, especially stringed instruments, are both expensive and fragile, and the strings require constant replacement. They also have to be carefully insured, as accidents are not infrequent, deliberate damage not unknown, and theft a commonplace. Exam fees increase dramatically as the pupil moves up through the grades, and accompanists have to be remunerated in some form or another. Orchestra membership entails another fee, and holiday courses are far from cheap. Sheet music can be more expensive than books — more than once I have been asked to pay ten pounds for a flimsy two-page affair printed by a foreign publisher. In addition to all this, it is important that the child should have as much experience of live music as possible, which means the cost of concert tickets, as well as that of the fare to reach the concert hall. Christa constantly urged me to take Joanna to hear some great cellist — I do not think even she realized how hard it was, when I had the boys to consider as well.

Whilst I agreed wholeheartedly with the head of music at school that music should be available to everyone, I was fast becoming aware that this was an ideal rather than a reality except at a very superficial level. It takes a great deal of energy as well as costing a lot of money. I had neither, but I did have a blind, grim determination that I would meet these needs or die in the attempt. The support of the rest of the family is also required, which meant in our case that we found ourselves being swept along in Joanna's wake to concerts, courses and music festivals. At least in the latter, everyone could find something to do — David managed to come runner-up in the verse-speaking class, his wide grin contrasting cheerfully with the grave faces of rows of prim little girls. Tom tried for the boys' treble singing class, and carried off the first prize. Even I found myself hanging for dear life onto my part in the recorder consort class, toes twitching to the beat, fingers slippery with sweat, vowing that I would never do it again until I found that we had won.

Christa, though disappointed, was not in the least disconcerted by her pupil's failure to obtain the County Exhibition, and promptly set about finding her fresh goals to aim at. She was given a concerto to play with her Friday evening orchestra, and performed it at a special small concert held in a local church. The occasion cheered us all up. She coped beautifully, and received many compliments. There were after all, we felt that evening, others besides ourselves who could see the budding talent that was there.

Christa took advantage of the increase in confidence which arose from playing the concerto, to suggest that Joanna should apply to audition for the National Youth Orchestra in the autumn. We gaped at her, thunderstruck. Young musicians from all over the British Isles compete fiercely for the privilege of a place in this superb orchestra. We were flying high indeed — higher than I had ever visualized. Somewhat disbelievingly, for it did not seem real, I sent off for the application form. I did not see how Joanna could stand the slightest chance. She was still only twelve, and she had, after all, just failed a very simple audition at a local level. Christa, however, kept her own counsel, and I did as I was told.

In all this welter of activity on behalf of Joanna's music, I was beginning to worry about Tom's. It was slowly dawning on me that I had committed a blunder of no mean proportions in giving him the same instrument as his sister. I had duly found a full-size cello for her, and he was now playing the three-quarter size she had vacated, but I could see that even the pleasure of owning his own good instrument was not enough to make him happy. He worked hard and faithfully, but he could not accept the feeling that Joanna outshone him at every step — the age difference he regarded as unimportant. There was no way, with such feelings, that he could develop any confidence in himself as a musician — he was defeated before he set bow to string.

For the time being, however, there was nothing I could do to help matters, as paying for Joanna's cello had made a large hole in my savings, all the larger because I had discovered that cellos, to be kept safe, require expensive hard cases. Tom duly sat for the grade exams, but on the cello, although he acquitted himself honourably, he did not do himself justice. He preferred the piano, and often went off to play it as a refuge from the difficulties of daily life. His results were much better on this instrument, and his success spurred him on. I regretted to see how essential this success was to him. Every small test, every music exam, was for Tom an agonizing life-and-death struggle to prove himself.

Everything less than perfection he counted as failure. No reassurance from me could modify this attitude, though I never gave up trying. He made life even harder and more painful for himself than it actually was, and I would have given a great deal to see him, too, at peace. His school did all it could to help, and at least he was very happy there in the non-competitive atmosphere.

The psychiatrist at the London hospital seemed, if anything, more concerned about Tom than about his sister, and I was to take him there many times for talks, long after she had ceased going. Neither of us liked these visits. We used to meet up again afterwards feeling that nothing had happened to justify the expenditure of time, energy and money. In the end I decided to try to improve matters so as to compensate Tom for missing the best part of a day at his beloved school. The British Museum was not far away, and I took him there. Together, we explored the Saxon treasures, and, favourite place of all, the Clock Room, where we paradoxically lost all sense of time, in our absorption in the intricate mechanisms. Long afterwards, Tom was to tell me how much these expeditions alone with me had meant to him, and I was extremely glad that I had thought to turn those days to profit.

One of the biggest difficulties in a large one-parent family is that the competition for parental attention is far more savage, in that there *is* only the one parent to give it, and the quieter personalities tend to become deprived. I frequently felt as if I were trying to keep a large raft afloat, dashing all the time from side to side to maintain the balance which alone kept it from sinking. There was no way, I knew, that I could do a perfect job. I was female, and could not be male, and there simply was not enough of me to supply all the demand. Since her return from boarding school, after all the trauma she had endured there, I had had perforce to give more attention to Joanna, for her need had been desperate. Tom and David had suffered, as I had foreseen, but there was little I could do about it except to seize every possible occasion to restore the balance a little.

I included Tom in as many concerts as possible. He was a delight to take, as he always sat as if turned to stone, totally rapt in the music. As a daring experiment, I had taken him to a performance of the Verdi *Requiem* in St George's Chapel, Windsor, shortly after his eighth birthday. The music is so dramatic, I thought it might well capture him, despite his tender years, and I felt it might have even more effect when heard amidst superb architecture. It was a huge success. The people in the next seats looked extremely apprehensive when they found they were sitting next to a small boy — but they ended up sharing their score with him when they observed the intensity of his concentration. Like Simon, and like his sister, Tom has perfect pitch, and does not hesitate to comment when a performer's intonation is not secure — no compromise is safe from that critical ear.

It always surprised me that this gentle, sensitive, reserved child should like judo as much as he did. Joanna had joined her brothers at the club on her return home, and for all of them the weekly session was a splendid opportunity physically to let off steam. All three were passionate in their love of the sport, and were fast becoming very proficient, moving steadily up the belts with each successive grading. We frequently attended the big contests organized in the area, so that the children could fight for the club. They put all they had into these fights, and I rejoiced to see the amount of aggression that was released, even from Tom — firmly disciplined by the sport. I enjoyed attending club nights and contests, and quickly learned to organize large supplies of food and drink for the latter, to last all day if necessary. Cheering the children on — albeit sotto voce to avoid disturbing concentration — released my own feelings no little. We all returned home exhausted but deeply satisfied. At judo occasions, I found I suffered far less from the 'single-parent syndrome' — largely, I suspect, because of the friendly support and understanding I received from the instructors, all of whom seemed to think it entirely natural that they should give up all their free time to work with children. Their friendliness made all the difference.

David, who had started when he was only five, was perhaps the most promising of the three, if only because his build was superbly adapted to the sport. As, indeed, it was to all athletic activity. At seven, he was tall for his age, as tall as his older brother, and lithe, with muscles already well developed. I loved to see him running at the school sports day, for he moved with an innate grace that distinguished him from his more stolid Anglo-Saxon fellows. He was passionately interested in all sport — indeed, in all activities which allowed freedom of movement. Perhaps it was because he could obtain more satisfaction in this way that he seemed to give me less cause for concern than the other two — except when he was struggling with the piano, which I knew he did purely to please me. I had still not come up with an answer to this problem. I was sure that if he simply stopped outright, he would be left with a keen sense of failure, with his brother and sister shining brilliantly ahead of him. Sue understood how I felt, and supported him patiently in his struggles to learn notes and time values. He was a very bright little boy, but he had the great handicap, common to all adopted children, of feeling himself different, so that he had to contend with himself, as well as the task in hand. It was very important to him, I felt, that he should find his own area of excellence.

I need not really have worried. David, who had had such a difficult and dangerous birth, and who had been a frail, premature baby, was one of life's survivors. His smile could always recharge my batteries. He showed something of his mettle this year.

Joy knew how much I encouraged the children to try their hand at all sorts of interests, and liked to join in the fun by supplying us with entry forms for a variety of competitions which she thought they might enjoy entering, cutting them out from newspapers and magazines. One day when she came in to join us for a cup of tea, she brought with her details of a painting competition she had seen in the *Observer*. It was from the "Young Observer" section of the newspaper, and was to be on the subject of the Olympic Games. Prizes were to be awarded in age groups. I saw David's eyes light up with interest, so I asked him to tell his teacher at school about it, in the hope that she would allow him to paint a picture in school time, using school facilities, which were, of course, better than ours. A few days later he came home carrying the result with great care, full of pride. I looked at it in admiration. It was remarkably good. He had painted a picture of a pole-vaulter flying through the air upside down — vivid, and as full of life as David was himself. I knew it would go in for the competition with a definite chance, and packed it up, and posted it with the utmost care. Then we all did our best to forget it. It was, after all, a *national* competition.

Well over a month later, when we had given up all hope, a letter arrived for David, with the *Observer* logo on the envelope. It burned a hole in my curiosity all day. At last he came back from school, and we all gathered round while he opened it. He had won first prize in his age group. The amazement and joy in his face were heartwarming. Even better was learning the glorious details of his prize: his painting was to be exhibited with those of the other winners in a London gallery; he was to stay overnight with me in a hotel in central London, with all expenses paid; he was to have his photograph taken shaking hands with the Olympic team; and he was to receive a sumptuous paintbox and a book of free ice-cream vouchers.

The whole family cheered. It was unbelievable. Things like this simply did not happen to us.

David and I spent a magical twenty-four hours. My beloved adopted son, blazing with pride, gave his mum a night out — and no mum could more have prized every minute of it.

We dined together in the hotel restaurant, and paid solemn attention to the selection on the menu, settling on an intriguing confection called a 'meringue nest' for dessert. David's appetite earned him great respect from a smiling waiter.

Our bedroom had its own bathroom with luxury fittings that were a far cry from our ancient bathtub at home, with its scratched enamel, and we each revelled in a huge bath. Best of all, from David's point of view, was the big colour television — we only have black and white — with a remote control switch so that we could watch in bed. As London was at that time sweltering in a ferocious heat wave I abandoned all idea of seeing the sights, and we settled down comfortably to watch a long film. It went on long after his normal bedtime, but on this night at least I knew my place, and we watched it to the bitter end, whereupon he fell at once into a blissful sleep.

Next day the magic continued. At the gallery, his photo was taken with his small brown paw lost in the huge fist of a real British Olympic pole-vaulter. Then he demolished a splendid buffet lunch, and received the beautiful mahogany paintbox that was his prize, along with the ice-cream vouchers with which he could placate the rest of the family, who had had to stay overnight with school friends.

I was so happy, I could hardly speak. I was happy at the effect of this success on him, for I knew he would always remember it—but what made me happiest of all was the love in his face as he watched me enjoy myself. That day I saw vividly that the caring and loving and giving in our family was by no means confined to me alone. I could see, plainly, that it was reciprocal, and the realization did more to strengthen me than any gift I had ever received.

We were light-headed with fatigue by the time we returned home, to face a barrage of questions from Joanna and Tom, who were very envious. It was all to prove, as I had foreseen, an unforgettable experience, one that helped David to forge his own, special, private bond with me. Years after the event, he still asks me from time to time, with a significant smile, "Do you remember the meringue nest?" As if I could forget. . . .

The free ice-cream vouchers gave a distinct fillip to our summer holiday, which we again spent at the cottage in Wales, for lack, really, of a better idea. Once again, it was a success for the three younger children, but a long, lonely fortnight for me. I was growing concerned again about Simon, who this year seemed to have retreated completely into his shell. I had duly taken him to the Maudsley for checks. They had given him two ECGs, one when he was awake and one when he was asleep (which involved having a special car to bring him home, for it had taken a very strong sedative to send him to sleep, and we could not rouse him). Nothing was found to indicate that fits might become a frequent problem, for which I was devoutly grateful. In fact, he has never had another. No doubt the onset of puberty was responsible for those he had had, as well as for his present changed behaviour.

It was making his holidays at home very difficult. Since they did not coincide with the school ones, he had willy nilly to be included in our high-powered routine of music runs and judo, and he had to sit through many a lesson, bored to extinction. He could not amuse himself, and no doubt felt very disorientated without the structured environment of Somerset Court. Our old rapport seemed to have gone, which made me feel guilty and miserable. Nor did he seem to have enjoyed the holiday very much. The heat wave, which this summer had left all other holidaymakers tanned and relaxed, broke the moment we set foot in Wales, and we had to make do with rain, wind, and an all-pervading chill. Simon clearly loathed swimming in these conditions, and there was little else to do but drag him reluctantly out on long, wet walks.

On our return, I poured out my woes once more to the patient Ray, for depression was thickening again like the Pembrokeshire sea mists, obscuring the sun. With Machiavellian cunning, he suggested by way of solution that I write a book about Simon and our life with him. I hesitated. I did not think that I could write anything that anyone would want to read — and also I was afraid of hurting the children. Unmoved, Ray suggested that I put the idea to them. He must have known perfectly well how they would react. Despite their encouragement, however, I still hung back. If I was to write about feelings as deep as mine were about Simon, it would be very hard to face a rejection slip. I needed interest from professional quarters.

Then, out of the blue, my agent, who knew nothing of these conversations, suggested that I might consider drawing all the articles about Simon that I had written in past years into a book — she felt sure it could be one of some value. This was all I needed, for I had a great respect for her professional opinion. As soon as everyone had gone back to school, I settled down to work.

Depression and loneliness vanished. Gone was the lethargy, the need to sleep in the afternoon, the heaviness in my chest when I awoke in the mornings. I had a job to do in which I could feel fully myself — and doing it did not in any way hurt the family. I felt needed, not only as a mother, but as a human being. After only a short time, I found that I was writing compulsively — the words were pouring out as I plumbed depths of feeling I had not known existed. I grew adept at fitting my writing into the gaps between our commitments. Although I have a desk upstairs in my room, I inevitably ended up at the kitchen table, where I did not feel cut off from the children.

I realized that this, and only this, was what I had been wanting to do all along. I had passionately wanted to speak out, not just on behalf of Simon, but of all those who were handicapped like him, to a world which was, in my experience, all too ready to sweep them under the carpet, and pretend that they did not exist. I had to find the right words, and I loved every moment of the search for them.

It was the busiest and by far the most positive autumn we had known since Paul's going. At the beginning of December, Joanna went for her first audition for the National Youth Orchestra. We both felt very intimidated as we entered the house in Hampstead where the auditions were held that year. Everyone else looked much older than my daughter, and more experienced, and the wait for her turn was a nerve-racking one. Christa had found a very kind and skilled accompanist for her pupil, however, and she did much to ward off the butterflies.

Only a week later, poor Joanna had to sit her Grade Seven exam. The date had clashed with a Covent Garden dress rehearsal — she was in *La Bohème* again — and I had had to swing all the weight of the Royal Opera House against the juggernaut of the Associated Board of Music's computer in order to have it changed. By the time I had finished, they must have thought she was a budding opera star. Even then, we had to struggle down country lanes uncleared after a recent heavy fall of snow in order to reach the examination centre, with the car waltzing from side to side amid fervent prayers that nothing was coming in the opposite direction. We had the same accompanist as at the NYO audition, and she told me when she came out that Joanna had played quite beautifully, which made it all feel worth it, even when we found we had to push the car out of the snowdrift in which it was now stuck.

She did not succeed in getting into the NYO, but the letter which came told her that her playing had shown promise, and suggested that she audition again the following year. Although she was disappointed, this was encouragement indeed, and she vowed to work extra hard. The disappointment, in any case, was forgotten when the result of her exam came through, and she found that she had won the highest distinction she had ever been given. She was radiant, and could not wait to see and thank Christa, who had prepared her so immaculately. What with this, and *La Bohème*, Joanna spent her Christmas holidays on a cloud floating high above the rest of us.

It was a happy time for all of us, with good friends making sure once again that we should not be too much alone. Even New Year's Eve was different. There was no chance to pour purple passages into my diary — I had enough writing to do without that, and, in any case, Marilyn and Peter took us all off to London with their family to see a Christmas play. The whole party saw in the New Year together in the vicarage, listening as the big clock struck midnight on the church tower nearby. Coming from this quarter, the sound lost its impersonality, and became somehow wholly protective — at any rate, for the first time in years, I suddenly felt safe.

CHAPTER SIX

Fourth Year: Moving On

We were only a week or so into January when the kind of mishap I had long dreaded befell me. Joan had come to spend the day with us. During the short winter afternoon we had gone for a brisk walk which, unfortunately for me, had involved climbing several stiles.

That evening, as we sat quietly chatting, I became aware of a small pain at the back of my neck. It gradually increased in severity until I was in a great deal of discomfort, with subsidiary pains shooting down my arms to my fingertips. I realized that somehow, during the activities of the afternoon, I had contrived to worsen an old injury sustained some fifteen years before when Simon was a heavy baby — so heavy that he was a great strain to carry, especially when doubly encumbered by a very heavy pushchair. The pain then had been acute for a few days, and then had gradually died away to little more than the occasional twinges. Busy as I was with the baby, I had never bothered to do anything about it. Now it had flared up with a vengeance.

Quite by chance, it happened that only a few weeks before a friend had been telling me about an osteopath in a nearby village, who had succeeded in relieving her bad headaches. Since I also suffered from them, I had been interested enough to take down his name and phone number. Now I decided to consult him. This was not because I did not trust my own doctor, but because I was afraid that the latter would order bed rest, or wearing a surgical collar, so that I would not be able to keep the children's activities going. I preferred to see if manipulation might solve the problem more quickly.

The osteopath examined my spine, and told me that several of the vertebrae of my neck were out of place, as was one in my lower back. I had forgotten all about the time when I had hurt that, decorating a room a few months after Tom's birth. The pain then had been bad enough to drive me to the doctor, but a few weeks of rest and heat treatment had quieted it completely, and life had gone on as usual. The osteopath decided that it would be prudent now to straighten it — and so my troubles began. His manipulation brought instant, sweet relief to my neck — and new, devastating pain to the lower back. I went back several times for further treatment. A nerve, it seemed, had been trapped. In the end, he succeeded in freeing it, and the pain went, but I was forbidden to lift heavy weights, dig the garden, or go in for any activity which might strain my now fragile back.

This was a harsh sentence for someone in my position. I could afford help neither in the house nor in the garden — except for the occasional hour from one of Joy's acquaintances when Nature threatened to overrun us altogether. Caring for flowers and vegetables had brought me a great deal of quiet comfort in the last few years, as had long walks in the countryside around our home. I was in no position to argue, however — I was far too afraid of the pain which, it seemed, could start up again at the slightest unguarded movement. The osteopath always managed to relieve it, but the relief rarely lasted longer than a month or two. The cost of the treatment was an additional worry, for repeated visits became a heavy drain on our income. Still, however, I refused to go back to conventional medicine. Many of my friends and acquaintances had had persistent back trouble, and went to the doctor only to end up having major operations. I was terrified of this, for I knew that during the period in hospital and the ensuing convalescence I could not care for the family. If I could possibly stave off such an eventuality by staying with alternative medicine, I was prepared to go on trying.

It was not easy. The back pain made me feel older than my years, and desperately tired. Standing in queues became an ordeal to be avoided. Upholstery suddenly assumed an importance in my life it had never known before — unseen menace lurked in the springs of soft settees and the springy plastic backs of the school chairs alike. A board had to be slipped under my mattress, and another on the driving seat of the car. I felt like a centenarian.

Since back pain involves no visible injury, the sufferer often feels suspected of malingering. I felt deeply guilty when I could not so much as help my mother to her feet when I visited her, or stood back and watched when others were shifting chairs and tables before a meeting. A cousin of mine recently said that she was glad in the end to have been operated on, if only because her disability now bore, as it were, an official stamp, and she could at last enjoy a little sympathy and understanding.

This sense of guilt now tacked itself on nicely to all the rest I carried on board, as if to load the ship down as far as it would go. My morale began to slip again. The long hours spent working on the book did not help the pain, so that I felt threatened in this, my very favourite occupation. I longed once more for someone to take just a little of the load off me, to allow me to rest up occasionally, to understand. Living in isolation is never easy, but living in isolation when in pain is one of the hardest experiences to come to terms with.

Yet this difficult period of back trouble was responsible for some very definite improvements in our way of life. It forced me, in a way that nothing else had been able to do, to look critically at our daily routine, to reassess it, and to take some positive practical steps which, as always, did a great deal to allay my anxiety over falling ill.

There was no way, now, that I could continue to perform alone all the hundreds of tasks involved in running the household. The only possible solution was to share them out among the five of us. Even Simon when he was at home was very capable of vacuuming the stairs and landing, for instance, even if the vacuum cleaner did become overheated before the state of the carpet could satisfy his meticulous mind. The younger boys, at nine and eight respectively, were well able to help in the garden. We grassed over the flowerbeds I could no longer dig, and, eventually, most of my beloved vegetable patch. Two small boys at the end of a garden roller, working with a will, can manage a great deal — though our lawns to this day remain picturesquely undulating. When they realized how useful the extra space was going to prove for cricket and badminton, they had all the incentive they could need. Joanna hated gardening, but took her turn behind the mower with everyone else.

The important step forward was not so much that the children performed these chores, but that they did so of their own volition after we had thoroughly discussed the matter in family conclave. They reacted enthusiastically to the adoption of this procedure, which now became standard whenever the family faced any crisis or difficulty. The result was that we began to pull together far more as a group than we had in the past, with each individual becoming increasingly aware of both the qualities and the needs of the others. It certainly helped in the present predicament. The old house became far less arduous to run, with willing hands taking the heavy lifting off me, and each child taking over the cleaning and maintenance of his or her own room.

Despite this new, adult attitude on their part, I knew I must remember that they were children, and had a right to childhood. I kept the chores to the basic minimum, and turned a blind eye to imperfections. If the mess in a bedroom became too great for someone to cope with, I carried out the necessary blitz, and wiped the sheet ready for a fresh start. Tom, with his collections of toilet roll centres, old cornflake packets, yogurt pots and shoe boxes, not to mention the burnt matchsticks, was the one who needed rescuing most frequently, and I still smile inwardly at the memory of his look of relief when he found that order had been restored.

Yet another step forward this winter was in the area of my own leisure. I had already discovered that the occasional short break was not just a luxury, but a vital necessity — the problem was in affording them. A friend who played in the consort with me suggested that we go to a weekend recorder-playing course at a centre of adult education. The children went to stay with school friends, and Marion and I set off together. It was held in a rambling old house with which I immediately fell in love, and I enjoyed every moment of the friendly atmosphere, the good food and the congenial company. My eyes were suddenly opened to the possibilities of these courses as a solution to the loneliness I felt during my breaks from the children. Examining the notice board, I found there were courses to suit every taste and interest, at extremely reasonable prices. I returned home determined to make use of what was being offered.

Recorder playing had by now become firmly established as my principal leisure interest. It was my own small niche in our world of music, and prevented me from feeling buried beneath cellos and pianos. Bookbinding had died a natural death as I discovered my own limitations when it came to dealing with small, precise measurements, and my total ham-fistedness when handling sheets of gluey material which week after week wrapped themselves round me, the workbench, the tools — everything except the cardboard book covers they were destined to adorn. It had all been something of a blind alley, but it had helped me to survive when things were at their most difficult, and it had, of course, led me to Christa.

The great advantage of belonging to the recorder consort was that, with the single exception of myself, it was composed entirely of teachers. Since these are essentially people dedicated to the wellbeing of children, they never allowed mine to feel totally excluded from our activities. Far from it — Joanna, Tom and David often accompanied us to concerts or festivals, and occasionally played with us. In this group I felt supported, especially in my efforts to keep the music going, and this meant a great deal to me.

We were often invited to play in schools, to demonstrate to the pupils how beautiful the different recorders could sound when played in harmony together. I loved these occasions, despite the inevitable nerves, as they gave me an exceptional chance to see many different types of state school from the inside, and to appreciate the work of my friends and their colleagues in using music to enrich the lives of the children, some of whom came from backgrounds of a deprivation undreamed of by my own family. The atmosphere at some of the concerts was electric. I shall never forget the steel band which performed at one school in Colindale with a skill and brio which put the nervous efforts of us mere adults to shame. The audience clapped, stamped and shouted itself frantic, and would not allow the young musicians to leave the stage. Joanna had gone with us to that concert, and her face was a study — she had never experienced such an audience reaction before. We left at the end hot and sweaty — and completely high.

We played our very best when we performed to children. My teacher friends believed that it was incumbent upon them to set the highest standards, a belief which I shared. Music is a marvellous medium for teaching many things besides the mere playing of notes, as I saw at those school concerts where children of all colours and creeds performed happily together — in harmony. "I'm not in the least musical," said one little girl to me as she climbed into our car in the early days of school runs. I smiled, and said nothing. A Beethoven slow movement was playing on the car radio, and by the time we reached the school I heard her humming the melody. There is music in everyone, waiting to be coaxed into growth.

I was having a problem coaxing it in David, nonetheless. I was certain now that we needed to find a different instrument for him, but I knew I must be very careful. Another mistake might put him off for ever. I was very puzzled to know how best to proceed.

It was Christa who came up with the answer. Her husband, Jim, was a professional flautist working in a well-known orchestra. He also took some pupils. She had met David, and thought that the flute might well be the right instrument to suit his bubbly personality. Better still, a pupil–teacher relationship with Jim, a big, gentle, patient man, might supply David with at least some of the male attention he so sorely lacked at home. I thought it an excellent idea — everything about the instrument seemed right for him.

So he began lessons with Jim on a borrowed flute — I had to make sure it was all going to gel before beginning the search for his own instrument. It was obvious, however, after the first few lessons, that this was going to be a great success. Pupil and teacher took to each other at once, and I rejoiced to see David receiving some of the adult male attention he needed. The only real snag was Jim's heavily charged, and somewhat irregular, rehearsal time-table, which clashed with my own by no means empty one too often for me to feel entirely comfortable, as regularity of lessons is vital if a child is to make progress. Both Jim and I did our best, but it was by no means easy for me when the lesson had to be at a different time each week.

The sound of the flute was now added to that of two cellos, the piano and the recorder in our house. It was just as well, I reflected, when everyone was practising simultaneously, that we lived in an old house with thick walls and a leafy garden — or we would have been receiving complaints from our neighbours. We could never have managed in a terrace house, or even on a housing estate, without considerable negotiations over practice hours, and a consequent sense of restriction. Once practice starts to become intensive, as it inevitably must with serious musicians, expensive soundproofing is the only alternative to lots of space. As I could not afford the former, I was more than lucky to have the latter. Even so, there were times when the noise became too much even for me, and I would take refuge at the far end of the garden until they had finished, though more frequently I was to be found going from one room to another to listen, comment and encourage. Musical though they were, all three tended to become dis-heartened when they could not get their fingers round a difficult passage, and needed all the support I could give — especially, at this time, Tom.

One day I received a message from the headmaster of his school, asking me if I would go along to have a chat with him about Tom. The memory of the interview with the headmaster at Joanna's boarding school still throbbed, and I presented myself at his study door in a state of acute nervousness, wondering what, exactly, could be going wrong now, just when everything seemed at last to be going better. He greeted me, however, with such a friendly smile that I was at once reassured, only to be very shaken when he told me why he had asked me to come.

It seemed that he had come to the conclusion that Tom was an exceptionally intelligent and artistic child, and he wanted to suggest to me that I allow him to sit for scholarships to major public schools — scholarships which were available to bright children in state junior schools in the Home Counties — rather than leave him to continue in the state system into comprehensive school, where he did not think he would flourish.

The comic side of the situation struck me at once. It seemed at the least incongruous for a state school headmaster to be suggesting to me, a graduate product of the state system and an advocate, in theory at least, of comprehensive education, that I send my son to a private, fee-paying school just because he was bright. It seemed even funnier when I thought how much happier Tom had been ever since leaving the independent system.

It was my sense of humour, in fact, which obscured what the headmaster was really trying to tell me. He was a very experienced and dedicated teacher, whereas my own experience, though wider than average, was still limited. In fact I knew nothing whatsoever about the reality of comprehensive schools. I had been educated in a small grammar school, with an upper sixth form which consisted, in my year, of exactly seven girls, so that we received what amounted to private tutoring. Tom's present school, with its caring, lively, family atmosphere, was a far cry from the big, impersonal, conveyor belt of the full-size comprehensive. His hypersensitivity and emotional vulnerability had been noticed by the headmaster, who had known how to shelter them, and he was trying to ensure that Tom would remain in an environment suited to his individual needs. I, with my good experience of state schooling and bad one of an independent boarding school, was hardly able to listen objectively.

Worse, the decision which I was now being asked to make was fast reducing me to panic as I realized the importance of its implications. It affected all Tom's future life. The dreaded sense of isolation descended on me again. I yearned for someone who both cared and understood with whom to discuss it — with whom, too, I could share responsibility. By now, Paul had become far too remote a figure to consult. He no longer really knew Tom as he was in everyday life.

I went home to try and work it out. In the end I decided that the wisest course would be to put the matter to three or four people whom I respected, and to weigh up their views, and also to consult Tom himself. If he were to win a scholarship, it would mean that he would have to board at a prep school for the next few years, and after what had happened to Joanna, I would never again send a child away from home until I was reasonably certain of his feelings on the matter.

The answers from my friends were predictable: those who had been to public school thought it would do Tom good to be sent away whatever his views on the matter, while those who had attended day schools were in favour of keeping him at home. Fortunately for my sanity, Tom himself was quite definite. On no account, he told me, after listening to my outline of the matter, did he want to leave home. Although he had been very young when Joanna had been sent to boarding school, he had been painfully aware of her misery, and now had no wish to share the same fate.

There was no way I could ignore this, the more so as my own feelings had remained mixed. If Tom felt so strongly, there was no way I could risk all the security I had so laboriously built up for him. An unhappy, disturbed child cannot benefit from even the best education. Tom was making it plain that right now he needed to be at home where he could see his family every day. He needed plenty of friends and activities to reinforce his sense of belonging, give him self-confidence, and help to heal the wound he had suffered. Only when he felt himself strong enough would he be able to contemplate flight from the nest, and that time, he was indicating, had not yet come. If our lives had not been damaged by divorce, he might already have had the strength — bitterness flooded me at the thought, for it seemed as if there was no end to the price we had to pay. But that lay in the realm of conjecture, and served only to twist the knife artistically in my own wound.

There was really, therefore, no option, and the decision to leave things as they were and to send him on in due course to

Joanna's school had to be the right one in the circumstances. The combination of a caring, stable home, albeit a single-parent one, a local school, a supportive church community and a rich musical life was, for the present at least, a winning one. It would be dangerous to upset it. I could not gamble it against a nebulous future.

The fact that I could not, even now, plan ahead was becoming ever more painfully difficult to accept, despite Ray's encouragement. The structure of our one-parent family life, complex though it was, and firmer though it now seemed, was not an erect, independent one. It hung suspended, swaying on fragile threads over which I had almost no control, from the shadowy, departed figure of a one-time husband and father. There was no way of changing that state of suspension. The price of independence was the sacrifice of all that gave stability to the structure — my constant care.

By now I had reached the last stages of my book about Simon, which is the stage I enjoy most. Only when I was writing could I feel completely happy and escape from all problems and pressures, more, even, than during my short, occasional breaks away from home, for writing brought its own sense of fulfilment, which no holiday could do.

It was spring when I finally completed it. By the time I had corrected the last page I was in a curious, uneasy state. I had been deeply moved when writing it, and it took all my courage to pack it up and send it to my agent. It was not, in fact, unlike sending a child away. If it was rejected — and I had had my share of rejection slips in the past — it was going to hurt very badly.

Once it was out of my hands I worked very hard at putting Ray's advice into practice, trying not to look ahead, living life a day at a time, immersing myself in the ceaseless round of judo sessions, music festivals and Covent Garden rehearsals (*Otello* this time). But I could hardly bear to pick up the post in the mornings.

It was, in fact, a phone call which brought me the news that the book had been accepted by the first publisher to whom it had been sent, and it took me completely by surprise. It was to be published the following winter.

When I put the receiver down I sat there quite unable to move. The news meant more to me just then than any other achievement, including my degree, for it had come at a time when I was so convinced of my failure in every area of life that I could hardly believe that someone should be enthusiastic enough about my work to want to publish it. And if, when it was published, my book could help, even a little, the plight of the autistic and their families, I could feel that I was not entirely useless.

It was as if there had just been a burst of fireworks in the night sky. I could not believe it — nor could I wait to tell the children. Their reaction was heart-warming. They treated it as a family success. Their delight made me see what a very close group we had become. At times like this we did not feel like a broken family at all.

The only one who could not share the general euphoria was the subject of the book himself. In case they should incur teasing at school, or be irritated in any way by publicity, I had taken the precaution of changing the children's names in the story, and this effectively removed the whole operation beyond the limits of Simon's comprehension. In the event, it was the only aspect of publishing the book at which the children carped, but once having decided on the change, I was saddled with it. I had discussed the matter of publicity with both Ray and Mrs Elgar, and both had reassured me that it would not hurt the family — but still I was bothered. Even though my love for Simon had been the mainspring of the work, I had not the confidence to believe that it would not in some way harm him or the others.

Although everything soon quietened down again, and normal life took over once more, the knowledge of the book's acceptance was to prove an inner reserve of energy and new strength on which I could draw in the next few months whenever difficulties arose. Not the least of these, however, was a strong sense of loss. My job was gone. I had absolutely no idea what I could write next. I only knew that I did not want to stop. As the weeks went by, and no ideas came, this sense of loss grew.

It was compounded by the deaths of two good friends — within weeks of each other. My neighbour, the old First World War veteran, who had given me a military escort to the divorce court, and who had often cheered the children up with small presents and tales of his far-off schooldays, died suddenly one night. So, too, after a small stroke, did Joan's mother, who had also taken me under her wing on that day, and whose kindness had been constant. These were losses which we all felt deeply. We mourned our old soldier friend who had been part of our daily life, and whose love of physical fitness, which had him weight-lifting when he was well into his eighties, had galvanized us from our lazy habits. The sudden disappearance of Joan's mother from the extended family altered its entire structure, for she had been the senior member, and was both loved and respected. Everything, I felt, was changing.

Not all the alterations were for the worse, however. One positive outcome was that Joan now decided to sell her London flat and buy a house in our area, so that I hoped to be able to see her more easily. Her father, an artist and writer, had died a few years before so that the loss of her mother altered her life too, considerably. I did my best to support her, but it was by no means easy to break away from my own demanding family. The two deaths left us feeling that nothing was quite real, much less safe.

The arrival of a letter from Canada announcing that Paul was coming over on business in July, and asking if he might take the children away on holiday for a week did nothing to lessen these feelings. The sense of solidarity which had seemed so strong when the good news about the book arrived appeared instantly to dissolve. Tensions appeared out of the blue. Joanna, who was booked to go with her form at school to a PGL adventure camp for the week in question, flatly refused to change her plans. The most she would consent to was a day's outing with her father after her return. Since Simon, too, would be at Somerset Court at the time, he would, perforce, have to share the excursion with her if he were to see his father — which would effectively preclude any possibility of real communication between Paul and Joanna. Tom and David, on the other hand, were only too delighted at the idea of an extra week's holiday from school — but in the face of Joanna's reluctance to go they felt guilty. We all felt guilty. With the exception of Simon, each one of us was ashamed of our feelings.

Mine were exceedingly painful. I had been completely alone with the children for so long that I was no longer used to the disruptions of access, and resented them bitterly. I felt that this stranger that Paul had become had no right to come and disturb the children I worked so hard to care for. Whilst I could hardly deny the existence of paternity, I argued about the reality of paternal rights, which I felt could not be bought with money or presents, but only came into being through the exercise of constant, loving, protective care. It was lucky that I had Ray to support me — it was a relief to pour it all out to someone who did not criticize, and who, on the whole, agreed with me. It also helped me to hide some, though not all, of my pain from the children. They cared about me too deeply to be unaware of it.

After their departure with Paul, I felt sick at heart. I had been invited to lunch at the vicarage — they had all gone off during a Sunday morning service — which helped, as I felt the strength of Marilyn and Peter's loving support. The trouble was that I did not want to behave in a civilized manner at all — I wanted to bang my head against the nearest wall and scream. Sitting over a delicious lunch, surrounded by a happy united, family, I struggled with the pain, and the anger, and shoved them back with all my strength, speaking brightly of the small holiday I was about to take in the New Forest during the family's absence. I tried my hardest to be as generous and forgiving as my hosts, but I knew I was different from them. I felt black and poisonous inside. There was no peace in my heart — nor had there ever been.

I worked very hard during the next few days at enjoying myself on my own in a small hotel in the New Forest. I was lucky, for an exceptionally friendly assortment of people was staying there, to the point where we ended up forsaking our separate tables in the dining room and gathering in one big group, which was very pleasant for me. During the days I walked in the Forest, and found much pleasure in visiting several of the old village churches. Those on duty to protect them from vandals were always ready to chat and tell me a little of their history. I made a sentimental visit to Lyndhurst, where I had been for a short time at school during the war, and was enchanted to find the grave of Lewis Carroll's 'Alice' there, behind the church. It was as if I were playing hide-and-seek with loneliness, only it was no game.

Despite all my efforts, the week seemed very long. At last, however, we were all reunited once more, and Paul vanished back to Canada. We eyed each other warily for a while, and the boys did not quite know how to relate the stories of their adventures. Joanna, too, remained very silent about her day's excursion. It took several weeks for us to settle down to being a family once more, and to get on with our lives together.

It was the journey to Wales at the end of August which completed the process. I had still not found the energy to change the old holiday patterns, though in view of the precarious state of my back, I viewed the long drive with considerable misgiving. The extra loop we had to make in order to pick up Simon did not help, for it meant that we could not help becoming entangled in the dense holiday traffic. Badly though I wanted to include him, doing so seemed to become a little more difficult with each year that passed.

Joan was to join us for the second week, and I greatly looked forward to her coming for I knew it would solve the problem of my loneliness, so that we might all enjoy the holiday.

It seemed, however, as if Wales was trying to tell me something, and was now resorting to her clearest vocabulary. It rained for the entire fortnight. Cold, blustery winds whipped up the Irish Sea and soaked us every time we set foot out of doors. The cottage reeked of damp clothes. The sun came out for a few hours when Joan arrived only to disappear again, for good. The children were happy enough, running round the dripping countryside, but for Joan, Simon and me the days were long. My back, resenting strange upholstery, became increasingly painful, and I was growing worried about the long drive home. Only the last evening saved it all from being a total disaster, at least in my eyes — for it left me with a memory I was to smile over for years to come.

As a special end-of-holiday treat I had booked tickets for a performance of Mozart's *Requiem* in St David's Cathedral. The rain had been coming down in sheets all day, and, as I did not know the way, I was becoming nervous about this drive, too. The car was parked in the farmyard which lay at the bottom of a very steep hill, driving up which when cold must have shortened the life of many an engine. It was pitch dark and still pouring with rain when we set off. The Escort was full of excited children and wet, tetchy adults — Jessie, the farmer's wife, was with us as well. The windows were steamed up, and I could not see a thing, which led to my backing the car into the stream which bordered the yard at one side. The farmer helped me, greatly mortified, out again, and eventually we made the main road — rather late.

Meanwhile, in St Davids, they were discovering that they had oversold their tickets. A flurry of excited Welsh greeted our arrival just before the beginning of the concert. Our tickets proved our right to seats — but by now there were only complimentary places left. So, soaked and dishevelled, our boots caked with farmyard mud, for there had been no time to change,

we were solemnly led to the very front row. It was only as I began
to recover my breath that I became aware that we were sitting
amongst all the local dignitaries, in their silks and mink, which
they were carefully twitching aside to avoid contact with us.

Simon, however, was completely at his ease, blind as always to
incongruities. He sat beautifully still at concerts, and here, being
in the front row, he could happily stretch his legs. They were
very long legs, and tonight they were encased in size ten
Wellingtons, badly stained with whitewash. They stuck out just
in the path of the tenor soloist as he made his entry, resplendent in
full evening dress. The flicker which crossed his tensely smiling
face as he caught sight of them, paused, and finally stepped across
them was, to me, unforgettable. It seriously disturbed my ability
to concentrate for the rest of the evening, but, on the other hand,
it had been one of those rare moments which illuminate the rest of
life, and I would cheerfully back into a hundred streams if I could
experience it again.

We all enjoyed the evening, and I felt, as we found our way
back to the farm, as if we had made a united gesture at the
elements. My own elation died down during the long drive back
to Hertfordshire next day, however, for by the time we reached
home I felt as if I had a knife in my back. The pain drove me once
more to a major decision: this was the last time we could go to
Pembrokeshire. No matter how hard it seemed, I must set about
trying to find a location for our holiday that was less of a strain on
me. I felt very sad, for the children loved the place, and were free
there in a way they could not be in more built-up areas. I could
not then see that such a decision was another step forward — a
letting go of the past. I only knew that I had been forced into it.

On our return I visited the osteopath once more, who managed
to make life tolerable again for a while, and we all settled down to
the beginning of the new school year. Joanna, in particular, was
working very hard at her cello, for she had three important
hurdles in front of her that term — an audition for the County
Youth Orchestra, followed by another for the National Youth
Orchestra a week later, and then her Grade Eight exam, the most
important of all the grades for a budding musician. All of which
involved a great deal of organization, most particularly in finding
accompanists. As we are a first-generation musical family we had
no relatives or friends to help out, and Christa was emphatic that
these pianists should not just be good pianists, but sensitive ac-

companists. I was, therefore, hard put to it. In the end, it was friends of Christa's who came to the rescue, but not without some difficulty, for they, for the most part, were busy professional people. Christa believed that all performance material should have the most meticulous preparation, which involved rehearsals with the accompanist — so that life became complicated indeed.

I did not resent this in the least, for it delighted me to see Christa passing on her own high standards to my daughter, who was never allowed to get away with the second rate. Watching Joanna as she worked, I rejoiced at the change in her. All the disturbance and anger seemed to have died completely away. This thirteen year old was full of fun, interested in everything around her, hard working and purposeful. She was very affectionate, and we enjoyed each other's company.

There was absolutely no sign of any teenage difficulties. She was still not in the least interested in fashion, make-up or boys — her whole being seemed to be given over to her music. I had been a late developer myself and therefore did not attach any particular importance to this slow advance into puberty. I felt sure that we would meet some rough patches as she grew up — I could still remember vividly the tears and tantrums of my own middle teens, when my father lay ill at home — but I felt that we had built up a strong foundation from which to meet them. It was as well, I think, that I could not foresee what form they were to take.

The auditions went off smoothly, despite nerves. She heard from the County Youth Orchestra first: she had been accepted for their reserve orchestra — standard procedure for the reception of newcomers, but procedure which did not please the ambitious Joanna in the least. Then came the letter we were all waiting for, with its telltale Croydon postmark. We all crossed our fingers as she opened it, and held our breath.

She had been accepted.

For the second time in a year there was a burst of fireworks in the sky. We went mad with delight. All the runs, the expense, the hours of practice were justified at once in that one short letter. Joanna, in fighting her way through fierce competition to join the ranks of some of the best young cellists in the country, in its top youth orchestra, had snatched our banner from my hand and run ahead with it, as if to prove that against all the odds we could win through.

We rushed to the phone to tell Christa. Her daughter had also been accepted in the auditions, and we could share our happiness. Marvellous musical experiences now lay ahead of them, Christa told me, for there was little so uplifting for a young musician as playing in an excellent orchestra under the baton of great conductors. It would be an experience which would stand her in good stead for the rest of her life. The head of music at school, when we told him, agreed — he had been a member of the orchestra as a boy, and still valued the training it had given him.

It was a happy time. The letter became dog-eared as we read and re-read it, still not quite able to believe in it, that such things could happen to us.

With such encouragement, it was hardly surprising that Joanna should sail through her Grade Eight exam to another high distinction. This was all she needed to crystallize her determination to make a career of music. Christa and I, anxious for her wellbeing in a profession so overcrowded and competitive, sought to dissuade her. The reality of a musical career is very different from the glamorous image it tends to assume in the minds of children. Music as a marvellous hobby is one thing, music as bread and butter is another. All arguments were in vain, however. At fourteen, Joanna knew exactly where she wanted to go, and her chin set in a way that was to become very familiar as time passed.

It had been an extraordinary year, I reflected, as I set about the preparations for Christmas once more — a year which had transformed the whole appearance of our world. Although we were still a broken family, still financially dependent, and still prone to days of sadness, we were, I felt, full of the elation of success, at last on the mend. As once again we joined our friends in carol singing, warmed by the faithfulness of their support, we were able to feel for the first time that perhaps we, too, had something to offer.

CHAPTER SEVEN

Fifth Year: Time Present and Time Past

Joanna went off to her first National Youth Orchestra course in a frame of mind bordering on pure terror, convinced that she had only succeeded in the audition by a fluke, and that all the other players would be far superior. Fortunately, Christa's daughter was in exactly the same state, so that they could prop each other up during the journey down to the general assembly point at Victoria station.

Just over a week later they both came back exhausted, but full of everything they had seen and done, deeply impressed by the orchestra's standards and atmosphere. Joanna went on chattering about it for days, both to me and to her head of music at school. I listened, thrilled to the heart that she should be having such an experience.

Not so Tom. This latest success on the part of his older sister sounded the death knell to his relationship with the cello. When I discovered him one day in the sitting room where he had gone to practise, collapsed in tears over his instrument, utterly defeated, I knew I could delay no longer. I had made a mistake that must now be put right, cost what it might.

Tom needed an instrument that was personal to him, on which he could develop at his own pace, without feeling constantly overshadowed by his sibling. I sat down beside him, and put the idea of making a change to him. He began to brighten as we discussed it, and before long we had settled that he should learn the viola. Its sound appealed to him, and so, significantly, did the idea of belonging to a minority group among string players.

Too much time had already been lost, so I went straight into action. Before anything else, I had to contact his cello teacher and explain matters to her. We liked her very much and did not want to hurt her feelings. She understood our difficulties, and we did not lose a good friend. Within a couple of days, the school of music had fixed us up with a new teacher and a new timetable for lessons. All that remained was to find an instrument. Thanks to my savings this was no longer the problem it had been when Tom first started the cello. Also, I was beginning by now to know the ropes, and the dealer who supplied us with all the cello strings, bridges, mutes and other accessories had become something of a friend. We explained our needs to him, and before long Tom was the proud owner of a small eighteenth-century viola, a copy of the work of a master, made by a craftsman from Doncaster. For its size, it had a strong, mellow sound, and Tom loved it at once.

The lessons were hard for him at first. He was unused to holding so heavy an instrument in so awkward a position, and this, coupled with the difficulties of reading a new clef, and acquiring a completely new technique, made the going heavy. Despite his fragile appearance, however, and the ready tears, Tom had a tenacity which equalled his sister's. It showed in his judo, where he won many a fight not through any elegance of style or neat throwing technique, but simply by holding on and refusing to give up. He worked with a will at his viola, for he was bent on catching up. Tom had secret ambitions of his own, which he confided to no-one.

I sighed with relief. The mistake had at last been rectified. Now, perhaps, I could relax a little.

So I did — but not for long. A hectic round of publicity engagements surrounding the publication of my book swept me right out of my domestic routine, to give me a heady breath of the outside world. Completely new to it — I had had no idea there would be so much excitement — I found it all very stimulating, and completely unreal.

I found it far from easy to talk about the book which by now seemed, with all the deep and painful feelings it contained, to have been left somewhere far behind me. Fortunately I was a relatively experienced speaker, as I had often given talks on the subject of autistic children to local groups, so that I was not reduced to total panic, but I found many of the interviews unnerving.

It was troubling to find that there was a discrepancy between the way I answered the questions that were put to me and my feelings about the experience I had been through. It was as if I was saying what people felt I ought to say, rather than what I really felt. I tended to sound bright and courageous, whilst all the time the memory of the long days of grief and near despair after Simon's diagnosis was very vivid. Somehow, the tears seemed to disappear in the telling. The book was acquiring a life of its own, quite distinct from mine.

Once, when I dared to voice my deeply-held belief, to a magazine editor phoning up for a story, that all families of autistic children need the regular support of a social worker, backed up by a psychiatrist, I received a severe snub. "You want the moon!" she said crossly, and rang off. Yet I was in fact speaking of an urgent need which at last is beginning to be acknowledged and, where government policies allow, answered. Only those who have experienced autism at first hand can know how deeply it affects the entire family.

Simon himself remained blissfully unaware of all the interest his story had aroused. His emotional withdrawal had, if any-thing, increased, though his practical skills were showing considerable improvement. He had developed a great interest in carpentry, and spent hours in the workshop at Somerset Court helping to make jigsaws, plant-troughs, stools, bird tables — a whole assortment of sturdily made goods which Mrs Elgar sold to swell the funds of the community. I liked to think that he was able to have the dignity of contributing to his own keep.

His only speech consisted at this time of fragmented phrases referring to past events, which seemed to have little bearing on the present, such as the name of the farm in Pembrokeshire, or that of the hotel where, when he and Joanna were very small, we used to break the journey to Wales (I always found it odd that "The Speech House" should, as a name, have so captured the attention of a non-communicating child) — and other odd snippets. He could not tell me anything at all about his life in Somerset.

As he was far away down there, the phone calls and the interviews did not disturb him — until, that is, Southern Television asked if they might make a documentary film about us. I agreed, provided that Joanna, Tom and David were kept out of it. I was still very dubious as to the effect publicity might have on them. This proved to be another mistake, for they have reproached me ever since, arguing with some justice that since we had done so much together, we should have done that, too.

They were thrilled when they returned from school one day to find the television team in our house. Their eyes widened at the sight of the kitchen full of bright lights, trailing leads, burly electricians and cigarette smoke. Their disappointment at being left out was so obvious that the cameraman took some extra stills, just for our family album.

The next day, the team and I drove down to Somerset to shoot some scenes on location. This was to be the greatest pleasure that the publishing of the book had given me, for, as the producer wanted to give some idea of the many activities of the community, I suddenly found myself sharing the very detail of Simon's everyday life there of which the nature of his handicap had deprived me. I loved every moment of the swimming session at the local baths, the rehearsal of the music group (so well trained by Mrs Elgar that they give concerts around the neighbourhood), and the skittles at the local pub. I watched avidly, storing away impressions, intent on remembering every detail so that I could use them when I tried to prompt Simon into speech during the holidays. The television team, which, for assignments such as this, had been specially picked, were deeply moved by all that they saw. I could see that they really cared, and felt, as a result, far more relaxed when talking to them.

All too soon it was time to part from these new friends, which was hard, though they left us with the promise that the whole family would be invited to the studios in Southampton to see the finished product, all expenses paid. It was hard, too, to return to my quiet backwater after so much excitement — but the backwater had a busy life of its own which soon caught me up again.

My back had begun to hurt badly once more — no doubt the publicity had been more of a strain than I had realized. I was growing anxious about this continual need for manipulation. I felt it could hardly be doing any good, especially as it was giving increasingly temporary respite from pain. It might be wiser, I thought, to go to someone eminent in the profession, rather than continue to seek treatment at a local level. A personal recommendation led to my making the transfer, and for a time, at least, there was considerable improvement. It entailed adding the cost of the fare to London to that of the treatment, but there seemed to be little option if I was to continue to lead a normal life.

Joanna went off to her second NYO course in the Easter holidays. I had been somewhat dismayed to discover that these courses, too, were very expensive, despite the NYO being a national orchestra, which I would have expected to be subsidized by the government. My relief was great to find that our county, Hertfordshire, awarded a grant to cover the costs, and I was very grateful for it, for it would have been exceedingly difficult to find the money three times a year.

As it was, I could watch Joanna go off, bubbling over with a mixture of nerves and excitement, dying to see all her new friends again, and feel no financial worries. I saw how much more easily she related to other musical children. In their company she felt understood and in her natural element. After this course letters began to come for her from all parts of the country — it was as if she had become a member of a huge, extended family.

The final concert was in the Royal Festival Hall. Joy and Joan went to it with me, and we all enjoyed ourselves trying to pick out Joanna amongst the big orchestra. She was in the back row of the cellos, looking very small, but she was undoubtedly there. I was glad of the company of my friends, for I was far too excited to concentrate properly on the music, and they helped me to believe that it was really happening. It did not seem possible to me, as I remembered all that had occurred in the last few years, that we could have come this far.

Soon after this, Joan moved out of London to the pretty house she had bought a few miles from ours. This was, in a way, the beginning of a new phase in my social life, for it was not long before two more of her friends, rather confusingly called June and Jane, came first to stay with her, and then themselves to buy properties in the area. They soon became my friends, too, and as all three were single career women, with jobs in the City, they were invaluable as a link with the outside world and helped to keep my single-parent hang-ups in perspective. I rejoiced to have Joan living nearby, even though I was unlikely to see very much of her owing to the demands of her job. Her solid support had come to mean a great deal to me, as well as to the children. It had been her arm that had supported me at my father-in-law's funeral — a gesture which I never forgot. I had been to her buryings, too. Shared grief forms a lasting bond.

Suddenly, we received the promised invitation from Southern Television. They had kept their word. Simon, unfortunately, was too far away in the wrong direction to be included in the treat. This time, it was the turn of the others.

The fun started the moment we left the house, for I had decided, as it was supposed to be a treat for me too, that we should go by train. This in itself was an adventure for children

accustomed all their lives to travelling by car. The glories of a full
British Rail breakfast took the day off to a magnificent start. I
watched in surprise at the amount the three of them consumed,
and wondered if perhaps I was not giving them quite enough to
eat at home. They chattered happily all the way, and, once again,
I felt warmed by the sense of our unity as a group, and of the
affection and care which flourished among us, encompassing
Simon who, on days like this, seemed almost a focus for it.

A royal welcome awaited us in Southampton. We were met at
the station, and whisked off to the studios' canteen, where the
three of them happily devoured a second breakfast of bacon
sandwiches. I began seriously to wonder if I was *starving* them at
home.

After this, came a tour of the studios, ending up in a small
room full of TV screens where the sound and vision were being
put together by our friend the producer. We gazed mesmerized at
the pictures showing on several screens simultaneously, and
approved the choice of music — Simon's beloved Bach. The job
done, we all went to the pub across the road for a slap-up lunch. It
was not so very long since breakfast number two, but the
children were in no mood to waste opportunities. As course
succeeded course, I could see respect for their prowess growing
on the faces of our friends — whilst I was beginning to wonder
about the consequences.

The next item on the agenda, though outwardly normal and
pleasant enough, was to prove fateful for me, though I had
no suspicion of it at the time. Graham, the producer, suggested
that his wife Jane should drive us round to see the sights of
Southampton.

I had, in fact, lived in Southampton until I was five years old,
when, on the outbreak of war, I was taken from my parents and
evacuated, first to successive families in Bournemouth, and then
to the depths of Somerset. Just after the war, I had spent another
year there, also in a foster family, while my parents fought, and
lost, a court case trying to regain possession of their house which
they had let during the last years of the war. So that this was a
very moving tour for me, the more so as I persuaded Jane to drive
us to see my old home. It was strange to show it to my own
children. I sat looking at it. Old memories, long dormant,
seemed to look back at me from the windows and beckon me in
as we drove off. It was good to recognize landmarks from my

childhood in the rebuilt, modern town — the monument to the engineers of the *Titanic*, the Civic Centre clock, and the Bargate. At least something solid from that far-off time before the bombs fell and shattered buildings and lives still survived — and comforted the inexplicable sadness that was growing in me.

At last, reluctantly, for I did not want this magic day to end, we boarded the London train, the children laden with keepsakes, and waved goodbye to our kind hosts. We were very quiet during the journey home, for there was much to think about, and we wanted to remember it all. It was one of the happiest days we had spent together and, for the first time, I had not been longing for a partner with whom to share it. For once I was able to accept it as something that had come about as a result of my own efforts.

Only a few days after our return, we received a visit from an American psychologist, Mira Rothenberg, who that summer had been elected "Woman of the Year" in the States, and who was in England for the publication of her book *Children with Emerald Eyes*. She had read my book, and had written to my publisher to see if a meeting could be arranged. I was, of course, honoured. She came on a glorious July day, and we gave her tea in the garden.

We took Mira to our hearts instantly when she spotted our raspberry patch and proceeded to raid it with rapturous little cries of "Berries!". We had never met anyone quite so direct before.

This was not without its disadvantages. During tea, as we casually chatted, she suddenly asked me how much we saw of Paul — producing a freezing silence round the sunlit table. I could not cope with such a question put on so short an acquaintance, and it angered me. But it was not possible to stay angry for long with Mira, and before long we were talking as easily as before. We took her out for a walk beneath the shady trees of the common, and she admired the countryside.

She looked at me very straight when the time came for her to take her leave, and thanked me for allowing her "this little glimpse of heaven and hell" — which floored me.

I pondered over her words for days after her visit. Mira worked with disturbed and deprived children in the States, and I respected her greatly. But what had she meant? Surely she had seen that we had struggled through and were once more a united and happy family? Whatever had prompted her to make a remark like that? I lacked the courage to phone her up and ask her.

Perhaps it was not so much the courage I lacked as the desire to know the answer. I ended up simply trying to forget her uncomfortable, disturbing words. There was too much to be done to waste time attempting to work them out.

They surfaced again, nonetheless, when the following month, August, brought a visit from Paul, with its inevitable disruption of our family life.

We did not meet. By now, I was deeply afraid of seeing him again, and rousing once more the violent, agonizing feelings which surrounded my memories of him. I wanted my life to go on as it had done of late, with lots of stimulating activities, and food for thought.

There was no longer any need to ask for help from Peter and Marilyn. The boys were by now old enough to meet their father at an agreed rendezvous.

Joanna had refused to go once more. Indeed, this year she refused to see her father at all. Her reason, when gently I tried to probe, was that it hurt too much to say goodbye again, and that she had had enough of being hurt. I did not know how to help her, though I could sympathize. I knew all too well, from the early days of access, what she meant about saying goodbye.

It was as if the wound were never going to heal. The slightest touch and it started to bleed again. I could not make Joanna go against her will. She had just reached puberty, and I did not dare to jeopardize a balance of mind so hardly won. I would have given much for her to be spared these conflicts, to be given a measure of peace in which to come to terms with her nascent womanhood. Watching her school friends laughing with their fathers, and caressing them, I was filled with inner tears. Joanna had lost one of the most important relationships in a woman's life.

History was repeating itself: my mother's father had died when she was only fourteen, my own father had fallen fatally ill when I was twelve, and now my own daughter, too, was suffering the same bitter deprivation, though for reasons that were harder to come to terms with. And there was nothing whatsoever I could do about it. I could only give her my love and support, in the full knowledge that it was not only not enough, but also that it was a gift which had its dangers. I knew that Joanna's life must not become too tightly interwoven with mine. This was another reason for being grateful for the NYO courses, which were an excellent way gently to begin the process of separation.

She had especially loved the summer one, during which the orchestra visited Scotland. Although it lacked the necessary funds for foreign trips, it travelled a good deal in Britain, which pleased me almost as much, for it meant that Joanna visited places she might otherwise never have seen. She returned home tired out as usual, and, as the boys had just departed with Paul and it did not seem a very good idea just to sit around at home missing them, I took her off with me to my retreat in the New Forest. She was crazy about horses, and I felt that the wild ponies might work their own soothing spell, as indeed proved to be the case. Our few days together, however, were suddenly transformed by the arrival of our fairy godmother in the shape of Southern Television, or rather in that of the research assistant who had worked on our film. She gave us two seats for Glyndebourne.

I had been there on several occasions with Paul. Opera lover that I am, those visits had been for me high-water marks in all my musical and theatrical experience. Cinderella at the ball has nothing on me the moment that I step out of the car in the Glyndebourne car park into that rarefied atmosphere. For me, the hours spent there, walking in the flower-filled gardens, spellbound by exquisite music exquisitely interpreted, are my personal experience of faery. Nothing there is real. Nothing has any relation to the outside world of cares and anxieties. The spirit, for that brief space of time, is free to range.

Now, thanks to Southern, I was to have the privilege of introducing my daughter to it, and enjoying her reactions.

The performance we were to attend was not, in fact, an ordinary one, for it was to be televised. At that time, Southern recorded one opera each season, and the resultant film was transmitted internationally, the next year. The audience was to consist of the company's directors and employees. Since they would be part of the film, they all dressed formally, as if for a real' performance. The small auditorium had to be shared with big, mobile TV cameras — though, as far and Joanna and I were concerned, this was all part of the fun.

Once in our seats, we discovered the bonus hidden in this type of performance. A television recording has to be perfect. All flaws have to be eradicated — a slip of the tongue in the foreign language, a wrong move, a trapdoor that fails to open — and the whole scene has to be shot again. In a poor production this would have been extremely boring — but this production was utter enchantment. Happily, for us, it contained many trapdoors and similar perils, so that we heard many arias, superbly sung, more than once. Joanna and I revelled in it, forgetful, like Cinderella, of all else.

The stroke of midnight found us, alas, completely lost in a wasteland of uncompleted motorway somewhere north of Southampton. I was so tired that my eyes would not focus on the map, and we only found our way back to the hotel by good luck — all judgement had long since collapsed. It was worth it, we agreed sleepily the next day, and as Cinderella would have told us. Joanna, I knew, would never forget her first Glyndebourne.

The adventure had given my self-confidence a considerable boost, so that when it came to the next major excursion a couple of weeks later, when we were to set out on our family holiday, I could plan the drive with much less apprehension. I had finally chosen a cottage in a small village by the sea in Dorset as the location. As this meant that we could easily pick up Simon on the way, it was likely to prove far less exhausting.

We reached our Dorset village without mishap, along a very beautiful route. The pleasantness of the journey was marred, unfortunately, by a traumatic arrival, for there was nowhere, in a village scored with double yellow lines, to park the car while we unloaded it. I ended up in a shouting match with a furious farmer, in whose adjacent drive I had temporarily, and neatly, parked. He could see my difficulties, but he must have been overcome by his own, for he threatened me with the police. Somehow we unpacked the car, soothed an anxious Simon, let out the cat, and finally parked the wretched vehicle a quarter of a mile away. I spent the first evening in tears, cursing all men, and all farmers in particular.

A sound night's sleep restored my perspective and my sense of humour. Delicately recounting the incident next day, in the post office, we discovered that my protagonist was famed locally for his volatile temper, which we had had the ill luck to arouse, but that his heart was in the right place, for he raised a lot of money for charity. I looked at Simon, with his sweet, placid, vulnerable face, and sighed. Sometimes he, and we who cared for him, needed something a little more difficult to give than money.

Despite this melodramatic beginning, this was to prove the most successful of our holidays so far. The village was still an active one, with a church, a school, and several shops. Although there were throngs of summer visitors, there were still plenty of 'real' residents, and they were very welcoming. The church was an active one, too, and we quickly made friends among its community. I felt far less alone. There was even a small but well-stocked library which opened several days a week, with a librarian to chat to. The beach, inevitably, was far more crowded than in Wales, and, since it was composed of the tiny pebbles of the Chesil Bank, was no use for games — but the crowd, on the other hand, in an away-from-it-all mood, was disposed to be friendly, and the swimming was good.

There was one major drawback, however — one which I shortsightedly had not anticipated. We had been going to Wales for so many years that I had forgotten our original reason for choosing it — which was the difficulty of caring for Simon in a strange place. In a remote cottage close to near-empty beaches, his eccentric behaviour had not mattered in the least. He could be as free as everyone else. Here, on a crowded beach where the stones hurt his feet, it was infinitely harder to keep him happy, especially now that the sea itself was less of an attraction than it had been when he was small. His swims grew shorter and shorter, and the time spent lying on the beach growing bored longer and longer. We also discovered that we had to keep a sharp eye on him in case he should suddenly want to change, for he had no concept of personal modesty and we had to descend on him in a flurry of towels before all was revealed. The only answer to that one, I thought grimly, was a holiday in a nudist camp, but the idea lacked appeal. It was as well that before long variable weather forced us to look for other activities.

Fossil hunting became a favourite of these. Tom and David, spurred on by some interesting finds, took it up enthusiastically. It has the great virtue of being absolutely free, once you own a reference book so that trophies can be identified. Even Simon at least enjoyed the walks.

We also attended every and any entertainment the village offered, from fetes to the amateur dramatic production which I watched with the vicarage cat asleep on my lap, feeling very much at home.

By the end of the fortnight, everyone voted that we should return the following year, and I accordingly rebooked. I was heartened by the children's enthusiasm, for, although I still had, from time to time, felt very lonely, it had been nothing like the bleak sense of isolation I had experienced in Wales. I was beginning, I felt, to know the ropes when it came to surviving.

Studying the map for the return journey, I had realized that, with only the slightest of detours, it would be possible for us to visit my foster sister in Somerset, from the happiest of my wartime foster homes. I did not then understand why I felt such a strong urge to do this — I had not been back to the tiny hamlet since I had left it in the summer of 1941. It was as if the day spent visiting Southampton had lit a slow fuse, with one memory igniting another. I only knew that I badly wanted the children to make the visit with me, to introduce them to Eileen, and her aunt Freda, who lived close by. They had both been very kind to the six-year-old waif Eileen's mother had picked out from the bunch of evacuees waiting for homes at the village Institute. My childhood, and that of my children, had suddenly become strangely interwoven.

It was an extraordinary experience, after driving the car through miles of unknown, narrow lanes, suddenly to come upon a scene that was poignantly familiar — the road which I had daily taken to school — a small school which stood beside the church just outside the hamlet. In the churchyard, I found the graves of my two foster parents, and grieved that I had never before found it possible to visit them. The children were very silent, deeply interested, absorbing the peaceful atmosphere of this quiet place.

I took them next to see the cottage where I had lived. It was empty now, and up for sale, for my foster mother had died only the previous year. I showed them the flower garden which, in a summer glory of blooms, had greeted me on my weary arrival, and cheered me. It was bare now, though well dug, waiting for the next gardeners to come and tend it. Its memory would always live for me in the scent of the southernwood which grew there, and which I grew now in my own garden.

Lastly, we visited Eileen, then Freda. They welcomed my children even more warmly than they once had me, and when at last we left for home, the car was full of fruit and vegetables, pots of home-made jam, and sweets. My heart was very full. It was as if they had once again done their best to comfort a very, very old sorrow. I was thoughtful as I drove back up the motorway towards Hertfordshire. I had just discovered what I wanted, or rather, perhaps, what I needed to write about next. I wanted to make some pattern out of the tangle of old memories which was fast appearing, it seemed, out of nowhere . . . memories that were pressing in upon me.

There had been something almost religious about this journey into the past. I had needed to find the hamlet still there, hidden away in its protecting hills, which once had protected me from German bombs. It was in some way a guarantee for the present, for the continuity of things — like the Bargate in Southampton. Perhaps that was why I had wanted my children to be with me. And also why I now felt that I had no option but to write about it.

As soon as the schools reopened, I settled down to work, resuming the simplified and much-loved routine that was necessary if I were to find the time. (The simplification, of course, was in the housework.) Once again, there was no room for depression, though I was a little worried as to the ultimate fate of the book. Publishers, I knew, were unlikely to be interested in yet another book about this period — there had already been many about the war. I pushed the worry aside. I was not writing it to please the publishers. I was writing it to try to understand those feelings which had come welling up when I saw the house in Southampton, and the cottage in Somerset — feelings of terror and bewilderment at the sudden loss of my parents and the familiar faces of home.

There were some interruptions, but they were welcome ones. The first was a visit from Bob, my brother in Brazil, who had come over to stay in London on business. He had staggered through Customs, and the airport crowds, with a huge watermelon for the family, fresh from the market in Rio. The children fell upon it. Indeed, they all but took a bath in it. Nothing so sweet and juicy had ever come out of an English shop. It was an imaginative gesture, and I loved my brother for it. I wished we could see more of him, but it was one of those things that, simply, could not be.

The other was an invitation to make a contribution to the BBC 2 series, "Light of Experience". This was rather more nerve-racking than anything else I had been asked to do, for it did not take the form of an interview, with a supportive questioner sitting by my elbow, but of a monologue direct to the camera, reading off an autocue. I discovered a new sympathy for newsreaders as I tried to resist becoming hypnotized by my own script. It was a fascinating experience, however, and a stimulating one, for it involved me with many thoughtful, interesting people. The trouble was that it made it hard to return to my solitary writing with any great enthusiasm.

The children, for their part, seemed happy and enthusiastic in all the activities of the new school year. Tom had entered the top class of junior school. This meant that he had a male teacher, and I was especially glad of this in our circumstances. He would come home full of endless stories of his doings, full of appalling puns and shaggy dog jokes. There was still not the slightest sign of boredom, and I felt more sure than ever that I had made the right decision over his education.

David was becoming increasingly respected in the school for his prowess in the sports field. He was bright academically, too, but I suspected that he was too much overshadowed by his gifted older brother for this to be very apparent. For the time being, there was little I could do about this, beyond making sure that he received his share of praise and encouragement at home.

It was hard for him, I knew, that he was at the time the only coloured child in the school — we live in a predominantly white area — and I worked at playing down the importance of colour as an issue, pointing out that anyone who is different, be they fat, thin, cross-eyed or red-haired, is a butt for teasing. This seemed to comfort him, and certainly he never gave a sign of being unable to cope. I knew very well that things would never be easy for him, but I felt that if he could feel sure of loving support from all of us at home he would have as much strength as the next child to meet the difficulties that came his way.

Joanna was faced once again with the yearly ordeal of the NYO audition. Although I regretted the pressure this put her under, I very much agreed with the system of holding annual auditions, which prevents the formation of a bottleneck at the older end of the orchestra, and allows a regular infusion of new blood. When she fell ill with 'flu, however, of a particularly savage variety, a couple of days before the audition, we both felt the end of the world had come. A phone call to the administration restored sanity: Joanna was not to fret — she could take her audition ten days later, among a different section of the orchestra. The caring, family atmosphere of the NYO came over strongly in this conversation. The competition might be fierce, and the orchestra big, but the players remained individuals, not mere cyphers, and no-one was to be penalized for an absence they could not help.

Joanna recovered, and took her audition among the oboes. To her rapturous delight she was readmitted. I heaved a sigh of relief. Better than anyone, I knew how much it meant to her, and how much it was doing for her.

She was preparing in a very business-like manner for her Grade Eight piano exam. Her relationship with the piano had been a stormy one ever since her return from boarding school. It had been the only music exam she had taken while she was there, and, not surprisingly, she had not done very well — a mere pass branded her as a failure in her own eyes. She could not forgive herself, and patient, gentle Sue had to bear with sulks, tears and tantrums as she gradually rebuilt Joanna's technique. At one stage, she had wanted to give it up altogether, and was only induced to continue when I pointed out that if she wanted to go to music college she would need a second instrument. Joining the NYO and a better mark in her Grade Seven exam had brought her to a more positive attitude, and now she was working with a will again. Her playing improved noticeably, and the piano received no more surreptitious kicks. I knew, from the set of her chin, that she would get the coveted distinction.

Unfortunately, the interruptions to my writing seemed to increase as the term moved on. Everything seemed to conspire against it, and I grew more and more frustrated.

Amongst other things, the administration of Simon's affairs had become increasingly thorny in the last months. He had now reached the age of sixteen. Since he was safely living in his community, school-leaving age bore no relevance to his daily life, but it greatly affected the matter of his fees. Until his sixteenth birthday, these were paid by the Department of Education and Science, which was all completely straightforward. Now, however, the buck was passed over to the social services — and my troubles began.

Since he was the first autistic child from our area to attend a community outside the county, we were creating a precedent — and no-one amongst the authorities seemed quite to know how to handle it, which created delays and hesitations. My anxiety immediately rose. I had visions of the money being refused, of Simon being sent home and myself trying to cope with his daily problems as well as those of the other children. I could make no sense of the forms that were sent for me to fill in. As they were often addressed directly to Simon, it was hardly surprising that I often did so incorrectly. No-one I turned to for help could understand them either. Fortunately, in the end, as for the umpteenth time I phoned County Hall, I spoke to an assistant director who had the humanity and the insight to realize my growing distress, and to reassure me, as well as to hasten along the long-delayed decisions. The reassurance was what I needed. Anxiety is always just around the corner for the families of the mentally handicapped and those in authority do not always realize how paralysing it can be, nor how easily it can be roused. I was exceptionally lucky to find someone who did understand.

My mother had also begun to make some extra demands upon my time. I had contrived to keep up regular visits to her over the last few years, though the distance had made this far from easy. Until recently, she had continued to play an active part in the life of the retirement home, helping out in the gardens and kitchens, playing cards with her friends, and enjoying the frequent outings and film shows. She had had one or two bad falls, however, and the last one of these had shocked her badly — a gash in her head had required several stitches. After this her mobility and her general interest in life had decreased noticeably, and she was spending an ever greater part of the day simply sitting in an armchair, watching the world go by.

Towards the end of October, I arrived at the home one morning to find her in bed. The matron had been, she told me, on the point of phoning me. She seemed very poorly. All her body was covered in large blisters. Later I learned that this was an unpleasant skin condition to which old people are prone. Eventually it was cleared up by cortisone, but on that October day no-one seemed to know precisely what it was.

I looked sadly at my mother as she lay in bed, curled in the foetal position, her eyes shut. Age had contracted her body until she was as small as one of my children, though far more frail. Our three lives — hers, Joanna's and mine — were likely to span the entire century, and still, despite my long education, I had not been able to break the chain of deprivation. At least, now that she was old and helpless, I could forgive her the unhappiness of our relationship, irretrievably damaged by that wartime separation, though I prayed that my relationship with my own daughter might be a better one.

I was resolved that Joanna should always know, as I had never known, how much I loved and valued her, even when the time came gently but firmly to push her from the nest. So far, it seemed, I had been successful. There had been no more major mistakes, and I had been forgiven by now for ever sending her away. There was a˜ strong understanding between us, and, provided it continued, I had no reason to suspect that anything could go wrong.

I still had a lot to learn.

The year gathered itself up into the usual pre-Christmas tidal wave, hurling us all limply onto the late-December mud flats. This year these were transformed from their usual bleakness, however, by a visit from my other brother, Ian. His company, for he stayed with us, banished loneliness and literary frustrations alike, and we both enjoyed the long talks we had together.

Ian's life, as well as my own, had settled down to some extent since his previous visit just before Paul's departure, and we could now begin properly to increase our acquaintance. He had always been kind and protective towards me as a child, despite — or perhaps because of — a large age difference. That memory made a good foundation to build on now.

It had been, I thought, as we saw in the New Year together, an extraordinary and confusing year, with much about it that I still did not understand, but I felt that it had been a positive one. All I wanted, as we raised our glasses, was that we might continue in the same way — learning, achieving, growing in mind and body and, above all, loving.

CHAPTER EIGHT

Sixth Year: Cracks in the Ground

My brother brought a spell of freezing cold weather with him from Canada. He, of course, was used to it, and was only surprised at the way everything in Britain came to a halt and fell apart.

He had made it clear that he felt strongly for us, and for our position, and I was deeply glad of his affection and concern. Distance, family commitments and lack of money had kept us apart for over thirty years, but now he was doing his best to bridge the gap that had grown, and I loved him for it. I longed to be able to visit him in Canada, but I did not have the money to pay all our fares, nor did he have the living space to house us all. But at least now he had shared our everyday lives for a while, and I could feel he was solid and real, and no longer just a name at the end of a dutiful letter. He was someone who really cared about us, even if he did live several thousand miles away.

His departure left me very tearful, and I was glad that I was booked to spend the following weekend at a music course at the same adult education centre I had been to with Marion. I went with another friend, whose husband had been sufficiently heroic not only to take over his own family but two of mine as well. We were both exhausted after the hurly-burly of Christmas, and found it an enormous relief to be away from our homes for a brief thirty-six hours. The speaker was witty and informative, the music beautiful, the food good, the house warm and the company pleasant — I could have stayed there a year. The grounds outside were deep in snow, and as the composer under discussion was Sibelius I had a strange sense of being part of some great, mysterious pattern.

We returned home lamenting only the shortness of the course, and vowing to return the following year, when the same speaker was to come again. This little break was, indeed, to become the most precious of all that I took, for it recharged my batteries at a time when they were always dangerously low, and when long months of winter still lay ahead.

The family routine this year seemed to be growing ever more taxing. Although Joanna had now finished all her Grade exams, the next step in her musical career was entry to college, for which she was still far too young. Christa, however, did not want her to stand still. To keep her on her toes, she urged her to enter for competitions and festivals of all kinds, so that she should acquire experience of performing to others in all manner of conditions. Whilst I wholeheartedly agreed with her policy, it made for many problems of organization, for each performance required its attendant rehearsals — with an accompanist. At least when Tom was performing, the problem did not arise, since his sister was by now a very competent accompanist herself, but the cello repertoire that she was now beginning to explore required a pianist of considerable ability, and these, I found, were thin on the ground. It was a problem which tended to grow out of proportion. I felt as if I were forever begging people to accompany my daughter.

As the winter drew on, I became very tired and low-spirited. Even the showing of the two television films made the previous year could not buoy me up for long. The finished product seemed strangely unreal. The pleasure, the satisfaction had been in making them — just as it had been in writing the book. I had loved working in a team with other people. Now, watching them, I was on my own again, and the book had become something in the past. It was rather like looking at butterflies pinned in a glass case. They were dead, and my vision of them was brief — and they had once been alive and vivid.

Eventually, as always, spring broke through the mud outside, and we began to liven up again. One of the disadvantages of living in a very old cottage is that the tiny windows, built centuries ago to keep out the elements, also keep out the light, so that by April we all feel like plants that have been kept for months in a dark cupboard. Easter daffodils seem like so many suns, and the children and I used to bring in great bunches of them from the garden, where they grew wild. This was one of Joanna's favourite jobs, and we realized now how badly we missed her when, for the second year in a row, she spent Easter away on her NYO course. Simon, in particular, home for the holiday, could never understand it when his beloved sister was not there. "Where's Joanna?" — his cry would echo plaintively round the house. "Gone away to play her cello," we would chorus in reply — we knew he could understand that much, at least. Five minutes later, "Where's Joanna?" would come again. It added somehow to our increasing sense of loss. Absences still made us very uneasy.

Her return cheered us all. Tom, safe now with his own

instrument, listened avidly to her tales of the orchestra's doings, and I could see determination to follow in her footsteps hardening with each successive story. Joanna, for her part, encouraged him, and spurred him on to ever greater efforts on his viola. He was, in fact, making considerable progress very fast, and was by now thoroughly in love with his instrument. I rejoiced to see how music, far from dividing them, as it had threatened to the previous year, was now strengthening the bond between them. Tom was, in fact, very proud of his sister, and loved to hear her play. David, as if he felt this was all a little too intense for him, held himself somewhat aloof— he was, after all, a wind player. He would, nonetheless, have hurled himself to Joanna's defence if he thought her attacked or criticized.

Joanna was delighted soon after coming home to receive an invitation to share first desk in the cello section of a very lively local youth orchestra which met during the school terms. Though pleased for her, since I knew she needed the experience, my delight was somewhat dampened by the knowledge that the commitment entailed yet more transport in the car. The timing of the runs rendered any other social activity on a Friday evening all but impossible, and it was difficult to avoid the feeling that my whole life was being taken over by Joanna. Although in the end I managed to share the runs with other parents, they came close to being the straw that broke the camel's back — especially when she begged to be allowed to stay on after the end of orchestra to play in the chamber music group, which made the run to retrieve her a late one. I could not, of course, refuse, but the request brought back in full spate the old longing to have someone, anyone, to help and to care for us.

The trouble was that the camel's back was by now in a bad way once again. A rash attempt at gardening had brought a return of severe pain. Throughout May and June I seemed to be forever travelling up to London to visit the osteopath, but, this time, manipulation brought no improvement at all, rather the contrary.

The osteopath's constant bills, the travel expenses — the costs were beginning to add up in a way that frightened me. Inflation had made a nonsense of a settlement made in 1975, and it was once again becoming very hard to make ends meet. Finally, though I hated doing it, I appealed to Paul, laying our difficulties before him. He had the grace to respond, and increased our payments slightly, but the total sum was still way below its original value. By now, he had bought his own house in Canada. I guessed that his expenses were heavy and pursued the matter no further, though friends assured me that he was prospering in his new environment.

Nonetheless, I still had, somehow, to meet the cost of Joanna's expensive cello lessons. In the end, swallowing my pride, I went to see the headmaster at her school. It so happened that, before opening as a comprehensive in our area, it had existed as a London grammar school, with a charitable foundation. This foundation still functioned in the new neighbourhood, and we parents had been told that we might apply to it if we needed financial help for any of the educational activities of the pupils. Very nervously, I asked if Joanna's cello lessons came into this category, and explained my difficulties. The headmaster listened to me with the utmost compassion, and promised to put the request before the governors. He felt that it was unlikely that there would be any difficulty — and, indeed, a grant was made to us very soon afterwards.

The feeling of being supported meant almost as much to me as the money itself. Knowing that the school was behind us took some of the weight of responsibility off me. It made me feel that someone thought we were of value, and that what I was trying to do for the family was understood and approved of. Even if complete financial catastrophe overtook us, Joanna, at least, would still have a chance of continuing her musical education. I could hold my head a little higher.

Metaphorically, that is. Physically, this was no longer possible. The pain in my back had reached an acuteness I had never experienced before. I could no longer possibly afford the amount of treatment I was having. I explained my difficulties to the osteopath who suggested, in disinterested tones, that I transfer to the physiotherapy department of a large local hospital, where, he said, I could be fitted with a surgical corset, and if necessary be given the spinal injections which would be too expensive coming from him. I returned home in tears. Sitting and standing had alike become torture, and I could only walk a few yards without becoming exhausted. There was now, it seemed, no alternative but to go to my doctor, and from him to surgery, if I was ever to have the least hope of living a normal life again. Then, as I sat in the kitchen, still in tears, thinking it over, an idea came to me. There might, after all, be just one last chance.

A friend, a few months previously, had spoken to me about acupuncture. Her husband, who had also suffered greatly with his back, to the point of having had a spell in hospital and being confined to a wheelchair, was now leading a normal life, thanks to the help of a particularly skilful acupuncturist. I had listened with some scepticism, since I could not see how being pricked by needles could possibly be responsible for such a recovery, but as my friend was a trained nurse I was in no position to scoff.

Suddenly, it seemed worth trying. Anything was worth trying. At least it could hardly do any further harm, and it was within the bounds of possibility that it might help. I rang my friend, and obtained the phone number of the practitioner who had helped her husband.

A few days later I found myself on my back on the acupuncturist's couch feeling self-consciously like a birthday cake. Gradually, I began to feel pleasantly relaxed. Details of my medical history were taken down, and the acupuncturist explained that it would be necessary for me to see him several times. He was a quiet, self-contained man, and I trusted him — partly, I think, because the majority of the medical books on his shelves were in French, and I had a great respect for French medicine.

The next few days brought no noticeable improvement, only sudden, sweeping waves of sleepiness which had me dozing off at all sorts of odd times. Since Simon was home for his July holiday, this was both inconvenient and difficult, but my eyes seemed to close of their own accord. I was glad when the other three broke up and could watch over him rather more alertly than I was doing.

This year, Paul's visit coincided with Joanna's NYO course, which meant that, with Simon safely returned to Somerset Court, I could once again manage a few days' rest in the New Forest. Just before leaving home, I went for another session of acupuncture.

At first, the result was similar to the preceding time. I spent the best part of the first two days of my holiday asleep. On the third day, however, I woke up and suddenly decided to go for a walk. This may not sound a very momentous decision — except that for months I had neither wanted nor been able to do such a thing. I set off into the Forest resolved to be prudent and not try to do too much too soon, but in the event covered some five miles. On my return, I slept deeply for another couple of hours, and awoke refreshed and invigorated — and, there was no doubt about it, the pain in my back had almost gone. I felt like cheering. It was unbelievable. I could not in the least understand it, but that did not worry me. I was simply content to be out of pain.

I was even strong enough to go into Southampton to visit the town archives in the Civic Centre. I wanted to see if I could find any information about the planning of the wartime evacuation in which I had played so reluctant a part. As I sat reading a box full of dusty letters that the helpful archivist had unearthed for me, letters which gave me more details than I had ever hoped to find, my anger and amazement grew. It was the surprise expressed in the letters which shocked me — surprise at the appallingly miserable state of many of the children who were to be sent away: verminous, rickety children, children with no boots or clothes to protect them against the winter, children from the dockland of whose existence and sufferings no-one it seemed had been aware until impending catastrophe drove them out into the open, beneath the averted noses of the worthy councillors. The stink of poverty rose from those yellowed pages. As I sat there reading, forgetful of hunger and the passage of time, I wondered how much things had really changed. Our children today might not, on the whole, be verminous or suffering from malnutrition — but they were still deprived, and still suffering. It was only the outward forms which had changed.

My reactions to those old letters were all the stronger because I was once more becoming worried about Joanna. Her tension had reappeared in the last couple of months. It had become very apparent in her attitude to her father's visit. She could not make up her mind whether or not she should go to see him at the end of her NYO course, when he came back with the boys. Her confusion was painful to witness. I turned to Ray for advice, and asked him if he could possibly come to our home to talk things through with her. He duly came, and they had several hours together. I was more than grateful. Joanna, I knew, needed someone she could confide in who was outside the situation.

In the end, after much deliberation, she decided that she would go to see Paul — but only to tell him that she did not want to see him again. She asked me to accompany her to this confrontation, but for once I refused my daughter. It was kindly Ray who took my place. He drove her over to meet Paul, who was staying with his mother.

I was none too sure what Joanna was hoping to achieve. She could have been simply wanting to punish her father. She could, on the other hand, have been indirectly appealing to him, hoping that he would override her decision with protestations of affection and concern — or she could have been frantically wanting to cut the threads of a painful relationship. Perhaps it was a mixture of all three. Whatever it was, I feared for her. I knew from experience how Paul met emotions as deep and violent as hers.

It was, therefore, no surprise when a very silent pair of people returned from the reunion. Joanna said little, shrugging the whole thing off as if it had been the most trivial of encounters. It was only as I walked with Ray back to his car that I realized the extent of his anger. I saw that, never having met Paul before, he had not understood the completeness of his emotional withdrawal from us. If Joanna had needed anything that August afternoon, it was hugging, and loving, and reassuring — and she had received nothing but politeness. It was the only time that I ever saw Ray shocked.

In the days that followed, she repeatedly told me that she was glad she had told her father that she did not want to see him again — as if to convince herself. Whilst I gave her all the love and reassurance I could, it was in the painful knowledge that I was the wrong parent. It was not really from me that she wanted it.

It was as well that we were all going off on our family holiday at the end of the week. It helped to put physical distance between ourselves and the scene of all this disturbance. Tom and David, excited again at all that they had done with Paul, became tense and worried by Joanna's attitude, which once more made them feel disloyal.

It was a great relief to take the road to Dorset once more, stopping off at Somerset Court to visit their Summer Fair, as well as to pick up Simon. He, I often thought, exerted his own healing influence on the family when it was troubled. His pleasure upon seeing us was simple and straightforward, and we could all respond warmly and naturally.

We wandered happily round the gardens with him, stopping at the different stalls and sideshows, licking ice-creams and greeting his fellow residents, before packing ourselves once more into the groaning Escort and proceeding on our way south. This year we knew where we were going, and could take steps to avoid encounters with fierce natives.

We enjoyed this second visit even more than the first. There were old acquaintances to renew, and favourite spots to revisit. Although I was still conscious of the sense of aching inner solitude which so beset me on holiday, I was by now more adept at living round it. I had brought books on wild flowers and butterflies, for instance, so that we might have the fun of identifying the many species new to us which abounded in the luxuriant Dorset countryside. The children's main interests remained swimming, fishing and fossil hunting. The latter received a tremendous boost the day when David and Tom came rushing home carrying an ammonite the size of a dinner plate which they had found in a nearby field. It was in good condition, and was given a place of honour in the kitchen. We joined with gusto in the Family Service at the little old church. Simon loved singing the well-known choruses, even if he was usually a beat behind everyone else. It was always his "Amen" that was the final word of the service.

The holiday served its purpose in giving us all a rest and a change, however occasional the sunshine, though in no way could it meet all our needs. It did, however, help us to grow together again after the disruptions of the preceding few weeks, and we returned home in a better state to meet the challenges of the new school year.

This began just after our return. It was an important time for Tom, who was now moving up to Joanna's school. He was less fortunate than she, in that by now, at the beginning of its fifth year, it was some six hundred pupils strong — already twice as big as my own much-loved grammar school in the forties — and he could not have the individual attention which had meant so much to her. He settled in quickly, however, for many of his friends had moved up with him, and the process was completed when he came home one day after he had been there only a few weeks, to announce, pink with excitement, that he was to sing in a Covent Garden production just before Christmas. Looking at his happy face, seeing how much interest and pleasure he was taking in his work, I could not think why I had even hesitated over allowing him to come to this school. The start could not have been more promising.

David, too, seemed to be profiting from his brother's transfer. For a whole year now he would be free to develop away from the shadow of his clever sibling and to enjoy the many projects initiated by an imaginative teacher. His superabundance of energy created problems for him when it came to academic work, though he had an excellent practical brain when he would consent to sit still for long enough to focus it. He still really only came into his own on the sports field — or when he was playing the flute. He had a naturally beautiful sound on this instrument, and he was making very good progress. Music, for my youngest son as well, had become an area in which he could shine. David, I felt, would hold his own, whatever the odds against him.

My own work, on the other hand, was going far from well. After incorporating the notes taken in Southampton into a preface, the book was finally typed and sent off. I was far from happy about it. I had come to the end of writing it without understanding what it was that had driven me to begin it. It had been the most difficult thing I had ever tried to write, and I did not know why that was either. Above all, the effort to order the jumble of fragmented memories had been unexpectedly painful. More than once, I had found myself in tears as I sat at my desk. All I did know was that it was desperately important to me — and from that I reasoned that it might be so to others of my generation as well.

Although, in view of their discouraging attitude when I had first announced my intention of beginning the work, it was hardly surprising when no-one showed any interest in the finished product, I was profoundly disappointed. Used as I was to rejection slips, this one was different. Not only did it shrivel the new shoots of confidence that had sprung from the success of the first book, it did far more serious damage. The book had been about my own childhood. The rejection of it was therefore another rejection of me.

The old, bitter feelings of uselessness and futility returned in a rush. All further writing became impossible. The smallest encouragement, the slightest sign that someone had a use for my pen, would have changed the situation in a flash, but this was not to be — not this autumn. Though it seemed now that I was making a reasonable job of caring for the family, I knew that I was failing totally to rebuild my own ruined life. This rebuilding was essential if the parting from the young was to be a normal, healthy one when the time for it came. I could not afford to fail. The only thing I could find to be cheerful about was the improvement in my back. After a couple more sessions of acupuncture, I-was now completely free from pain, and could function normally providing I avoided lifting heavy weights. Yet I was too depressed to be adequately grateful even for this almost miraculous relief.

All the same, it was a good thing that the treatment had been so successful, for Joanna was now begging me, on top of cello lessons, piano lessons and the two orchestras, to allow her to play in a string quartet that was being formed from among the best players in one of the orchestras. This met on Saturday mornings. There was, of course, no way I could refuse, for I knew the experience would be invaluable to her, but it was one more strand to be added to the complexities of the week. I was glad, too, that the opportunity had come along now, after the disturbances of the summer. Joanna needed her music more than ever. At the same time, I felt it was taking us over, and it made me uneasy.

Luckily, I was able to share the transport on Saturdays with another parent, but even this left me needing to be in two places at once on a Saturday lunch time. It was David who came to the rescue by suddenly developing a distinct talent for cookery. By taking over the preparation of the bangers and mash that, owing to paralysis of the imagination, was our inevitable Saturday meal, he allowed me time to collect his sister at leisure without pressurizing her in my guilt over the two hungry boys at home.

One Saturday, I inadvertently arrived early to collect my cellist, and walked into the end of a rehearsal. As I sat listening, all my growing uneasiness died away. I realized that there was something very special about these four young players. I forgot about the time, and the boys, and the sausages, and listened entranced. This, I felt sure, was giving Joanna something unique, something that could come from no other source. I could only be thankful that she had found it.

She was far less happy at school this year, and it was fortunate that at least in this one area she could feel secure. Part of the trouble was that, at fifteen, her dedication to music was isolating her more and more from her peer group. Some of her friends in school were also very musical and talented, but none of them worked at their musical studies to the exclusion of almost everything else as Joanna did. Pop music, discos and boyfriends were for her part of a foreign world — and it was the world of school. Although her performances in school concerts won her a great deal of respect, she felt cut off from the others. Members of staff tried to dissuade her from giving so much time to music, and this alienated her still further, serving only to increase her determination to make it her life. She longed for Fridays, when, in the youth orchestra, she felt she had friends who understood her.

The time of the NYO audition had come round again, and the apprehension told on us all. I was devoutly grateful for the fact that Joanna's godmother lived in a flat in the street next to the audition rooms. We used to stagger in to her for refreshments after the audition. Judy was something of a fairy godmother to Joanna. As a ballet critic, she was in a position to introduce her goddaughter to yet another area of the music world which, on our slender budget, she might never have encountered. Joanna was very fond of her, and the sandwiches and cakes she always had ready for us turned the ordeal of the auditions into a treat, spiced with tantalizing glimpses of a very exotic world.

The auditions were successful, and an ecstatic Joanna found herself a member of the NYO for a third year. She could feel now that she really belonged, and was one of a nationwide family. She had developed a great affection for the musical director, Ivey Dickson, and often wrote to her, as did many of the other players — I often thought how Miss Dickson must treasure those letters from the young people for whom she worked so hard. I had already noticed how old members of the orchestra turned up to support the concerts. There are those who criticize the discipline of the NYO, saying that it is overdrilled; yet all the young musicians that I met loved and responded with their best to the high standards and ideals that were expected of them, chiefly, I suspect, because they were aware of the excellent results that were obtained. All were proud of belonging to such an orchestra, and Joanna was no exception.

The row of cups from local festivals had taken over our kitchen dresser. The boys eyed it without enthusiasm, for Joanna had somehow contrived to bribe them into cleaning them for her. For me, they seemed to symbolize the way music dominated our family life. I was beginning to query the wisdom of this complete takeover — there seemed to be something almost obsessive about it. Where I had instigated and encouraged it as an activity that would give direction to our life together, it now seemed to have swept us away, and we were racing on almost out of control — with Joanna rather than me at the reins.

Tom, moreover, had taken his place beside her. He had obtained a good distinction in his first viola exam, and this had stimulated his enthusiasm. I was devoutly grateful for the portable nature of the viola and the flute. The boys, at least, could do their practice upstairs, almost out of earshot, which was a help on the growing number of days when I needed a spell of silence. It was no use sending Joanna up there, as the powerful sound of the cello made the exposed beams vibrate, sending down showers of centuries-old dust about our heads.

Tom also had a very pure treble voice, soon discovered by the head of music at school, so that he ended up with a solo in the Christmas Carol Service, as well as having all the excitement of the Covent Garden experience, in which he became totally caught up. His piano continued to flourish and altogether, at twelve, Tom seemed to be almost more involved with music than his sister had been at the same age.

It was David who, in a sense, had remained the most balanced of us. Whilst he enjoyed his music, there were other things he enjoyed equally. I felt that in his case, at least, it had remained the therapy I had originally intended it to be. He and his teacher had both made a heroic effort to reach the standard required by the Grade One piano exam. When he emerged from it with a distinction we all heaved a sigh of relief. Now, at last, he could give up the instrument with honour, with absolutely no feelings of failure — merely the acknowledgement that he did not enjoy the piano enough to warrant continuing with it. With the flute it was a completely different matter — this was his own special patch, where the other two could not make him feel threatened. Many a time I blessed Christa for having thought of it.

All the same, the place where he enjoyed himself the most, and tried his hardest, was probably the judo mat. There everything — his muscular build, his speed of movement, his quick eye — seemed to come together for him. Not that he always won, indeed there were long periods where he seemed to stand still, but he was a quick learner, and was showing great potential. By now, all three children were respected members of the club, with green belts adorned with many tabs. It was sad to realize that Joanna's sixteenth birthday was approaching, which meant that she must now move up to the senior club, and so break up the family group.

This proved, in fact, to be the end of judo for her. A long talk with the club coach left her reluctantly agreeing that senior judo, where she would have to fight on equal terms with men, was not really the wisest choice of sporting activity for a future professional musician. Whilst she by no means wanted to live wrapped in cotton wool, it did not seem too sensible to invite disaster in a sport where pulled tendons, dislocations and broken bones were regular occurrences.

She was very sad to give it up. I, too, was sad that she should lose such a valuable outlet for anger and aggression, which I was convinced had played no small part in restoring her emotional balance after her return from boarding school. It had provided a useful counterweight to the intensity of her musical life, and I wished I could think of something with which to replace it. We simply did not have the money to allow her the horse-riding which was her other great love, discovered when Simon learned to ride. No ideas occurred to me, however, and Joanna's world narrowed a little further. Tom and David, of course, could carry on, as they still had several junior years ahead of them.

The world I had struggled so hard to build for the children was beginning to seem a very lopsided affair. The rejection of my book had sapped both my confidence and my strength, and I was constantly questioning my own motives and the wisdom of my decisions. The happiness and elation following the success of the first book had long since vanished — by now, it might never have happened. The desire to sleep began once more to dog me through the day, dragging at my feet. Once again, I was waking in the mornings with the familiar pain in my chest, and a feeling of being unable to face the day. Worst of all, I could not so much as sit down to write. The discovery of real lumps in my breast sent me flying to the doctor in a panic, ready to plan my funeral. They turned out to be nothing more than accumulations of fluid which, the consultant reassured me as he drew it off with a syringe, was common enough at my age. The menopause, with all its unpleasant symptoms, was beginning to prove something of a handicap in our struggle for survival. Touching ground again after this shock I told myself fiercely that if I was becoming paranoid, or even merely neurotic, it was not without some justification.

Events seemed bent on proving me right. Joy, my close friend next door, suddenly phoned me one morning and asked me to go in — she was not well. I found her in severe pain, her hand pressed to her face. I summoned the doctor, and was relieved when he came promptly.

This was, in fact, the beginning of a long and serious illness, necessitating many hospital visits, which was to continue throughout the whole length of the winter. She was extremely brave, for the pain, when it came, was acute, while the only drug which relieved it had a long list of side effects which severely limited her activities. I could only admire her courage, for not only did she never complain, she somehow managed to continue with her writing throughout, so that few of those who knew her outside the medical profession suspected how very ill she had been. Somehow, this very courage of hers made me more aware of what I saw as my own failure, for I no longer had the will, let alone the desire, to write. Joy's illness was one more proof of the hostility of the world, and, facing it, I no longer had the strength to hold on to the activity that was my own lifeline.

More and more I turned to religion to supply me with this strength, but here, too, my growing depression seemed to block the way. My real needs seemed to be unanswerable, and I could not even begin to articulate them. I met with such constant kindness at church that I felt guilty for being unhappy, and struggled to preserve a façade of cheerfulness and acceptance. It was a very brittle one, and it disintegrated the moment I reached the reality of my loneliness at home. Even so, I headed for church each Sunday as if to the one safe haven I knew. One day, I felt, if I persisted, I might find the same simplicity of faith I so envied the others, and the same peace of mind. At least as I sat among the warm colours and glowing wood, polished and smoothed with faithful love, I could find a refuge, however temporary, from the pain that was always there, just below the surface, at the beck of a familiar hymn tune, or the wording of an old prayer.

Until, that is, one Sunday morning early in December, when the churchwarden, in the vicar's absence, mounted the chancel steps and quietly told the assembled congregation that Peter and Marilyn were to leave us the following March, to go to Paris. The building around me seemed to give a sudden, ominous lurch, as if something had given way deep in the foundations. I stood there helplessly, fighting back the tears. This place, then, was no safer than any other. Here, too, like anywhere else, people I loved could leave me and go their way, smiling, to live their lives elsewhere. Although I knew that this particular departure was unlike all the others that marked my life like standing stones, it felt the same, as the pain and misery and rage began to churn inside me. Misery and pain are totally egocentric, and there was no way that I could view things rationally or generously.

To me, Marilyn and Peter were lighthouse keepers guarding the entrance to the only safe harbour I knew. They had saved me when I had been in danger of drowning. In saving me, they had changed my whole outlook on life, and I loved them with all the gratitude of which I was capable. Now they were leaving the lighthouse to stand empty, at least for a while, and I was afraid that, without them, I would never be able to find the harbour again. I began to wonder if it had all been another illusion — like the happiness of the early days of my marriage.

The ground seemed to be crumbling beneath us, yet somehow ordinary life had to go on. I did not dare to allow it to do anything else — we were running in order to stand still.

Christa had urged me to allow Joanna to sit for the scholarship examinations to the Royal College of Music and the Royal Academy of Music that winter. Although it was highly unlikely that, as she was only sixteen, she would be awarded one, Christa felt that the auditions would be valuable experience for her — and there was always the outside chance that she might, in fact, carry off a scholarship. I was a little dubious, for, in the event of this happening, I thought that Joanna was too young to give up her general education and specialize entirely in music. There was certainly no harm in her trying the auditions, however, and getting some idea of what she was up against.

So, on a clear, sunny morning a few days before Christmas, Joanna and I made our way to the Royal College of Music. We travelled by a combination of tube and taxi, as driving in London was still a prospect which reduced me to a state of witless panic.

When we came out again late that afternoon, after a gruelling day, it was to find that the sunshine had vanished, and the heavens had released a deluge which showed no sign of abating. All taxis, of course, had disappeared from the streets. Too tired to think clearly, we set off across the park in the forlorn hope of finding a stray one. Soon, dazzled by the headlights and the reflections on the wet roads, we were completely lost. Joanna, carrying the heavy cello, was desperately tired and, with my back problem, I could not help her. We both longed for the sight of a friendly face, or a helping hand, but none came — everyone else, it seemed, was busily rushing about their lives.

Joanna did not complain, but I was close to breaking down. Only the knowledge that I must not make things even harder for her steadied me. Finally, we stumbled out onto the Bayswater Road, and took our place in a bus queue. Ten minutes later, what must have been the only empty taxi in London delivered us from it, the driver startled by the amount of enthusiasm with which we greeted him, and we reached Marylebone in time for the last of the pre-rush-hour trains. Safely in it, we could laugh at our bedraggled state. My laughter, however, had a brittle note about it. Somehow, for me, the whole incident had thrown into sharp relief our vulnerability, and our isolation. Lost in the dark in the great park, with the rest of the world rushing past unnoticing, uncaring — it seemed to me an exact image of our situation.

Fortunately, Christmas was upon us soon after, and there was no more time to think about it as once more we went through the motions of rejoicing. This year my heart was not in it — it felt, as it had once before, like a charade. I never had known how to rejoice when someone was going away.

Just before she left to go on her NYO course, Joanna received a letter from the College. They were not offering her a scholarship, but they were offering her a place for the next academic session on the results of the audition. At sixteen, this was no mean achievement, but I could see from the set of her chin that for her it was not good enough. "I'll try the Academy," she announced.

My heart sank. The Royal Academy of Music auditions were held only a couple of months before her O-levels. I would have preferred to avoid anything stressful around that time, but, as I looked at my daughter's determined face, I realized that this was not my decision. Not any more. Joanna was growing up, and my role in her life, almost imperceptibly, was changing. Our hitherto clear-cut relationship was clear no longer, and in this, too, I felt confused and lost, afraid of hurting, yet wanting to help. My own experience had taught me only one rule of which I could feel certain: whatever mistakes either of us made, Joanna must be sure that she had, always, my support and my love. There would always be that, however little else I might in the end have to give, and I wanted her to know it. At a time when everything seemed to be shifting around us, one small certainty could make a resting place for the spirit, and something deep inside me was telling me, insistently, that she needed this now, more than ever before.

(

CHAPTER NINE

Seventh Year: Landslide

I had no particular desire to welcome in the New Year. The digestive trouble which had begun in the days when I was at my most anxious about Simon, before his diagnosis, and which always returned to plague me in times of stress, was making life very uncomfortable now, and robbing me of what little energy I had. I was worried, too, at my continuing dependence on Librium, for which I had a repeat prescription. It was time now, I felt, to be free of it, and my acupuncturist, when I returned to him, encouraged me, but this was easier said than done. When I tried to cut down on it, I became even more irritable and jumpy than usual, and had difficulty sleeping — all of which seemed hardly fair on the family. There was, it seemed, no comfort to be had anywhere.

Joy's illness, though now under control and no longer painful, had left her very weak, and she was making only slow progress back to full health. In the vicarage they were busy packing up and making all the innumerable arrangements involved in moving a big family from one country to another, and I did not want to witness that. Ray was always there at the end of the phone, and he always helped, but I needed a human presence, an encouraging arm, not a disembodied voice heard through a machine.

It did not improve matters greatly when Joanna returned from her NYO course looking very serious, and stating her intention of putting in many, many more hours of practice a day. She had, she told me, been doing far less than her fellow cellists, and needed to catch up. I could not see how, with the approach of O-levels, she was going to fit everything in, for she was very conscientious about her school work, and could not bear to be given bad marks — but I knew better than to object. Her day, in fact, became rigidly compartmentalized, and the rest of us were obliged to live with hours and hours of cello scales, arpeggios and exercises. I used to dread the scales in thirds and octaves, where the beauty of the instrument vanished into an appalling caterwauling as the musician struggled with difficult feats of intonation to the point where the hair rose on the back of my neck.

Neither Joanna nor Christa could understand my reactions. To them, scales were fascinating, even beautiful. To me they were fast becoming a form of daily torture. My post-Christmas weekend break at a music course seemed like paradise after home. There at least I could enjoy the music without having to endure the practice, and this winter I was more appreciative than ever of the company of other adults.

Tom, singing with his schoolmates at Covent Garden, gave me another brief escape in the shape of a dress rehearsal ticket for Verdi's *Otello*. I had learned the ropes by now, and set off early to be near the front of the queue, armed with my thermos and my packet of sandwiches, to be enchanted once again by the sight of my own child moving around the magnificent opera set.

He poured out wine in the opening scene with such aplomb and displayed such convincing fear at the savagery of the storm that I began to wonder if here was not yet another talent, hitherto unspotted. I put the thought from me. By now I was beginning to feel that I could not face the nurture of any more talents — it was too much like running Kew Gardens, orchid house and all, single-handed.

Ray, knowing how low I was feeling, did his best to encourage me — above all to get me writing again. We discussed a project for a book together — I even went up to London to see if we could obtain the support of his colleagues, but we could not get the necessary backing and it came to nothing. I could not hold back the humiliating tears when I left the interview, and I wandered into All Souls, Langham Place, to look for a moment of quiet in which to try to come to terms with everything. They were, unfortunately, tuning the organ. It was not very different from a cello practice, and I left in a hurry. There seemed to be nowhere at all where I could find peace.

By early March I was lower than I had ever been before. Everything seemed to be blurred in a grey, exhausted fog. My solitude hung around me so heavily that all I wanted to do was sleep. The vicarage family were now about to depart. I did not go to the farewell party the parish held for them. I could not. I hated myself for feeling as I did. I even wished they had never acted lovingly towards me. I hated the church, and I certainly hated everything I knew about God. I was certain I would never feel the same way about religion again. I had thought to find my own approach to divine love through the medium of loving human acts, but this now seemed merely a dream. I was once more out in the cold.

The coming of spring revived me: the pace of events accelerated, and I responded mechanically to the demands which every year increased at this time.

Joanna took her audition at the Academy. It was a far less strenuous and more relaxed affair than the dramatic day at the College. Once again she missed the scholarship — but was offered a place. She received the news philosophically. By now she had accepted that her age was against her. She was uncertain, however, whether to take the place, or whether to stay on at school and put in some time in the sixth form, so as to grow up a little more before beginning college life.

In the end she decided on the latter course, though with no great enthusiasm. She was no longer enjoying school as she once had, and she bitterly resented the well-meaning attempts of her teachers to dissuade her from a career in music. They only served, in fact, to increase her determination — and her hours of practice. Unfortunately, they also made her feel still more isolated. No-one, it seemed, understood her — except her fellow musicians, many of whom suffered at school in the same way. I, too, since I did not appreciate the practice, and was undecided as to the best course of action for her to adopt, was somewhat suspect. I, in fact, was completely out of my depth.

Happily, there occurred next one of those extraordinary pieces of magic which have lit up my life at intervals over the long years alone, and which helped, I truly think, to keep me alive and sane. One of our churchwardens phoned me out of the blue to offer me a free place in a block booking travelling to Paris to attend the institution of our vicar in his new church. It entailed going over one day, by a combination of train and boat, and travelling back the next — staying overnight with members of the Parisian congregation. Two years previously, with the pain in my back, I would not have been able to accept. This year at least that part of me was strong enough to allow my sense of adventure a little play. In any case, the offer was deeply comforting. Someone, somewhere, it seemed to say, had some inkling of my feelings of loss, and was trying to help.

The journey reminded me of my student days, when I used to make the trip to Paris regularly by the cheapest routes. I had never travelled as one of a group before, and this was a very oddly assorted one, but there was much laughing and teasing and I enjoyed the whole trip. Seeing Paris again, however briefly, woke me up to the fact that not only it, but a whole wide world still went on living its life outside our home — and that one day I, too, might yet be free to partake of that larger life. The family was, after all, beginning to grow up. The whole visit was a powerful stimulant — though it still hurt to see my old friends' new home and new commitments.

The trouble with the family growing up was that the cost of feeding and clothing them was increasing frighteningly once more. The school's help with Joanna's cello lessons had released a little more money to help with everyday expenses, but this, as inflation increased, was no longer enough to feed the boys' enormous appetites — nor was Joanna's far behind. Everyone was growing fast, and though there were fourteen months between Tom and David, they were exactly the same size, so that there could be no handing down of clothes. Our income was simply no longer adequate to meet their needs, and these, I knew, were not going to grow less as they advanced into their teens. Friends had told me that Paul was now doing extremely well in Canada, and assured me that he could afford to give us more, though he had always denied this to me. Reluctantly, and only because I could see no other way, I resolved to go back to the court to apply for an increase in maintenance payments. If the judge, on seeing the evidence, believed that I was acting correctly and in the best interests of the children, I could hardly be doing wrong. A few days after my return from Paris, I went to see John, my solicitor, to begin preliminary negotiations.

This entailed, of course, listing all our expenses — a logical enough requirement, but one which plunged me back once more into my winter depression. I loathed this financial dependence on Paul with all my heart and soul, for it maintained links with him which I longed to break. Yet because our children had exceptional needs, there was no way I could properly care for them without this vital income. Both Ray and John supported me solidly. Both regarded supplying the needs of the children as an obligation which a father should not disregard, the more so if that father enjoys a comfortable income.

In spite of their support I felt bitter and humiliated as I listed the number of times our piano was tuned and the children's teeth painted with fluoride. It seemed a violation of our privacy. I had worked hard to save the money for the down payment on our first house. I had worked even harder looking after the children and our home. Now I was being called upon to account for every penny in order to beg for our basic keep. The hurt of the rejection which had put me in this plight was redoubled. So was my anger against a society which, despite the findings of the 1974 Finer Report, still all but disregarded the plight of the thousands of one-parent families who now form the new poor. It is very hard to care properly for children in a society which does not recognize the importance of doing so. Because I cared, cared passionately, I now found myself in a position of total weakness. My sole asset was that I was articulate enough to fight, to plead my cause.

Being articulate, however, was not enough. Physical stamina was also necessary, and I felt that mine had gone. I did not think that it was ever going to be possible for me to recover from the breakdown of my marriage. I wanted to forget Paul, but I was not allowed to. I was still obsessed by him. If I succeeded in banishing him from my days, he returned to haunt my dreams. By now I had managed to cut right back on the Librium, but my sleep was anything but peaceful. The drug had dealt effectively with the symptoms, but it had not touched the feelings of anger, grief and failure which produced them. I had the sensation that everything was slipping gradually out of control — it was as if I were clinging on to safety by my fingertips — and they, too, were weakening.

As if to test this, my last strength, Joanna seemed to be demanding — and needing — more and more attention. She had done extremely well in her mock O-levels, from which she had concluded that, as she had done no work for them whatsoever, none was necessary when it came to the real thing. As a result, inevitably, cello practice filled every last minute of the day.

In the meantime, I had written off to the Royal Northern College of Music at Manchester for information. The daughter of a friend had opted to go there, and we were attracted by her glowing reports. I thought, too, that it might well be better for Joanna to spend her college days at a distance from home, so that she might fully enter into student life. That had been my

brother's wise advice to me when I went to university, and I had
always been glad that I had followed it. Provided that she could
find a good teacher there, Manchester might well be better for
her than London.

Music festival time had come round again, with all the
rushing around and extra rehearsing that this entailed. There
was an additional event to attend this year, as Joanna's quartet
was competing in the string ensemble class.

It was a popular class, and many groups had entered. Joanna
and her friends were playing part of Haydn's "Kaiser"
Quartet, with its beautiful slow movement. They had taken
the trouble to dress alike, in simple black and white, and I
thought how professional they looked as they tuned their instruments.

The crowded room became very still as they began to play.
Everyone, I thought, seemed to be experiencing the *frisson* I had
felt when I heard them rehearsing. There was something very
special, very moving, about the performance of these four
young people. They had the musicality, the rapport and the
control of far more experienced musicians, only it was applied
with the freshness and vitality of the young. It was for me one
of those occasions when I knew without a doubt that all the
fighting, the struggle and the heartache were justified — not just
because the quartet won the class, which meant nothing in
terms of their careers, but because each had been empowered to
give all that was unique in him or her to create something which
transcended their individual selves, something of rare beauty. I
was somewhat shaken. I felt more strongly than ever that I had
been entrusted with the nurture of something very rare and
delicate, and this evening gave me the certainty that this was not
just maternal bias or a bad case of ego projection. I had been
given a treasure to carry.

The happiness of that evening was, had I known it, to be the
last for a long time. As O-levels approached, Joanna's effervescent, affectionate personality seemed to change. She withdrew
into herself and her music in a way I had never known her do
before. I had been unaware that in the schools of today it is
customary to send the pupils home on 'study leave' during the
weeks preceding public examinations — as Joanna's year was
the top one in the school, there was no precedent to warn me. It
was, therefore, quite suddenly, after the end of the half term

holiday, that I learned there was to be no more school that term, not even after the end of the examinations.

I was shocked and angry about this. I believe that children facing the stress of public exams need the support of their peer group and of the structured school day more, perhaps, than at any other time. Finding themselves suddenly deprived of these two sources of security leaves the vulnerable teenager feeling excluded and uncared for. I am convinced that in Joanna's case, the loss of her friends and teachers contributed significantly to the crisis that was now approaching. While her schoolmates lay around at home, morosely watching TV or finding themselves part-time jobs, Joanna, far from studying, devoted all the hours that would have been spent at school to cello practice. The entire day, and the entire house, was thus dominated by the cello. It was clear to me that there was a strong obsessive element in this, even though I knew that musicians have to practise long hours.

In the end I consulted Ray. He came to see her, and talked with her at some length. He, too, was very concerned, and arranged to come again.

Meanwhile the head of strings from the Royal Northern College of Music had replied to my letter of inquiry. She had, she explained, a flat in London, and invited Joanna to go and play to her there. We went for what we expected to be an informal interview — only it turned out to be a searching audition. The outcome was the offer of a place at the College after Joanna had put in a year in the sixth form at school. She was also given a list of those teachers at the College who lived in London, so that she might visit them for consultation lessons and so decide with whom she would eventually like to study.

This third offer decided matters. Joanna decided to forget about scholarships and accept the place — largely, I suspect, because at that time she needed more than anything else to have a clear idea of where she was going.

Such a positive step towards planning her future should, I felt, have given her some feeling of security, but this was far from the case. The once good relationship between us was coming under increasing strain. Tensions were multiplying and outbursts of anger were frequent on both sides. The least sign of maternal authority from me provoked bitter resentment. I tried frantically to readjust to this new state of affairs, but I could not change my ways quickly enough, nor even always understand what I was doing wrong.

The fact that in our family I was both father and mother exposed me to a double ration of criticism. It was almost a relief, paradoxically, to notice that in cello lessons the same tension and hostility characterized her reactions to Christa's comments and corrections. Christa was Joanna's 'cello Mum', but the once happy relationship was deteriorating before my eyes. I was glad that Christa had teenage children of her own and was able to understand.

Joanna now started to visit the teachers from the College for consultation lessons, and before long she made her choice. She made it, however, somewhat drastically by declaring that she wanted to change teacher the very next term, and not wait until she reached College. She wanted, she said, to progress faster, and would listen to no argument. Etiquette demanded that we give Christa a term's notice, but my tense, volatile daughter had no time for such niceties. I was faced, therefore, with the unpleasant task of telling Christa that the pupil on whom for five years she had lavished such care now wanted — almost at once — to move on to someone else. I was too concerned about my plainly unhappy daughter to oppose her, but I hated having to hurt Christa. The last lesson was a miserable one. To her everlasting credit, Christa understood, and accepted the situation, but we both felt very sad.

For eight, nine hours a day Joanna now drove at her practice. I was beginning to fear for my sanity, for the constant noise deprived me of any possibility of quiet thought. I could not even hear when anyone spoke to me on the phone. In the end, I asked the churchwardens if she might work in the still empty vicarage. I was not sure it was good for her to spend the whole day alone in an empty house, but I was at the end of my wits. I had no idea how best to act. I was growing very frightened, for I sensed Joanna's own fear. I felt that she was even more lost than I was. The repetitive, never-ending exercises on the cello reminded me vividly of Simon's compulsive swinging of cupboard doors when he was little — that too gave him a sense of safety in a world over which he felt he had no control. I was acutely aware of my disadvantage in not being a professional musician — for I had absolutely no experience to guide me when it came to helping Joanna. My brothers and I had been given piano lessons because this was considered a good thing to give your children. We all three loved music, but this love had been neither developed nor educated. I was, as a result, trying to care for a talent which I did not really understand — and it did not make for easy communications between us.

She now saw little or nothing of her schoolmates. Her only outings were to the occasional concert and to her beloved orchestra on Friday evenings. She came alive then, and the droop which of late had become habitual left her shoulders. I could see that with her musical friends she could relax and be herself. She liked to linger in their company, whereas when she visited school to sit her exams, she came straight home again. She did not belong there any more.

In July, Paul came over from Canada. This year, since his visit coincided with Simon's long annual holiday from Somerset Court, Simon was to go with his brothers for a week by the sea. As Joanna had decided that she would spend her one year in the sixth form taking a single A-level — French — I had arranged for her to spend a couple of weeks with Anne Marie in Metz, to improve the fluency of her spoken French. She had firmly stuck to her guns over not seeing her father, and the visit to France seemed a good way of giving her something fresh to think about. She could not take her cello with her on the long journey by train and boat, and privately I rejoiced at this. The rest, I was sure, would be good for her. The novelty of living in a French family might well rouse her from the apathy which seemed to lie over all her activities other than music — and the family were old friends of ours, not strangers.

I felt quite pleased with myself for arranging matters so tidily, and was hopeful that Joanna might yet readjust to the new patterns in her life. It was not the first time in my life that I had blinded myself to the real gravity of the situation — but I had very little resilience left with which to meet anything more serious than the superficial symptoms which I had noticed. I was quite cheerful when I saw Joanna off.

The more so, as nearly a week of freedom from family cares now lay before me. Rarely had I needed it quite so badly. Longing as I always did for the company of my own kin, I was to travel up to Cumbria to visit my uncle and aunt — my father's younger brother and his wife. It was a very happy visit, which left me wishing that the distance between us was less. My

uncle bears a strong physical resemblance to the father I lost
as a teenager, and being with him made me feel less alone.
They drove me round the beautiful Cumbrian countryside and
generally did all they could for my comfort and amusement, so
that I relaxed, and for a few days succeeded in forgetting my
troubles. It was fortunate, it turned out, that I had that brief
respite.

The boys, back from their holiday with Paul, were in a state
of mingled anger and anxiety. Usually, they enjoyed their time
with him, but this year the enjoyment had been spoiled by their
concern over Simon. Their placid, easy-going, autistic brother
had shown signs of great disturbance during his week away.
Both the younger boys felt intensely responsible for him, and it
had frightened them to see him crying, or urinating in the
garden — something that never happened at home.

Simon's autistic fear of change, coupled with his total in-
ability to understand why his father no longer lived with his
mother, had rendered him unable to adapt to the new situation.
He had been, obviously, very confused and unhappy, and this,
naturally, had made his brothers unhappy too. They had not felt
able to talk to Paul about it, so that they returned home in no
peaceful frame of mind. They begged me not to allow Simon to
go with them again. I promised to think it over — the request
held more implications than they were aware of.

It was a relief when Simon returned to Somerset Court — not
because I wanted to be rid of him, but because there he would
have a chance slowly to recover his balance after the upset.
Somerset Court was his safe world, where he was not subject to
the confusing behaviour of the rest of us.

Soon after, Tom and David went off again themselves, this
time to an orchestral course and a Church Pathfinder Camp
respectively. Joanna returned immediately after their departure,
and I thanked my stars that I was able to give her my undivided
attention, for even I could not hide from myself the fact that she
was in a very disturbed state of mind.

The visit to France had certainly dispelled her apathy — but
only to produce an explosion of rage such as I had never known
from her before. Most of it was directed at Isabelle, Anne
Marie's fourteen-year-old daughter, who had been so good with
her guests when we visited her before. This time it had been
different, according to Joanna, who was veritably seething with

fury at the French girl's behaviour, making no allowances whatsoever for differences of culture, language or age — and without the least vestige of her usual sense of humour.

The absence of any form of music in the household had left her both bored and without defences. I began to feel decidedly sorry for Anne Marie, who must, I felt, have had a trying fortnight keeping the peace. Joanna, it seemed, had been determined to dislike everything. The French, she declared, thought of nothing but food, and most of them were appallingly overweight. I had to smile at the grain of truth in this exaggeration. Anne Marie fought a perpetually losing battle with her comfortably rounded figure, and if Isabelle took after her mother she was no doubt having similar troubles. Anne Marie, too, was an excellent cook, and I remembered how we had all, Joanna in particular, enjoyed her culinary achievements when we had stayed with her.

My smile faded in the course of the next few days, however. I was puzzled by Joanna's vehemence. Her anger was both real and deep. It was no passing teenage explosion. Again and again she told me how she could not stand fat people, or people who spent too much time thinking about food. She herself, she announced, was too fat, and intended to lose some weight. She, who had always eaten with relish anything I placed before her, suddenly now refused to touch all but a bare minimum of salad and fruit.

I heard this with dismay. She is of a very similar build to me — and I have never been in the least fat. Our diet as a family, moreover, had always contained plenty of brown bread, fresh fruit, yogurt and honey, with only a sprinkling of convenience foods, so that there was not too much room for manoeuvre. Even the small helping of food on her plate Joanna now picked at as though it disgusted her. In noticing this I found it difficult to hide my irritation, but I gritted my teeth and managed to say nothing. I was resolved to play the whole thing down.

As I saw it, my daughter had now succumbed to the teenage rage for slimming. I had not expected this to happen in view of her declared aversion for fashion, make-up and boys. I was, if anything, relieved that she should at last be showing an interest in matters feminine, even if her priorities did seem a little odd. All the same, I sensed that the matter needed careful handling. As an advertising copywriter I had worked for a while on a slimming product account, and had written of the dangers of slimming without proper medical supervision — though in fact I still had no real idea of the nature of the dangers involved.

I decided to try to talk it over, woman to woman, with Joanna, and told her what little I had learned. She responded, I thought, in a very adult way, and we worked out together how she might safely lose a little weight by cutting down on certain foods, whilst still maintaining a balanced diet. She seemed sensible about it, and I breathed a sigh of relief. I could see that she really did think herself too fat. At least she was taking an interest in her appearance.

By the time she went off to her NYO course at the end of the week, she seemed a good deal calmer and more cheerful. The course overlapped this year with our family holiday, and I had been forced to ask Joan to come to our rescue by collecting Joanna from the last concert for me, and putting her next day onto the train for Dorset.

After a good deal of agonizing, I had finally decided not to include Simon in the holiday this year. Although the short break in Cumbria had helped, I was still feeling desperately low, and extremely tired, too much so to face the extra demands of caring for him as well as the others. It was the first time I had ever left him out of our summer holiday, and it was a very painful decision.

Trying to be adventurous, I had this year chosen a cottage in a different place. It was not many miles from the one where we had spent two successful holidays, and it had the advantage of being situated further from the busy coastal road. We had not been there long, however, when I realized that I had made another mistake. It was, of course, too late to do anything about it.

The cottage itself was very pretty and clean, and stood in a narrow, leafy lane, which was all quite delightful. The flaw, from our particular point of view, was that the village to which it belonged had none of the community life which had made us feel so welcome before. Bisected, indeed killed off, by a busy main road, its empty church and meagre shops left us isolated once again. We worked hard at enjoying ourselves with cliff walks and swimming, but somehow, for me at least, the heart had gone out of it. Tom and David had reached an age where all they wanted in order to be happy was freedom for physical activity, whereas all I wanted was to rest — to sleep and forget everything. They were very affectionate, and caring with me — but our needs were not exactly compatible.

We were all glad when the day came to meet Joanna off the train. She seemed even more tired than usual after an NYO course, and she explained that she had been very ill during the days before the final concert. Most of the orchestra, it seemed, had been felled by a particularly unpleasant gastric virus, and she herself had been confined to bed for a couple of days. I was glad that she had a week of sea air in front of her, to help her to pick up again before the beginning of the school year. She seemed curiously languid, and withdrawn, most unlike her usual holiday self.

As the days went by, however, there was no sign of returning vitality. She remained quiet and listless, content to lie on the beach while her brothers splashed around in the chilly waters of the Channel. This was even more strange. In all our previous seaside holidays it had been Joanna who led the way into the sea, however wet and windy the day, hurling herself through the breakers, jeering at her cowardly mother, laughing at grey skies and icy waters. Now I had to chivvy her into the sea, only to have her run out again almost immediately, blue and shivering with cold, protesting that she was too tired. The sea air failed lamentably to restore the colour to her cheeks or to remove the dark circles from under her eyes — or, above all, to restore her missing appetite.

She was continuing to display the same ostentatious disgust for food which had so struck me on her return from France. Every crumb of pastry would be left on the side of her plate, every scrap of potato, and every grain of rice. She would take lettuce, but she would meticulously shake every drop of vinaigrette dressing off it before eating it — she who, when she was little, used to lick up the dressing and leave the lettuce. I could not understand it. It was as if we had never discussed the matter together. Joanna, apart from the almost forgotten difficulties at boarding school, had always been an intelligent, rational person. She now seemed suddenly to be acting quite out of character. She had agreed with me that it was necessary to maintain a balanced diet whilst cutting down a little on the quantity she consumed — yet here she was shrinking back from essential food as if it was laced with weed-killer.

I had not the least idea how to handle this situation — except that instinct told me to continue to play it down, which I did. Eventually, as the week approached its end, and she was still refusing to eat, I felt I must try to broach the subject again with her, for I was beginning to be seriously concerned about her health. For some reason it was hard to be casual, and I felt oddly nervous as I reminded her of our previous conversation on the topic of diet. I was very taken aback when she did not offer any argument or opposition. She merely smiled at me — and agreed with everything I said. This disarmed, indeed routed me. I turned away in relief that she was, after all, being perfectly sensible. Only the relief was short-lived, for she continued to behave as if nothing whatsoever had passed between us, rejecting every food except egg yolk, citrus fruit and raw vegetables, apparently unaware of any discrepancy between words and deeds.

The arrival of her O-level results, forwarded from home, did not mend matters. She was aghast to find that she, who had never had anything but As right the way up the school, had now only managed to achieve one — for music, naturally. Until this year she had always worked hard and conscientiously, taking immense pains over the presentation of her work, and this perfectly respectable crop of Bs was to her an appalling failure, which did nothing to lighten her present dark mood. Nothing I could say comforted her.

Fortunately for our sanity, a phone call from an old friend of my father-in-law announced his imminent arrival "to take us fishing". A vague project aired months before during a visit had become a concrete actuality. Nicky's coming was like that of a kindly magician who, by waving his magic wand, transformed the last two days of the holiday. Suddenly we found ourselves eating fish-and-chip suppers, fishing for mackerel, visiting Lyme Regis — doing all the things which make holidays special and which I found so hard to organize amid the general shortage of money and energy. For thirty-six marvellous hours the load was taken right off me and I could be happy watching my children enjoying themselves — even Joanna. The memory of it was to lighten that of the whole sinister fortnight.

School started again immediately after our return home. It was none too soon. By now I stood in desperate need of a few hours a day of quiet. The burden of my responsibilities seemed to have become heavier than ever this summer. Never before had I found the children so emotionally demanding. I felt I had nothing left to give anyone. Isolation, loneliness, exhaustion — my old enemies hemmed me in, and I felt at bay.

Then Joanna came home to tell me that, since she was only studying for the one A-level, French, she was only required to spend a few periods a week at school.

My stomach turned over. I knew all too well what that meant. The vicarage was now occupied by the new vicar and his family, so I would be shut in again with the scales and exercises and a daughter once more cut off from friends and school routine, a daughter who seemed completely lost and unhappy and whom I no longer had the least idea how to help.

At the end of the first week of term I had to attend a dental appointment. Unfortunately, or perhaps, as it turned out, fortunately, the dentist had to do a very big filling, which took a long time. He did not actually hurt me, but somehow the long spell in his chair, with tense muscles and aching jaw, was the last straw. Something deep inside me seemed to snap. I left the surgery with my face numb, and the tears held back by the last of my control. I could stand no more. Everything was finally too much. The task of bringing up the family alone was too great, and too long in duration. I needed help. I had to have it — *real* help, regular help.

During the drive home I reached a level of desperation that I had never known before, and the force of it took me past the last remaining barriers of pride and fear, and into the local social services department. Shaking all over, vainly trying to stem a tidal wave of tears, barely able to articulate my own name, I asked to see a social worker.

This local office had not existed when I was first on my own. If it had, we might have been spared much misery. I knew of it now because workers there had contacted me occasionally for information about autism. Now it was my turn to ask for help. A social worker came and sat quietly with me, and I talked until my tears ceased, and I could talk no more.

Somehow, even then, I could only pour out the topmost, superficial layer of troubles — the day-to-day anxieties which formed really only a small part of this terrifying chaos of emotion. I could not touch on the deeper things — the endless solitary misery that gnawed away daily at my very roots, the frightening situation with Joanna. Instead, I found myself telling her about David starting this term at secondary school, and my worries about him. Nonetheless, the interview acted as a safety valve — the flood of talk eased some of the pressure, and eventually I recovered myself enough to resume the journey home. I could hold on a little longer.

That weekend, while shopping in the village, I asked Joanna to weigh herself on the scales outside the chemist. I had never bothered to buy any for the family, as I had never attached much importance to weight. Now we both received a shock. In a month, she had lost over a stone.

I was desperately worried by this, for I knew it was far too drastic a reduction. If it continued, she would soon lose all her remaining stamina and vitality — and she did not have much. Summoning up every last scrap of patience I tried to explain this to her, this time appealing to the musician in her, pointing out that considerable reserves of strength were necessary if she was to survive long hours of rehearsal and performance. She agreed with me sweetly once again, smiling kindly at my overanxiety, but this time it was not to be so easily allayed. Sure enough, the days went by and she continued to reject everything I gave her to eat. We might never have spoken.

The situation at school was contributing its own share of tension. Joanna had chosen French as her one A-level subject chiefly because it was one which it seemed possible to cover in a year, since it involved comparatively little reading. As there was, all the same, a great deal of grammar to be learned, I offered to give her extra coaching at home, with the approval of the head of department at the school. I little suspected just how unfortunate the proposal was to prove. It was, in fact, a dire mistake. The last thing either of us needed was any extra strain upon our relationship. I had thought the work might give us some reciprocal pleasure, as Joanna is intelligent, and has a musician's ear for languages, whilst I very much enjoy teaching on a one-to-one basis. I was soon disillusioned. She was suffering from so acute a sense of failure after her O-level results that corrections upset her to the point of tears, and every piece of work set seemed to weigh her down with all the cares of the world. Far from enjoying it, she made it clear that she hated working with me. After a couple of weeks I saw there was nothing for it but to acknowledge my mistake and back out.

On a rational level, I realized that we were far too closely and, at the moment, painfully involved to be able to sustain a teacher-pupil relationship, but for all that I felt hurt, and rejected. I felt I could not communicate with my daughter any more. The only area in which she seemed unchanged was her music. She had recently started lessons with her new teacher in London. Although she was enthusiastic about them, I suspected that she found it all very strange, and somewhat bewildering, after the long years of Christa's watchful care.

At least the new teacher discouraged the long hours of practice which had become the pattern over the last year. He preferred far shorter periods of intense concentration. Instead of devoting the free time to her French, however, Joanna mystified me still further by spending all available hours in the kitchen — baking. Big cakes, little cakes, iced cakes, fruit cakes, biscuits, scones — in the most cornucopian of my earth mother days I had never produced as much as my daughter was doing now. At first I interpreted this sudden interest in cookery as a good sign — until I noticed that she never touched any of her handiwork herself, but sat smiling benevolently while her brothers devoured it delightedly. I was less enthusiastic. I had never cared for rich cakes, and the many ingredients made significant inroads into the housekeeping budget — but I had not the heart to stop her. It was good to see her actually looking happy. Giving her her head in the kitchen was one of the few ways in which I still felt I could reach her.

Her weight continued to drop inexorably, no matter what we said. A frightening suspicion was forming at the back of my mind. The local library contained a couple of books on the subject of anorexia nervosa. I borrowed them, and, concealing them from Joanna, proceeded to read them. I had barely heard of the illness before, and knew just enough to have a vague idea as to what it consisted of. Now I wanted, needed, to know the details. I returned the books far from reassured, but feeling that at least now I had a few facts to steer by. I still hoped that if I went on playing the whole thing down, the problem might resolve itself; but I had read enough to worry me deeply.

Suddenly, like a life belt thrown from a ship passing in the dark, a letter came from the social services department. It was from the senior social worker, whom I had not met on the afternoon of my desperate visit. She had, the letter said, read the report on it in the case book, and wondered if it would help me to discuss my problems further, with her. She even offered me a date and time when she could come to the house.

The extraordinary thing was that I did not at once grasp the importance of that letter. I had, after all, been waiting for it for fourteen years, ever since the diagnosis of Simon. Its arrival was to prove a major turning point in my life — and I was too low to recognize it. If anything, my first reaction was one of wariness, for it was typed on official paper, and nearly all my encounters with officialdom had only ever caused me further pain.

No doubt the wariness showed when Helen came to the house a couple of weeks later. I was very nervous, but her down-to-earth, businesslike manner soon reassured me. This time I did not even know how to start to talk about our problems, but she led the way gently, and, as she glimpsed their complexity, began to work out a plan of action. I could hardly believe my ears when she told me she would come to see me once a week — except during the school holidays, for she had children of her own. This miraculous visit, therefore, was not to be unique. There was no need to try to cram into it everything that was troubling me — Helen was caring enough to give me time. I realized then that I was actually being offered the support which I had craved for so long.

Very quickly, as I became aware of her professionalism and her experience, I grew to trust her. With her help I began to uncover the roots of the depression which disabled me so continuously — roots which sank deep into my war-shattered childhood, with its desolate experience of evacuation and deprivation. Paul's rejection and desertion of me had reinforced and extended that old pain, and profound depression was the inevitable result. I realized how writing my ill-fated second book had been my own attempt to lessen the hurt, rather as one rubs at an aching tooth — but I had only succeeded in irritating it. I had, sure enough, disinterred a number of old, dark memories, but I had neither the skill nor the objectivity to perceive the effect that those unhappy experiences had had upon my life, nor how I might modify it. I had simply left them lying around like victims after a major road accident, with no doctor at hand to know what to do with them. Now, at last, with Helen's help, I began to put things together.

The comfort which I drew from this work with her was altogether extraordinary. I wanted, badly, to get better, to function once more as a whole, healthy human being instead of the zombie I felt I was fast becoming. Unfortunately, circumstances were once more against me. The therapy had to be interrupted before it had really got under way — for Joanna's needs suddenly began to eclipse mine with the result that I had to lean on Helen in a different way.

She had only been to visit me three times when I had to take Simon, home for his autumn holiday, for his routine visit to the psychiatrist at the Maudsley Hospital. Apart from the guilt I felt at not including him in the summer holiday, there was little I needed to discuss, and somewhat to my surprise I found myself talking about Joanna instead. In fact, I poured out all my worries, worries which I had not yet even confided to Helen. The psychiatrist listened to me quietly, and asked a few general questions. Then, however, he put the one which suddenly, for me, lit up the whole puzzle as if with a brilliant flare. It was simple enough: he wanted to know if her periods had stopped. As it happened, they had not — not entirely, but I now remembered a fact which I had so far overlooked. Joanna had told me herself that the August one had been somewhat late. The next had been later still, while this month's had not yet arrived, and was by now long overdue. I told the psychiatrist, aware of the significance of what I was saying. I had read in the books from the library that girls who contract anorexia nervosa stop menstruating. I suddenly felt sure that the missing one would not arrive. The whole delicate mechanism of menstruation had been thrown out of gear by the dramatic weight loss.

He asked if I would like to take Joanna to see him. I protested, as I had four years previously, that the distance was too great for the regular visits Joanna would surely need — I simply would not, I felt, be able to cope. Time, energy and money were all in too short supply. I did not really know what I was saying. My mind was stupefied by the impact of the discovery I had just made. I thanked him, and stumbled out of the hospital with Simon to begin the weary journey home.

That day had all the dreamlike qualities of a Cocteau film. I was so silent as I sat in the bus and the train beside my big autistic son that he kept turning to me and saying "Mum?" with a puzzled smile on his face. He could not know, much less understand, that I was struggling to come to terms with the most horrific blow of all that I had ever received. My normal, beautiful daughter, the cherished sister of this autistic son, was anorexic. She was mentally ill, of an illness which, unless I could find someone to rescue her from it, consisted of a slow form of suicide. It did not seem possible that it could be true, but deep inside me I knew absolutely that it was, and I was filled with a slowly gathering panic. I did not know what to do — nor, since I had refused the help of the Maudsley, to whom to turn. This time, it was not the dank fog of depression that hid all the answers from me — but the tormented darkness of a nightmare.

CHAPTER TEN

Seventh Year: Continued

As I lay in bed that night, I wondered what I had ever done to attract the attention of the Furies and provoke so concentrated an attack. I wondered even more a couple of days later when they launched yet another missile in the shape of a phone call from the matron of the home where my mother was living, requesting me formally to find a nursing home for her as soon as possible. She had not, she told me, sufficient trained staff to continue to harbour someone who now needed full nursing care.

I nearly laughed down the phone, so impossible was the timing, but I managed to check myself. I was the only person around to do the caring, and it simply had to be done. I obtained a list of nursing homes in our district from the deaconess at church, and began the job of phoning round. At least in this area it was possible to take practical steps with the feeling that I knew what I was about. And while I concentrated on this, I reflected, I could hardly worry simultaneously about Joanna. Also, thanks to the Benevolent Fund which had financed my mother until now, I would not have to contend with the sole responsibility of the nursing home fees. I blessed the day my father had gone to work for that caring Corporation.

Helen's visit that week was a comfort beyond price. Never had any social worker taken on a family at a more timely moment — at the approach of battle, it now seemed, and a battle which to me looked suspiciously like Armageddon.

Joanna's weight continued to drop. The following week, when it seemed reasonably certain that the missing period was not going to show up, I made an appointment with our family doctor — it was as if I had felt that I needed to be sure of this last symptom before taking action.

I took the precaution of phoning him beforehand to explain the reason for our visit, and to ask whether, in fact, he wanted me to be present at the interview. When, having heard me out, he remarked matter of factly that it sounded like anorexia, and asked me to come with Joanna, I could have hugged him for his directness.

He was very gentle, yet completely frank with her. He told her that she was, indeed, suffering from anorexia nervosa, but that there was nothing he could do to help her, for this was an illness of the mind, not of the body. She would need, he explained, the help of a psychiatrist — and this, at least, was something he could arrange. I had been making inquiries, and had come to the conclusion that a certain clinic in north London might be the best place from which to seek help, since it was easily accessible from our home. So our doctor agreed to write there for an appointment. He told Joanna to come and see him if ever she felt she needed someone to talk to, and, somewhat sadly, saw us out. He probably had a good idea of what lay ahead of us. I, however, felt a good deal relieved as we left the surgery. At last we were doing something.

On the way home, I suggested to Joanna that it was time now to be open about our troubles. It was only fair to Tom and David, who were bound to be closely involved, to explain to them what had happened, and what the situation was — and I also wanted to tell our family and friends. Not unnaturally, she was tearfully reluctant. She was feeling guilty and ashamed. To reassure her, I told her what I knew about the illness, emphasizing that she must not blame herself, for it was no more her fault than if she had contracted some serious physical complaint. I told her how large numbers of girls suffer from it, and that most frequently it arises from the emotional difficulties of growing up. I warned her, however, that the road to recovery was likely to be a hard and a long one, and that it was for this reason that I wanted to be open with everyone about it, for I was absolutely certain that we could not carry this particular load on our own. She was not happy, but she saw my point, and resigned herself — she saw, in any case, that I had made up my mind.

When we told them the bad news that evening, sitting in family council round the kitchen table, Tom and David did their best to understand. I felt that if they realized that their sister had a serious illness they would better tolerate her strange behaviour, and act protectively towards her when difficulties arose in the presence of outsiders. I softened the facts as much as I could, but I could see that they were very frightened. Still, telling them had the desired effect: they were ready to help Joanna in every possible way. We were, in fact, all very frightened. Facts culled from books can seem curiously irrelevant in real life. It helped us greatly to share our fear, at least to some extent, and to feel that we were facing it with a united front.

I never subsequently had cause to regret this decision to be completely open about the illness with anyone I encountered. The years of living with a mentally handicapped person in the family stood us now in good stead. Since we all loved and accepted our autistic Simon, we could see no particular stigma in mental illness — to us it was simply a sign that someone needed help. Such an attitude helped us to withstand some of the more hurtful reactions from other people, though, fortunately, there were not too many of these. Many friends went to the trouble of reading up about the illness in a recently published book★, and they were able to be of considerable help. The hardest to contend with were those who blithely assumed that anorexia was merely a form of teenage silliness, which the sufferer could snap out of with an effort of will — a common misapprehension about depression, too. Yet others — and these were the ones to whom I was the most vulnerable — thought that all Joanna needed in order to recover was extra loving care and a continuous supply of irresistibly delicious food, which implied that I, the mother, had given neither. There were some bitter laughs in the family when such well-meant efforts to tempt her appetite failed.

Despite her increasing thinness and decreasing vitality, Joanna continued to give all she had to her music. In this alone did she seem to want to go on living. Once a week she went off to her lesson in Hampstead, promising me faithfully that she would have lunch at a pizza bar afterwards, before attempting the journey home — a promise that I was beginning to suspect she did not keep. Her cello lessons were now entirely her own affair and I felt that this was a good thing, though I longed to be reassured that she was really happy in them.

The NYO audition had come round again — too soon after the change of teacher for comfort. This year, Tom went off with his sister to make his own first attempt at gaining a place in the orchestra. He, like her, had tried for a County Junior Music Exhibition the previous winter, and he, like her, had not been given one. Nothing daunted, Tom had set his sights firmly on a place in the NYO. We warned him that at thirteen he was unlikely to succeed, but he went off determinedly, dogged as always. I was

★R. L. Palmer, *Anorexia Nervosa — a guide for sufferers and their families* (Pelican Books, 1980)

glad that his audition had fallen on the same day as Joanna's, so
that he could keep a brotherly eye on her — I was beginning to
worry about her physical stamina.

She came home in tears. It had, she told me between sobs, been
intimated to her that as she had now had three good years with
the orchestra, it was time for her to make way for someone else. I
looked at her hunched shoulders, thin white face and wet cheeks,
and my heart felt as if it would burst with pity. There was no
comfort I could give. We both knew that the NYO was run in a
very fair way, and it was quite true — she had indeed had three
marvellous years in it. It was just the timing of the blow that was
so sad, when she was ill and growing worse. Tom, for his part,
was reasonably happy about his audition. There was nothing we
could do but wait for the results. All was still not entirely lost.

The days passed slowly, and still no communication had come
from the clinic in London. Hoping to speed up the process of
obtaining the first appointment, I had sent them a long letter,
giving many details of Joanna's history and background, but still
no reply came. I tried phoning, only to be told that nothing could
be decided before the meeting of a certain committee, and that
this was not yet due. I had hoped that as Joanna was continuing to
lose weight with each day that passed, and as the level of anxiety
in the family was obviously very high, the appointment might
have been given to us with some promptness, but this, it seemed,
was not to be the case. The days dragged on.

The three week wait for that first appointment was one of the
worst times in my entire life. The clinic's refusal to acknowledge
our plight heightened my anxiety to a level that was intolerable.
It made me feel that nobody really cared whether Joanna lived or
died. In more normal circumstances, such a wait would be
inconvenient, perhaps exasperating, but still bearable. In ours, as
I watched my beloved daughter fading away before my eyes, it
was not. During those three weeks, the atmosphere at home
deteriorated violently, as the strain told more and more. Both
Joanna and I were growing desperate, as we tugged in opposite
directions — I trying to pull her back into life, and she determined
to sink yet further away from us.

She resorted to lies and subterfuge to get rid of any food I tried
to give her. Snacks to eat at school would be thrown over a fence
en route. The hot drink and biscuits for the break during
orchestra rehearsals would be given away to friends. Tom

reported all this, for he now attended the orchestra with her, and so was with her a good deal of the time. The lying — for she would always say she had eaten the food I gave her — hurt me abominably. People usually lie out of fear — and I could not bear to think that our relationship had sunk to that.

I began to resort to subterfuge myself. On a nurse's advice, I mixed Complan with a jar of Horlicks I had hopefully bought for late night drinks. I felt comforted if she only drank a little of it — at least some essential nutrients had found their way into her. I bought bigger eggs. For some reason, she would still eat half the yolk, though she invariably left the white. Another friend gave me a recipe for a health drink which was supposed to be particularly fortifying. I faithfully mixed up a weird and wonderful list of ingredients. The expression on Joanna's face when I persuaded her to sip a little of it was comical. Nothing would induce her to take more, and when I tried it myself I could see why. It was so disgusting I burst out laughing — and Joanna joined in. As laughter was rare at that time, I was grateful to my friend for giving us that, at least.

These pathetic attempts to make her take food were useless, and I knew it. I was fighting something stronger than me, and I was only making matters worse. Yet for the life of me I could not stop trying. My efforts to keep her alive were every bit as compulsive as hers to starve to death.

Remembering the fear, the anger and the terrible scenes of those weeks — scenes such as we had never known before — it strikes me that anorexia is an illness which arouses peculiarly violent emotions in those who are closely involved with it. Before Joanna became ill, I had never paid more than purely practical attention to the importance of food in our lives. Suddenly, I found myself forced to think about it. Offering food is a positive, friendly and placatory act. It can express love, concern, friendship, protectiveness, celebration, cessation of hostilities. Rejecting this offer is likewise a negative act, an expression of hostility or, at the least, indifference. The mother, offering in her milk the gift of life to her new baby, becomes distressed and confused if for some reason the baby cannot accept it. The offer of food is of the very essence of maternity — which is why the action of the anorexic in refusing it is so traumatic. The whole child–mother relationship is blown apart. For a family such as ours, which had already been through such an agonizing experience of rejection, Joanna's denial of us was as painful as it could possibly be. Nor was she unaware of our suffering, but, unable without help to free herself of the terrifying compulsion to lose weight, her awareness merely added to and compounded the guilts that already racked her.

We were, I found, by no means the only victims of the illness in our neighbourhood. Anorexia, unlike autism, is very common. Friends, trying to help me, put me in touch with the mothers of other sufferers, but, far from supporting me, this only scared me more. Some had daughters who had been ill for several years and were still not recovered, others were full of bitterness and anger. It was rather like trying to find comfort in single-parent groups all over again, and with the same result. I became more and more afraid.

When the silence from the clinic reached its third week, my conviction that we could not possibly survive this disaster grew and spread into all areas of my life. My guilt matched Joanna's. I felt that all my efforts over the past seven years had been worthless. The only result was total failure. All the laboriously accumulated small achievements seemed a mockery. Whilst I thought I had been encouraging and helping the children, I had been destroying them. I had read that a frequent cause of anorexia is a too-close relationship between the mother and the daughter — which to me meant that all the love and extra care I had heaped on Joanna when she came back from boarding school so grievously disturbed had only served to disturb her more. I disinterred every mistake I had ever made throughout the years of my daughter's life, and used them to lash myself with. I began to hate music — to hate it for its competitiveness, the lack of compassion in the pressure which it put on children — I forgot that I had ever believed it to have healing powers. I stopped going to my recorder consort. I no longer wanted to play. I would no longer even listen to my beloved records — with the sole exception of Richard Strauss's "Four Last Songs", which I played over and over again, the tears running down my face, finding some inexplicable comfort in their heartrending sadness.

I believed that if help did not come soon, Joanna would die. The fear was not groundless — I had read that many died of anorexia. Once the body runs out of certain essential minerals, such as potassium, for instance, there is real danger. In my terror, the delay in giving me the appointment seemed like the purest cruelty. Her weight loss continued steadily.

The only people who were really able to be of help during those dark days were other women who revealed to me that they, too, had had anorexia when they were girls, and had not only re-covered, but gone on to live full lives. One of these was a doctor, and it was perhaps her realistic optimism which did most to keep the panic at bay.

On top of everything else, my mother was now claiming my attention again. I had been very lucky in finding an extremely good nursing home for her at the first try, and the time had now come to transfer her.

This meant that I was now faced with a fearsome amount of administrative work, which proved to be much harder to cope with in my panicky state of mind than merely transferring my mother from one place to another. Banks, lawyers, the DHSS and the Benevolent Fund — I had to correspond meticulously with all of them to set all the available funds, pension and benefits flowing in the new direction. I had to apply for power of attorney in order to pay the bills and manage the bank accounts. I listed the things to be done — the forms to be completed, the appointments to be made — and wept. An official is the last person, and an official form is the last thing, that anyone wants to see when in a state of severe stress. I could not cope. I sat and stared blankly at the pile of papers to be dealt with, and went under. In the end, feeling every bit as lost as I had six years before, I phoned the vicar, whom, once again, I did not know, for I had only seen him from a distance, in church.

It was the start of a new friendship. David came round to see me, and his clear explanations reduced the problems to their real size. Soon, it was all sorted out, and my mother's affairs began to tick over smoothly once more. At least it had taken my mind off Joanna for a space.

At last, at what seemed an eternity after visiting the doctor, we were given our appointment. I was asked to attend with Joanna, whose weight had dropped a further half stone in the interval. I was at screaming pitch. I went to the appointment wanting one thing, and one thing only — the practical help which alone could bring some relief from the strain.

After so long and so tense a wait, it proved an extraordinary interview. It was one of the most superb examples of a failure of communication I have ever encountered. It must have been intended to help us, or there would have been no point in offering it, yet it ended with me rushing from the building inarticulate with rage, dragging a dazed Joanna in my wake, and vowing I would never set foot in the place again. The social worker who saw us made a tactical error when she began the conversation by accusing me of being very angry. She was, of course, absolutely right, though I did not know it — but I was in no state to receive accusations. She then improved on the initial mistake by querying both the diagnosis and the need for worry — and I exploded. I wanted help, immediate help — not an intellectual argument. I realized that we had gone to the wrong place.

Yet, indirectly, we had been helped. For the failure of that interview drove me to the furthermost point of despair — the point at which I could at last accept that if I was to save Joanna I had now to attempt what I had always regarded as impossible. There was nothing for it but to go back to the Maudsley, the only hospital where I was certain that our needs would be understood. By now, I was ready to go and set up house in neighbouring Brixton if it was necessary to bring Joanna back to health. As soon as we reached home, I phoned Simon's psychiatrist, told him what had happened, and begged him to help us.

There were no more delays. We were at once given an appointment for a few days later. This response in itself calmed me. There were no suggestions that I was angry or neurotic, simply a tacit recognition of our distress, and an offer of help.

Even those few days seemed like centuries, though fortunately they were filled with a rush of events. Wraithlike though Joanna now was, she still insisted on continuing her music. I had entered into complicated negotiations with a dealer friend to buy her a really good bow. A first-class instrument was, we thought, completely out of our reach, but a bow would go some way towards meeting her needs. I raised the money by dint of selling both her first cello and her first bow. The timing was just right. I saw by the way she held it, and stroked it, what it meant to her. It even brought a little colour back to her cheeks, especially when her fellow musicians admired it. By now I felt that she sat upright in orchestra or string quartet by sheer willpower — everywhere else she drooped, or simply lay down.

I knew that both Tom and David were suffering greatly. Both did their best to be supportive and understanding, for they both adored their sister, but they were hurt by her strange behaviour and by the tensions at meal times. At thirteen and twelve respectively, they were being asked to show the maturity of adults, and the strain on them was very great.

Tom, at least, had many resources in his own musical life. Not only was he again singing at Covent Garden, but he had also recently been given the beautiful though taxing part of Amahl in a local production of the Menotti opera, with Jean Rigby, a young professional singer, taking the part of the Mother. The rehearsals for this, now under way, gave him some escape from the stress, and at least when he came home from them he looked excited and happy.

Even so, he paid dearly for Joanna's illness. He was due to take his Grade Seven viola exam, with her accompanying him at the piano, exactly two days before the appointment at the Maudsley. At breakfast time that morning, she and I had our worst ever confrontation over her refusal to touch her meal. We shouted and wept, and hurled abuse at each other in a manner hitherto unheard of in our family. Tom and David looked on, pale and horrified, and guilt at what we were doing to them only increased our violence. It was hardly an auspicious prelude to a music exam. There was simply no way sensitive Tom could play his best. Poor Tom — he deserved a gold medal for his brave performance that morning, had the Associated Board of Music but known the facts.

David, too, was very much at sea. It had not been the best atmosphere to help him off to a good start in senior school. He was saved from shipwreck by his sporting abilities, for he soon began to shine on the football field. Even so, he must have felt that the world he knew was crumbling about his ears. He, too, had been about to take a flute exam, but I had the wit to cancel it in time — I did not want him to suffer as Tom had done. Luckily, his flute lessons with Jim were calm, happy affairs, and it did not matter in the least that the exam was delayed.

Still no tidings had reached us from the NYO, and my heart began to sink. Sure enough, both letters, when they reached us, were negative — though Tom had made a good impression, and had been asked to audition again the following year. Joanna's was a kindly but definite goodbye. At first she was brokenhearted

— but there was still some fight left in her, for within a couple of days of receiving the letter, her chin was stuck out once more in the manner I knew well, and she was vowing she would audition for other orchestras. By now, if my chin was stuck out, it was only to await the next blow.

On the day of the appointment at the Maudsley, we were both silent and apprehensive. We did not know what to expect. We were travelling by train and bus. It was a cold, grey, blustery day, and as we stood near Waterloo, waiting in the bus queue, I suddenly saw Joanna's colour drain away, and realized that she was on the verge of fainting. I hailed a taxi, and hustled her inside. She was better by the time we reached the hospital, but I was relieved to be amongst doctors.

On arrival, she was given a thorough medical check which indicated that we were being taken seriously. There was no questioning of my anxiety, or of the diagnosis. Joanna was suffering from anorexia nervosa, and it was natural that everyone was tense and worried. Her weight, in fact, was approaching a dangerously low level.

The doctor who saw us asked her if she could keep a contract. It was to guarantee that she would increase her weight by two pounds during the following week, at the end of which he would see her again. She glibly promised to try. He also suggested that, since meal times had now become fraught with so much tension and pain, she might like to try eating by herself in a separate room, choosing her own menu from a list of foods which she felt still held some appeal for her, and which I would buy. She agreed to this, too. He promised to ring me in a few days, to see how we were making out, and to tell us the outcome of discussions at his end.

We did our very best, though I had little hope that Joanna would or could keep her contract. The boys and I strove to ignore her at meal times, though each of us was aware of every item in her strangely concocted menus. She ate alone in the dining room, which lifted some of the strain, but was not a very happy arrangement.

All the same, I no longer felt so frightened. I was no longer alone. Someone cared — someone, above all, who completely understood and who had experience in treating this terrifying illness. The doctor kept his promise, and phoned for news of our progress.

We met again a week after the first appointment. He looked serious when he weighed her this time. Far from increasing her weight, she had lost a further couple of pounds.

Upon this, he suggested to me that the best course of action would be to admit Joanna to hospital. He explained that the Maudsley had a sister hospital, the Bethlem Royal, which the staff called their 'country hospital', for it was situated in spacious, beautiful grounds in Beckenham. At the Bethlem there was a special unit for adolescents, and this he thought might be the best place for Joanna. He needed to know if we agreed, so that he might set the admission procedure in motion.

Joanna and I looked at each other. We both knew that there was no option. The alternative was unthinkable. We agreed.

The doctor promised me to phone again when he had made the necessary arrangements for a preliminary meeting with the medical team at the unit. Helen would also be invited to this, as she was now our official social worker. It occurred to me to wonder if Helen did not sometimes regret her original offer to visit me — she could not possibly have foreseen the dramatic succession of events which lay ahead, events so numerous and so complicated that we could only tackle the immediate crises in our weekly sessions. She certainly could not have guessed that she would be required to attend a meeting at the distant Bethlem.

Travelling home once more, Joanna and I tried to come to terms with the new situation. I could not believe that she was really going to leave us to live in hospital for an indefinite period. There seemed to be no end to the nightmare. I could not imagine my sensitive, freedom-loving, artistic daughter confined in a hospital unit.

She had persuaded the doctor to allow her to play in one last concert. The now ever-present danger of fainting was eliminated in her case because she was a cellist — the fact that she gripped the instrument with her knees prevented her blood from all flowing down to her feet and causing a blackout. Her quartet was to perform the Dvorak "American" Quartet to an audience of parents and civic dignitaries at the local school of music.

Once more they played outstandingly, and the tears stung my eyes as I listened. I wondered what Joanna was feeling as she sat there with her friends. She looked so frail that a gust of wind would have carried her away. Around me, I heard people commenting on her emaciated appearance, and the panic leapt in me.

I had warned the orchestra that this would be the last time that she would be playing with them for some time. She had been very happy with them — in fact they had given her the only real happiness she had known in the past few months, and it grieved me that she must give it up. I had, of course, also told her teachers at school, all of whom had been extremely kind and sympathetic — many of them going out of their way to help and talk to her. She had continued to struggle on with her French, but it was dubious now whether she would sit the exam in the summer.

The preliminary meeting at the Bethlem was set for a week after the last one at the Maudsley. Reaching it seemed an all but insuperable problem, for it was even further away than the Maudsley. I could not risk taking a now very weak Joanna on public transport, and I was in such a state of nervous tension that I was even more frightened than usual of the idea of driving across London. In the end, summoning up my courage, I approached our patient vicar once more. Again, he made it all seem very simple. An appeal from the pulpit on Sunday on our behalf brought in half a dozen names of volunteer drivers, ready and willing to take us to Beckenham and bring us back. The spontaneity of the response moved me deeply. Everyone seemed to think it the most natural thing in the world to give up what amounted to a whole day of their time to help us out. The feeling of being supported doubled my own remaining strength.

We had to be at the Bethlem by nine-thirty in the morning, which involved a laborious crawl through rush hour, and a painfully early start. I was navigating from a large street atlas for our driver, and, as we picked our way across south London, my fears about driving began to assume more realistic proportions as I realized that they arose chiefly from not knowing the route, the one-way systems and the lane positionings, rather than the driving itself.

At the hospital we were introduced to the psychologist and the social worker who would be involved in Joanna's treatment. I was too dazed at this first meeting to take in much more than the fact that there was an essential condition to her admittance: I had to agree to bring the whole family once a week to the unit for the family therapy which was considered to be vital for her recovery.

I gulped at this. The sheer length of the journey — it was an eighty-mile round trip through dense traffic most of the way — meant that, if it was to be accomplished both safely and sensibly, Tom and David would have to be taken out of school.

There was, however, no option, and I knew it. Joanna's life mattered more than any school work, which could always be made up, even if with some difficulty. Nor did I really think that I could manage it, week after week, without cracking up, but I knew it was no use thinking about that. I just had to try. So, shutting my eyes to the problems, with a feeling that I was taking a blind leap into the dark, I committed us.

We were shown round the unit, which was very bright and modern — it had in fact only been open a short time — and which contained its own school run by the Inner London Education Authority. Joanna would be able to continue working for her A-level there if she wanted to. She, of course, was desperate to know if she could take her cello into hospital with her, and if she would be allowed to continue her lessons. The cello, came the canny reply, could indeed be admitted with its owner, it could even live in its own room, but permission to practise and to attend lessons would depend on her ability to gain the necessary strength by putting on weight.

I saw at once which way the wind was blowing. The importance of music in the life of my daughter had been quickly picked up. Far from being destructive, as I had feared of late, its healing role was being extended — it was to be one of the levers used to prise Joanna free of her deadly compulsions. I suddenly felt sure that we were in the right hands, and the best possible place.

Even on this bleak December day, we could see that the grounds of the hospital were indeed spacious and well tended. Joanna need not, I told myself, feel totally imprisoned. Her room, though in complete contrast to her cottage bedroom at home, was pleasant, and she was encouraged to bring cards and posters with her to pin on the walls, so as to make it her personal haven. We were introduced to the ward staff, who would have the physical care of her — the gritty job of actually inducing her to eat. I felt reassured because, unlike us, they were not emotionally involved and had plenty of experience in the treatment of these difficult, disturbed patients.

The only feature of the visit which gave me real pain was the fact that the outer doors of the unit were kept locked. It was carefully explained to me that they were always opened at the request of the patients. The measure was necessary because some of the teenage residents were extremely disturbed, and could harm themselves and others if they were allowed complete freedom. I could see the sense of this, but no amount of reasonable, rational explanation could hide the symbolism of those locks. Yet they had an extraordinarily positive influence on Joanna — for they at once stiffened her resolve to get better and get back to freedom as soon as she legitimately could. I had long experience of her willpower. I felt now that if it were once set in this positive direction, we might indeed begin to hope for a complete recovery.

In fact, though at the time I was in no state to perceive it, the tide had turned.

Now, at last, we had found the skilled, caring support we had needed all along. Now, at last, someone was prepared to help us come to terms with all that had happened to us. I knew that Joanna's illness was not the result of some transient teenage upset, but of long years of emotional distress and confusion. This had been shared by her brothers, and, in helping her to get better, they would be helping themselves too. Far from being afraid of the forthcoming family therapy, I welcomed the prospect, despite all the attendant practical difficulties.

The inner circle of help, moreover, was a complete one, for Ray, whom I had kept in the picture since his visits to Joanna in the summer, now asked to be put in touch with the hospital team. He, better than anyone, knew the history and nature of our struggles. Helen, however, warned me that once the family therapy was under way, she would have to cease visiting me, as she did not want to risk her work with me interfering with that of the other therapists. This was a blow. I knew that I still needed her personal help, but I could see the sense of the decision. The important thing was that I no longer felt I faced all the problems alone.

It was settled that morning that Joanna should be admitted to the unit three days later — the day after my birthday, as it happened. I could still not believe, as we drove home through the dark and the wet, that any of this was real. My deep relief at having at last found help was mixed with a sharp sense of loss. Joanna would once again be leaving the family. It was unbearable to think that she could not get better while she was living with us, when we loved her so much. I had made a fine hash of things, I reflected — and directed us down yet another wrong turning.

The three days between the meeting and Joanna's departure to hospital were some of the most bitter, and the most bleak, of all this bitter time. Our broken family was about to be broken yet again — and for the cruellest of reasons. I could not forgive myself. I had failed my children, to the point where my daughter's life was in danger.

It was Tom who, without knowing it, once again freed me from this self-made rack. The production of *Amahl and the Night Visitors* was to open in the great chapel of a nearby independent school on the evening of my birthday. We were all going, Joanna included, each one of us more than grateful for the distraction.

Tom *was* Amahl. He had put his whole being into the character. His voice, though beginning now to soften round the edges, prior to breaking, and not of the strongest, was just big enough to sustain its relationship with that of the Mother. His pitch never failed, and his intense, innate musicality shaped every phrase. All the loving tenderness between the mother and son shone out. The pair of them gave a performance which was like a gentle, healing hand on my aching heart. As I sat watching them, I felt that Tom was acting out something he knew all about. He was reassuring me that love indeed existed, and always had existed for him, and by implication for each child in our family. All was not lost. Tom, with his bright face and silvery voice, challenged the darkness, and drove it back.

It was perhaps the most valuable birthday gift I had ever been given.

The next day, I took Joanna to the hospital, and kissed her goodbye. It would not be long before I saw her again, because we were all to visit the unit for our first session of family therapy four days later, but, somehow, I felt that this parting marked the end of a phase in our lives. A change was coming, and I sensed it, though I could not have described it. In any case I did not dare to try to look ahead.

On the way home, though tears were not far away, the sense of relief was uppermost. We were now going into battle, and I felt that we had a chance of winning it, though it was likely to be a long and desperate one. I could not begin to guess the depth of the fear and pain which Joanna herself must have been experiencing. Her sensitive musician's temperament was about to be subjected to a discipline such as it had never faced before. In the unit she would witness unhappiness and confusion greater than any she had ever dreamed of. The experience would, I thought, give her insights possessed by few other people of her age, and endow her with a rare maturity. I could not bear to think of what would happen if she did *not* get better — I could not afford to entertain so much as the possibility. We all of us now needed every last scrap of strength to concentrate on what had to be done.

As yet another of our friends drove us down to the hospital for the first meeting with Joanna and our two therapists, I tried to communicate some of these feelings to the boys. I knew it was going to be very hard for them to meet their sister in the hospital setting. I was beginning to see the reasons for the insistence on family therapy.

Joanna's illness had affected each and every one of us. When she greeted us with the news that she had already begun to eat again, for instance, Tom and David were deeply hurt that she should be able to eat only when she was away from them — they felt it must have been their fault that she could not eat at home. Everyone felt guilty in one way or another. They were awkward and inhibited in their first meeting with the two therapists — we all were — but they began to relax a little as they discovered the relief that comes from airing pent-up emotions.

Although it was so soon after her admission, it was decided that Joanna should spend Christmas at home, as it would have been too demoralizing for her to feel excluded from what is so essentially a family occasion. I was rigid with fright at the prospect — and it showed. Gently and firmly I was reassured: she would certainly lose weight again during the four days of the holiday, but she could not possibly lose enough to endanger her life. I was given phone numbers to ring in the event of an emergency. The responsibility was no longer mine alone. This effectively diminished our anxiety, and we could contemplate the festival with at least an approach to pleasure.

Friends rallied round during this, the most difficult Christmas yet. We were invited out to many meals, and this was valuable help, for it enabled us to take less notice of what Joanna did or did not eat. She was very weak indeed by now, and suffered greatly from the cold, for so great a weight loss affects the circulation. The central heating in our house is very efficient, but she still needed extra clothes, especially on hands and feet.

Even for the length of those four brief days, it was hard to control my fear, as each successive pound lost showed in her increasing pallor and languor. At church, we were surrounded by love and concern — and now Joanna, too, was glad that we had not tried to hide her illness, and drew courage from all the support.

Two days after Christmas, we took her back to hospital. She was, if anything, thinner and paler than when she had first been admitted, but she, and we, had survived, and there had been no painful scenes.

This Christmas had been the first skirmish of the great battle. Small as it was, we had won it, and we could advance with slightly more confidence. We were at war. Tom, David — even Simon in his own way — and I were linking our arms around Joanna, and pooling our strength. Together with our powerful new allies, we were united against a common enemy, and we were ready to give everything we had. We had never before faced anything so terrifying, and so incomprehensible — but on the other hand we had never before felt so utterly and completely together.

CHAPTER ELEVEN

Eighth Year: Building Again

Although for six days of the week Tom, David and I went on with our ordinary routines at home, the focus of our lives had shifted to Beckenham, to the hospital which had become in our eyes the arena of battle. Our visit there, with its session of family therapy, was the high point of each successive week, and all our other activities faded into insignificance. We very soon found, in any case, that we had little energy to spare for them. The long drive through heavy traffic, the strains of the meeting with Joanna, and the tensions of family therapy left us, by the time we reached home in the late afternoon, limp and exhausted — an exhaustion which, where I was concerned, lasted well into the next day.

I did all I could to lessen the rigours of the exercise. We packed a picnic lunch which we could eat in the car, parked beneath the trees in the hospital grounds, before the meeting. I am a firm believer in confronting challenges with the inner man well fortified, and a big flask of milky coffee always went with us, to be brought out on demand.

Anorexia seemed to dominate all our living. We were aware of food and other people's eating habits as we had never been before. We were angry with the vicar for preaching about fasting, and angry with the media for the ubiquity of slimming advertisements. Nobody but ourselves seemed to be aware of the dangers of experimenting with diet — and this tended to make us feel isolated once again. Fortunately, the boys themselves gave me no cause for concern in that direction — they both had healthy appetites, and a healthy disregard for personal beauty. We were in danger, nonetheless, of becoming almost as obsessive about food as Joanna herself.

Soon after Christmas, I felt that I was familiar enough with the route to the hospital to undertake the driving myself. Tom took over the navigation, and even managed to find us some short cuts. Deeply grateful though we had been for that generous initial help, it was good now to be alone together in a family group as we made our way to and from the unit. We often found that we needed to go on talking over together matters that had come up during the session, and it was difficult to do this in front of outsiders, however close they were. Coping with the drive proved a considerable boost to my morale, and before long I actually found myself enjoying the challenge of it.

For some weeks, we continued to find it difficult and painful to meet with Joanna only in the alien surroundings of the unit. We felt cut off from her — as one does visiting anyone in hospital — and hardly knew how to talk to her. The family therapy session gradually helped us over this. The first subject to come up each week was invariably Joanna's weight, and as this gradually began to increase, it led us easily into discussion and the voicing of anxieties.

Not that she could articulate all of hers at the time. It was over two years, for instance, before she could tell me why she had been able to begin eating again the moment she found herself alone in hospital. That moment had been, she explained, the first of real consciousness of just what she was doing to herself, the moment when she knew she had to focus all her willpower on the struggle to get better. She was to need every ounce of it for, as the flesh began to reappear on her wasted body, and her ideal of absolute emaciation faded, this struggle was to grow fiercer, not easier. It was at the time almost impossible for us to understand this, as it was for her to tolerate our jubilation as her weight went up. We were people standing on opposite sides of a deep gulf. Only with the help of the therapy could we hope to reach each other again.

Each week we saw a change in her — a change it was not always easy to adjust to. Tom and David listened wide-eyed to her tales of life on the ward. There she was allowed and encouraged to be as much of a child as she wished. As in some other forms of adolescent disturbance, anorexia tends to have the effect of causing the sufferer to regress to a far more childish level of behaviour in panic at the terrifying prospect of entering the adult world. Joanna was now playing this out to the full. Practical jokes seemed to be the order of the day, and my hair stood on end at some of the indignities inflicted on the staff, who richly deserved to be paid danger money. The young people in the unit had many grievances against the adult world that had hurt them, and against which they felt themselves powerless. Practical jokes were a harmless way of venting their feelings, and, simultaneously, of discovering that not all adults were hostile or censorious.

Joanna who, at school, had always been amongst the most saintly, after the traumas of boarding school, now joined full-bloodedly in the hunt. Her former apathy towards her physical appearance disappeared, and she began to experiment with clothes and hairstyles in a way that had her brothers' eyes out on stalks. Away from home, in an entirely supportive atmosphere, seventeen-year-old Joanna at last felt free enough from all the family worries to begin to explore adolescence.

This awoke guilts in the rest of us that were not easy to allay. It took all the therapists' tact and patience to convince us that her illness was nobody's fault, but had happened as the result of our circumstances and the pressures upon us. As each week brought perceptible changes in her, we could draw comfort and strength from the realization that we were working towards her recovery with Joanna, walking beside her, as it were. The rifts that had opened in the family as a result of the anorexia could begin to close again. We could see, for instance, how her passionate love of music was being utilized positively to keep her weight rising slowly, under careful control. (Any too-rapid increase would have distressed her unnecessarily, and weakened her gradually increasing confidence in being able to control it herself.) A positive force was set directly against a destructive one. The cello had duly gone into hospital with her, and lived royally in its own room — but the right to practise had to be earned, by keeping to a strict diet. The same rule applied to the resumption of lessons: she had to reach and maintain a stipulated weight before being allowed to make the journey from Beckenham to Hampstead for her weekly hour. She finally achieved this at the end of January, and it was a red-letter day for everyone. Her piano teacher, unfortunately, lived not far from us, which was too far to be practicable, and Joanna resigned herself to solitary, intensive practice of scales and exercises at the unit's piano.

The cello made its own contribution to the difficulties with which we were contending by being almost as temperamental as its owner. Despite its size, the cello is a very delicate instrument, as I knew to my cost. The temperature of the ward, as always in hospitals, was far higher than that of our home, and this did not suit it at all. All Joanna's attempts to keep its room humid proved inadequate. Within a month of its entry to hospital, its glue dried out and it split at the seams, to the despair of the musician. Kind local friends lent her another cello so that she might continue to play while hers was being reglued — but that one split, too. We were at our wits' end. I realized there was nothing for it but to purchase an expensive electric humidifier — which effectively solved the problem. The hospital eventually allowed us a grant towards the cost of this but, at the time, it was one more pressure. The price of petrol was beginning to rise, and the weekly journey was making savage inroads into my budget, which could ill stand it. I was devoutly grateful that her second instrument was the ubiquitous piano.

As her weight slowly rose again towards normal, Joanna's behaviour towards us became more and more unpredictable. In many ways, this was probably the hardest phase of the recovery for her. We never had to witness the times when she sat for hours before a plate of food, loathing it, disgusted by it, yet knowing that she had to eat it. The slightest increase of weight over and above the agreed amount upset her, and had to be offset by a corresponding decrease in the target for the following week. There was no chance of subterfuge in the ward, for meals were supervised.

We tried very hard to understand, and to see the struggle from her point of view — as did all our friends. Her room was filled with cards and flowers, including a giant valentine made by Simon for her at Somerset Court, which made her cry. A huge bouquet arrived for her from the school governors, in the school colours, and, as evidence of caring and compassion far beyond the everyday, brought a huge lump to *my* throat. I felt I could never repay the kindness that surrounded us. Even her French teacher at home continued to watch over her progress, and encourage her, though she was now having lessons in the unit's school. Everyone, it seemed, was bent on doing all they could to help. Our two therapists had carefully explained our target to us. We were aiming at a recovery timed so that Joanna would be able to take her place at music college in September as planned. This, to her, was a blow — she had not foreseen anything like so long a stay in the unit. I, who had read more about the illness and had spoken with other parents, had had my doubts. I knew that recovery entailed far more than merely regaining the ideal weight for her height and build. That, in fact, merely marked the beginning of the real work of healing, which could not be undertaken while the body weight was low, since this in itself adversely affects the personality. In this vital second stage, Joanna would need to work through all the disturbed feelings which had brought on the illness, so as to reach a stability of mind which would enable her to stay in control of her anxieties in the face of all the strains and stresses of everyday life. For a music student, struggling to build a career, these would be considerable. The therapy had to be very thorough.

By the end of a couple of months, we had all grown deeply to value the sessions with our therapists. Even Tom the super-conscientious no longer complained about missing school. One of the most painful effects of the illness had been the destruction of all our confidence in ourselves as a family, and in the love we felt for each other. We were so badly scarred by the trauma of Paul's departure that we were inordinately fearful of all quarrels and outbursts of anger. To us, these signified the ending of a relationship — someone leaving us. We had spent our days apologizing to each other, racked with guilt for the most normal and ordinary of feelings — and this had all been made worse still by the terrifying experience of seeing Joanna wasting away before our eyes.

Patiently, but firmly, our faith in our own worth had to be restored, though it was to be months before we could begin to believe in ourselves again. We had to be taught the normality of angry feelings — to understand that they do not necessarily mean the cessation of love. We had to learn, too, to accept mistakes for what they are — mistakes, and not symptoms of moral iniquity. Always the love which we felt for each other was emphasized, and reinforced, as gently we were shown how often we misread one another. We saw how it was necessary not only to be open in our communications — we had already tried hard to be that — but also to make our needs quite clear so that others could respond to them appropriately. As, gradually, we began to understand what had been going wrong, and stumblingly to put it right, so the support we drew from the sessions increased, along with our strength.

Family therapy suited and worked well for us, largely because in the past we had been accustomed to trying, at least, to work as a group. Our councils of war round the kitchen table were paying dividends now. We had not always made the right decisions, and we had often sorely misunderstood each other, but we had laid a foundation for the present work that was invaluable.

Nonetheless, it was far from easy for us to talk about painful feelings, especially in the case of the two youngest, who were not always sure what the feelings were, only that they hurt. Even when we wept over them, which happened many times, we discovered a comfort never before experienced, as the group learned how more effectively to come to the support of the individual. Thus, we dared to venture together into areas of pain which, previously, it had been too frightening to explore — the pain of our individual relationships with Paul, and our separate reactions to the marriage breakdown. As I at last looked squarely at the depth and intensity of this pain in each of us, I understood the meaning of Mira Rothenburg's parting words, two years previously. She had indeed, perceptive lady that she is, caught "a glimpse of heaven and hell". At the time, we could not acknowledge the existence of the hell. Now, with our two therapists beside us, we ventured to look at it and see it for what it was. As I looked, I could only marvel that the fragile crust of rational behaviour, on which I had worked so hard to build our new lives, had stood the strain for so long, constructed as it was over a veritable cauldron of anger and misery.

I was appalled, for instance, to hear Joanna say that she felt I had used her too much as a confidante, for all my financial worries in particular, worries which she had felt unable to bear. She had resented the fact that while in the privacy of home I, in talking to her of these matters, treated her as an adult, when it came to outside affairs, such as visiting the solicitor, I denied her this privilege, and turned instead to Joan or Joy. I felt hurt, angry and, of course, deeply guilty. Here was yet another sign of failure, with the very one of my children whom I had tried my hardest to help. As I thought back over all the years of struggles on her behalf, it was a bitter wound. We glared at each other across the meeting room. Neither of us could accept the other's feelings. Once again a gulf opened between us. But within minutes the first threads of understanding were being deftly thrown across it by our 'umpires' as they showed us how these unhappy feelings had arisen, and why, in our circumstances, it was almost inevitable that the eldest of my normal children should share my anxieties, since there was no-one else at home who could do so. Even with this help, however, I found it hard, almost impossible, at that time to see Joanna's point of view — I was too blinded by an overwhelming sense of weariness and

futility. It was, in fact, to be more than two years before I had
sufficient strength to acknowledge her right to those feelings, and
the part I had played in contributing to them — without feeling
guilty.

As the sessions progressed, I was beginning to be aware of a
personal difficulty. While they helped enormously in all the
situations which arose in our lives together, I was by now aware
that I had deep problems of my own, dating from before the
existence of the family, which I could not possibly discuss in front
of the children — and I had lost Helen. She had barely started the
work of helping me when the crisis with Joanna had put an
effective stop to it. Depression was beginning to settle again, and
to thicken — and, I felt, to hamper the work we were doing
together. In the end, in desperation, I asked the therapists at the
hospital if I might see Helen again, and to my relief they agreed.
She was contacted, and began once more to visit me regularly.

The whole landscape of my life thus now came under the
plough. I was glad. The depression was to me like the locked doors
of the ward to Joanna, and I, too, wanted to be free. It was a relief to
be working with Helen again.

It was hardly surprising, in view of all this, that all our other
interests fell into a distinctly secondary role. We were like a group
of scientists bent over a microscope, trying to recognize and
understand what we saw — which was hidden from the rest of the
world. We became completely indifferent to our surroundings. I
cut out all the driving I could during this period. The boys
transferred to a judo club at school. I just managed to keep the flute
and viola lessons going — and Tom's piano, though I fell asleep
while it was going on. My recorder consort had become a thing of
the past, and so had writing, and even serious reading. There was
only sufficient energy for the lightest of fiction and the most
comfortable of television.

At the end of February, we reached a milestone: we were
invited, instead of attending the usual therapy session, to lunch at
the hospital with Joanna and our two therapists. At once our
anxieties flared up. Meal times had been the scene of our greatest
distress. All pleasure in eating together as a family had been
destroyed — which meant that one of the focal points of our family
life had disintegrated.

This first meal together, after so bitter a separation, was
therefore an important stage both in Joanna's recovery and in ours

as a family — one which had to be negotiated with the utmost sensitivity if there was to be any hope of reintegrating us.

Tom, David and I were very nervous as we drove to the hospital that day. I was even worrying in case I should not be able to eat the hospital food, for I have a finicky appetite and dislike stodge, in case my leaving anything should upset Joanna. The boys' worries were less concrete, and were much offset by the pleasure of having a change from the eternal picnic.

I need not have feared. The hospital had gone to considerable pains on our behalf, and the lunch that was served was not only well cooked, but appetizingly presented — I could see Tom and David licking their lips out of the corner of my eye. Joanna was tense and withdrawn. She sat at table — we were in a private room — with the boys on one side of her, myself on the other, and our two therapists opposite us. As we ate, I tried to keep up a patter of conversation to relieve the tension. Tom and David responded gallantly, but there was no word from Joanna. She sat in stony silence between us, eating steadily. Like us, she finished every scrap of food on her plate, and, when the last of a mountain of chips had been cleared by a willing David, plus a very acceptable dessert, we all sat back in some relief to consider the experience together.

By now I had learned enough about being open to remark how hurtful I had found my daughter's total silence during the meal — and Tom and David had felt the same. She, for her part, had also come far enough to be able to explain that all it had signified was the intensity of concentration required to accomplish the still difficult act of eating. We looked at one another in surprise — and smiled.

It was the first time we really understood what our therapists were constantly trying to show us: how, despite, or almost because of, our deep love for each other, we constantly misunderstood each other. We hurt each other, not deliberately, but through a simple lack of clarity in our communications. Many other examples of this subsequently turned up throughout the course of the therapy, but this one remained in all our minds as the most vivid — perhaps because it had arisen in the very area where we were the most nervous. It shed a great deal of light over the way in which we behaved towards each other, as well as over that of most families we knew.

That meal eaten together was a most important step in rebuilding our shattered confidence. Accomplishing it successfully meant that we were now ready to attempt the next: Joanna, having regained her calculated ideal weight for her size, was to make a twenty-four-hour visit home.

We panicked again at once. By this time we were leaning very heavily on the hospital, and this was the first intimation that such total support would not go on for ever. We were taken patiently through our anxieties and reassured. The visit, made at the weekend, would be followed by family therapy the next day, so that we could work over anything that went wrong. Joanna herself was to be responsible for the amount she did or did not eat — it was no longer anything to do with the rest of us. This, of course, freed us from a heavy burden of responsibility, and eased most of the strain.

The visit, which took place in early March, passed off without incident. She came and went on her own, by public transport, so that there was no extra load on me. It all went off so smoothly that she now pressed hard for a 'real' weekend at home, with permission to attend orchestra on the Friday evening thrown in for good measure. Before she was allowed to do this, however, she had to earn the privilege — by proving that she could keep her weight stable, which she found was by no means easy.

Almost imperceptibly, we found we had moved into a new stage in Joanna's treatment, with her spending five days in the unit, and the weekends at home. Happy as we were to have reached such a stage in her recovery, reintegrating this new, far more outspoken Joanna into the family was a task full of pitfalls. I felt that living with her was not unlike walking through a minefield — one false step and the roof blew off, so volatile was her temperament. As with any other adolescent, I never knew from one day to the next whether I was dealing with the child or with the young woman, for either could appear with disconcerting suddenness, and all my normal reactions were inhibited by the seriousness of her illness. More than once we were devoutly grateful for the therapy session after the weekend visit. We would go into it announcing that we did not see how Joanna could possibly ever live at home again — and come out of it laughing at our own melodramatic reactions.

At the end of April, she was given permission to travel up to Manchester for her formal interviews at the Royal Northern College of Music. We were beautifully on schedule. She was now, in fact, entering the last phase of her recovery — and we knew it was both a difficult and a crucial one. Her weight remained stable, but still showed a tendency to sidle downwards at the first expenditure of unusual amounts of energy. She had to learn to balance this, and at the same time to try to adopt a more relaxed attitude to the whole matter of diet — no easy undertaking for a girl who had known by heart the calorie content of every single item of foodstuff for at least a year.

She felt better, and she looked better — with the result that she began to put pressure on every member of the medical team who crossed her path, as well as on us and on our two therapists, in her longing to be discharged. She was *not* yet better, however, and all her hints and direct requests met with a gentle but firm negative. She only subsided when she was told that if she were discharged then, she would find herself back in hospital in September, instead of in college. This was the ultimate threat, and it helped her to be patient.

Her life in the ward had opened out considerably since she had regained normal weight. She was allowed to groom and ride one of the ponies that were kept in a paddock in the hospital grounds. Horses, after music, were Joanna's chief passion, and I suspected that the companionship of the pony was playing no inconsiderable part in her emotional recovery. She was making up for all the riding lessons she had missed since Paul's departure. She also went out on shopping expeditions, and all manner of excursions. She was even working for her A-level again, though she did not make up her mind to sit it until the very last moment. She was, of course, none too pleased with the 'D' she obtained — an incredibly good result given the circumstances — but her pride was salved by a splendid 'A' for the oral. She had made friends among the girls in the unit — as well as among the boys — and was, in fact, extending her whole range of contacts. All of which was contributing to her desire to move once more into the wider world outside.

My range, by contrast, seemed to have contracted. There simply was not time for anyone or anything. The hospital visits, the sessions with Helen, the weekly visit to my mother in the nursing home and the remaining music runs took all my strength. I smiled somewhat cynically when I caught myself indulging in my favourite daydream of finding a new partner to love and be loved by — he would have had to be a determined man indeed to find himself a corner in my life as it now was. All

the same, the work with Helen was beginning to bear fruit in that
at least I was beginning to want to spread my wings a little,
whenever possible.

I had decided to try my hand at painting, since I still neither
wanted to write nor to play music. My father had been a
competent artist, and I, too, had always enjoyed art though I had
not really touched it since I was at school. I decided, since there
was little prospect of any other type of holiday that summer, to
snatch a week or so at a course while the boys went off to their
different pursuits — and booked myself in. It was not exactly
revolutionary by way of gesture, but it was better than nothing.

In May, my two brothers visited the country. Bob and his wife
stayed in London, and I saw very little of them, but Ian came once
more to stay with us. We all loved this visit. Although it was a
wet and chilly spring, there were still the odd days when it was
possible for him to play games of cricket out in the garden with
Tom and David, and to win their respect with some very stylish
batting, and for us to enjoy long talks sitting together among the
lilac and the apple blossom. The work with Helen had loosened
all the old, tight knots and I felt an extraordinary sense of freedom
to enjoy this relationship — an enjoyment to which he responded,
so that we spent a very happy time together. It was the first
positive result of all the time spent with her, and it gave me real
encouragement.

Joanna, too, for some time now had been having sessions with
a social worker in the hospital. At first, for some reason, she had
been completely hostile to her, and had refused to cooperate.
Then, quite suddenly, the hostility dropped, and all the barriers
with it, and she began to talk — talk which increased weekly in
volume and depth until one day it reached a fortissimo, a volcanic
eruption of rage and pain which continued for long hours
afterwards in her room. It was like the lancing of an abscess. She
told us about it later, and showed us the marks where she had
kicked the wall. We could see that she was still shaken. We held
her tight then, all of us. I felt sure that she now had a chance of
being at peace. We all stood a chance — we were all ready to begin
rebuilding — this time on a real solid basis of understanding and
acceptance.

We were all ready, but for me at least the process was about to
be deferred. Helen came to me one morning as usual, and gently
broke the news to me that after only another three or four

sessions she would not be able to come any more. Her husband was changing his job, and she and her family would be leaving the area.

It was another heavy blow. I was filled with an indigestible mixture of anger, deep gratitude and affection. It seemed as if all those most capable of helping me were fated to go away before completing the job. I had grown to trust and rely on Helen as an intimate friend, and the prospect of losing her frightened me. I knew that the months which followed Joanna's discharge from hospital were likely to be difficult ones, and I did not want to find myself once again without support at the home end. The last meetings were sad ones for us both, but she gave me one last gift before she left, in the shape of another social worker who was prepared to come and take Simon out for me twice a week during his longer stays at home, so that I might snatch a small break.

Simon had come and gone much as usual throughout the months of visiting the hospital — except that I had opted out of his long weekends at home, since they involved me in still more driving. If a family therapy session occurred during his visit, he simply came with us, and sat talking, quietly on the whole, to himself while it went on. I think that coming to the hospital with us, and actually seeing Joanna, lessened his confusion, though he could not, of course, possibly understand what was wrong with her. He was very sensitive to atmosphere, and he knew perfectly well that something was wrong in the family, and that we were all very worried. Unfortunately, it upset him greatly to see her crying during therapy, and we had to listen to long, repetitive tales about it afterwards. Simon, in fact, needed as much reassurance as the rest of us, possibly more. Dearly though I loved him, I was dreading his long summer holiday this year. We all were. We had been, in the past months, stretched until we felt that there was no more elasticity in us. I no longer had the inventiveness, the resourcefulness that I had had when I was younger — so that now I welcomed Barbara, the new social worker, with open arms.

Joanna was discharged from hospital exactly six months after her admission. The date had been much discussed beforehand, and we had spent a long time talking about our anxieties. These, inevitably, were legion. Family therapy, we were told, to our great relief, was to continue for a further six months, though at a less intensive rate.

We felt that we needed it more than ever, for Joanna had told us that she did not feel that she could come at once to live at home, which was very hard to accept — even though in many ways we were as apprehensive as she was about living together once more. Together we had worked out a plan of action and, after a few false starts, succeeded in getting it ticking over smoothly.

She was to stay during the week with June — one of the two new friends to whom Joan had introduced me — who had declared herself ready and willing to give Joanna a room in her flat. It proved to be exactly the right solution. June had had much experience with teenagers as a youth worker, and was less likely than most to be worried by my daughter's recent history. As she was away at work all day, Joanna had a good degree of independence, whilst June was there, and caring, during the evenings. At the weekends she came home to the family, as she had been doing since March. June's flat was in a nearby town, far away enough from home so that Joanna and I were unlikely to meet, without being too far, and situated close to transport and shops so that she could be fully mobile.

To celebrate her coming out of hospital, Joan took us all to see the Royal Tournament. The galloping horses and crashing cannon were the perfect expression of our jubilation and sense of release. It seemed now that the illness and the months of separation, far from breaking up the family as once they had threatened to do, had actually brought us closer together. The bands played and the instruments flashed in the bright lights. Even Simon seemed to share our feelings. Contrary to expectation, his long summer visit home was proving a very happy one. He seemed to be aware of the relief which pervaded the atmosphere, and was responding to it after his own fashion. "Joanna's all better now," he kept assuring us. "Joanna come home at the weekend."

The patterns to which we had become accustomed were changing, however. The school year was drawing to a close and the holidays loomed ahead. Tom had pleaded to be allowed to sit his Grade Seven piano exam. I had only agreed with reluctance, for the memory of his bad experience with the viola still throbbed. It turned out that it was as well that I did agree, for he obtained his distinction, which did much to help him forget past hurts.

We had all come to accept that there could be no more family holidays like the one in Dorset the previous year. It was time now to adopt a different approach to the problem. Paul, in fact, had

written to invite the boys to visit him in Canada, but I had vetoed
the proposal for this year at least. I felt that we had all experienced
too much disturbance in the past months, and that it would not be
fair to anyone to add still more. We had talked at some length, as
well as at some depth, about the young people's relationship with
their father, which we all found very painful. Although I could
understand on a rational level that it was necessary now for me to
stand back and let them run things themselves, it was not easy
when it came to putting this into practice. Still, I felt reasonably
certain that it was better this summer to have a respite from that
particular situation.

I had written to one of our former au pairs who, married now
with two children of her own, lived in a small village by the lake
near Lucerne, asking her if she could possibly put Joanna up for a
couple of weeks, explaining about the illness and the long stay in
hospital. The reply was a warm invitation to Joanna, which
proved to be the beginning of her love affair with Switzerland.

She set off on the long journey by train and boat, and I,
remembering the previous summer, crossed my fingers for the
success of the project. There had been some discussion as to the
length of her stay, for we were all anxious about her, while she
wanted to go for as long as possible, scenting freedom at last.
Christina had been one of the liveliest of our au pairs, and I
thought it was very likely that she and Joanna would take to each
other, but I could not be sure, especially as Joanna had only been
seven when the Swiss girl left us.

Once she had gone, Tom, David and I turned to our own
occupations. Tom went happily off once more to his beloved
orchestral course, while David headed north to another Pathfinder camp, where he hoped to do some serious fossil hunting. I
dug out my father's old paintbox and headed joyfully for the art
course I had booked, in the country near Oxford.

It was an extraordinary and valuable time in which I learned
absolutely nothing about painting beyond being vaguely encouraged to get on with it, but found myself flourishing in the
atmosphere of a strange, offbeat community living in a decaying
country mansion. The place seemed to be set in a time pocket,
suspended way outside reality, and inhabited by a gallery of
characters who might have stepped straight from the pages of an
Agatha Christie thriller. I painted a lot, read a lot, and observed
others to my heart's content. Mentally and emotionally, it was a

breathing space. Painting, I found, freed me from stress more than any occupation I had ever found. I loved the immediacy of it, and the way it forced me to look properly at the scene before me. I returned home refreshed and invigorated, if little the wiser when it came to technique.

We were glad to see our therapists when finally we all met up again. Joanna's departure for college was now very close, and our anxieties had begun to rise, though we had all been cheered when she announced that she wanted to spend the last ten days before departure entirely at home. They were not groundless fears, for although she was now out of hospital, she was still officially a patient. I was glad that she was to live in the college's hall of residence, so that she would not be isolated, and would be spared the chore of buying and cooking food.

The trip to Switzerland had obviously done her a great deal of good. She could talk of nothing but the lake and the mountains, and she and Christina had become close friends. The experience of independence had increased her confidence and sense of adventure just in time to help her make the next, big step into adult life. She was tanned and glowing with health and vitality. The illness had left no physical ill effects behind it. The only mark of it was that she seemed to have stopped growing, and was, if anything, slightly smaller than when she had first been taken ill. Her blood pressure was rather low, which is not really a disadvantage, and she tended to feel the cold somewhat more than average. Menstruation had still not recommenced, but we had been told not to worry about that. We managed not to, but she and I both felt that its return would set the real seal upon her recovery, and longed for it to happen.

Despite all these reassuring signs, both she and we were very apprehensive when it came to the last family therapy session before her departure. I knew that it was the end of another phase. Tom, David and I would be attending them alone until they ended at Christmas, apart from the odd occasion when Joanna would be at home and able to come with us. It was not easy to talk about her going, but it helped when we discussed the amount of comunication that we would maintain — which reinforced in everyone's mind that this was not the end of a relationship, only the beginning of a new stage in it.

Even so, it was desperately painful to say goodbye to Joanna. We escorted her to the station, and saw her off in style, but we all three had tears in our eyes as we turned for home without her. It is difficult in every family when the eldest child leaves home. It had been hard when it was Simon, but with Joanna's going the whole structure of the family was changed. For us, after the intense experience of the previous year, not to mention the years before, the change was far more frightening and disorientating than is usual.

We were not too aware of it at first. Dimly realizing that there was a gap in my life which had not been there before, I signed up for local authority painting classes for one afternoon a week. I was also fiddling with a project for another book, but as, even with the help of my agent, I could not find a publisher who was interested, it was without much enthusiasm.

It was when Joanna had been in Manchester for a fortnight or so that I was suddenly swamped by a wave of depression more violent than any I had known in the past year. Nor was I the only one — it swamped both the boys, too. Both seemed to have become restless and unhappy at school, though the signs were more pronounced in Tom, who kept coming home and telling me that he was bored — a word I had never heard from him before. David, for his part, seemed completely at sea in his academic work, which was not surprising in view of the number of lessons he had missed during his first year at the school. Here at least I could be of some practical help. The drive down to the hospital became littered with French irregular verbs, in which I rehearsed him relentlessly in a successful attempt to rescue him from the bottom set into which he had been relegated after a disastrous exam result. I had also been reluctantly forced to change his flute teacher, for Jim's timetable and mine had ended up by becoming completely incompatible. David now learned at school and, with regular lessons, soon began to progress quickly.

Even so, however much I busied myself with the boys and tried to fill my days positively, however happy the letters which came from Manchester and effervescent the phone calls, nothing seemed to dispel my growing unhappiness. I felt old and worn out. Friends at church tried to counsel and help, but in vain. My feelings about religion had gone back into the melting pot along with all my other feelings during the work with Helen, and I no longer knew where I stood. Everything, and everyone, it seemed, was changing, including myself, and it was a frightening sensation. Even family therapy, to which we now went fortnightly, could only reassure me that this confusion was normal after the great trauma we had been through. The reassurance helped, but did not stop it from hurting.

I longed for Helen. I felt desperately alone again. I knew that the work we had been doing was not finished, and that I could not accomplish it by myself. I asked the social services department if another social worker was available, but Helen had not been replaced and they had little help to offer. Our two therapists at the hospital promised to try to think of somewhere I could go, but the days went by, and inspiration was not forthcoming. In the end, I found it for myself. Thinking that he, surely, must know a solution, I phoned Ray.

Which was how, a week or so later, I found myself sitting in his office in Chiswick — his newest client. He was due to retire the following year, but the NSPCC had finally allowed him to take me on, since I was able now to reach his office. The drive down the North Circular seemed a mere trifle after the pilgrimage to the hospital — by now I was ready to go twice as far.

Ray began where Helen had left off. She had put the landscape under the plough, he set about rebuilding — and my depression lifted, as suddenly as it had come. I had a sense of purpose again, and no longer felt alone.

Tom, about whom I was far from happy, had, during this time, taken his second NYO audition. His viola lessons were in the doldrums, along with all his academic work, and I prayed that this year he might be successful, for I knew what a boost it would give him.

Joanna came home for a week at half term, looking rosy and well, and full of tales of college life. Whilst it was lovely to see her again I realized that this reappearance was very difficult for the boys and for her. She wanted to find home unchanged, and to fit into it as she always had, while they had during her absence grown into a more senior position in the family. The pecking order was upset, causing tensions and the occasional firework. We were all glad that the family therapy had been extended to cover this difficult period, so that we could grow to understand what was happening.

Soon after her return to Manchester, we learned that Tom, in his turn, had been accepted into the NYO. He was deliriously happy, rushing from one instrument to another in his joy. I, too, was radiant. I knew that the experience would be of even more value to him than it had been for Joanna, for he believed in himself less than she did. More important still, it would give him the chance of mixing with other musical boys and men. He was intensely deprived in this respect, more so than David, who found much masculine company on the sports field. Both boys, as they grew older, were feeling the loss of their father more and more.

At last, just one year after it had started, family therapy came to an end — soon after Joanna's return home for the Christmas vacation. Very gently and carefully Tom, David and I were prepared for the coming withdrawal of support. We all became tearful at the prospect. Partings still frightened us. Our two therapists had become good and trusted friends. We did not want to lose them — yet it was important, and we knew it, that we should begin again to stand upon our own feet. Even so, I dreaded the last meeting.

Yet when the day came, I suddenly saw that it should not, after all, be an occasion for tears. Joanna's periods had finally returned and she had been discharged as a patient — which made it surely a time for celebration, and for thanks for all the help we had received. So we packed the much-used picnic basket with freshly baked mince pies, an extra flask of coffee and a miniature bottle of brandy to lace it with — a small but apt symbol of our feelings.

As we sat together, enjoying the token feast, I looked around the group. It hardly seemed possible that only the year before we had come to that place with our hearts full of despair and the fear of death. This Joanna, bright-eyed and glossy-haired, full of her new friends and the work she loved, was the same girl who had arrived fainting and emaciated on the hospital doorstep. We had changed with her. In the space of twelve months we had all travelled a long journey. It had cost us pain, fear and hard work, but our guides had supported us over every careful step of the way. I felt that I would never be able to express my gratitude to them — but I knew that they understood.

No-one had dry eyes when we finally said goodbye, and it did not matter. Afterwards, all of us were able to look back on that as our first good parting — the first one that we had been able completely to accept.

Five days later, we were celebrating again. As it had been Joanna's eighteenth birthday at the beginning of the month while she was away at college, I had offered to hold the family party this year in our rambling old house. It was a way of thanking everyone for years of loving support, and of celebrating both her coming of age and her recovery.

It was one of the happiest days I had known for years. I was by no means left to run the party alone, either financially or practically — and it turned into the kind that simply takes itself along, with the house bursting at the seams with uncles, aunts and small cousins. June was there, as an honorary aunt, and so, of course, was Joy. As I rushed around, trying to look efficient, I knew that Ray was right when he assured me that we were coming through. I looked at Joanna, flushed and happy, and was suffused with gratitude that this infinitely precious relationship had not only been rescued from destruction, but strengthened so that it could develop into a lasting friendship.

Even Simon, usually uneasy at parties, seemed to have grasped the point of this one with unusual clarity. He wandered round telling everyone that Joanna was well again and playing her cello. Complex details may have been beyond his powers of understanding, but Simon had what amounted to a definite gift for homing in on essentials, and he was making quite sure that we appreciated them, too.

CHAPTER TWELVE

Ninth Year: Tom

Tom went off to his first NYO course in exactly the same state as his sister had before him — convinced that he had only succeeded in the audition by a fluke, and that everyone else in the orchestra was far more talented than he was. He returned dreamy-eyed, and with exalted ideals, but still with absolutely no faith in his own abilities.

His viola lessons, instead of being a source of enjoyment, had become a battleground of conflicting tensions, where every correction drew blood. Worse, all the happiness he had experienced at school during his first two years there had given way to restlessness and — the word kept recurring in his conversation — boredom. He was currently reading, or rather devouring, a book about a gifted young mathematician whose talents were neglected, even mocked, at his comprehensive school, and from the way he told me about it, I could see that he was identifying strongly with the hero.

Maths was Tom's delight. At his junior school he had been allowed to go at his own pace, his programme discreetly enriched by the understanding headmaster. Now, in the setting of a big comprehensive school, this was no longer possible. Far from proceeding at his own pace, he was feeling held back and frustrated. The choice of O-level options, already far more restricted than it had been in Joanna's time, was forcing him to drop subjects which he enjoyed, and in which he was keenly interested. As he was extremely bright right across the board, and as yet had no idea what he wanted to do by way of career, there was no clue to guide our selection and to help us avoid making bad mistakes. The system did not seem to be designed for people like Tom.

In an attempt to establish some priorities, I took him to see and talk to the music consultant for the National Association for Gifted Children. He wanted to take music as one of his O-level options, and I wondered if, in view of the severely rationed choice, this was entirely necessary. She listened to Tom playing and talked to him for some time. Then she sent him away and called me in. Music, it seemed, would have to be one of our priorities, for he really was intensely musical, and might well end up making a career in this field, though not necessarily as a performer. I sighed. I was not inexperienced any more. I now had a very realistic idea of just what this entailed for the rest of the family, and no longer felt warmed by a rosy glow of enthusiasm. She ended up by remarking that she thought Tom depressed, particularly about his school life, and suggested that I might consider making changes that would help him.

This observation, coming from an outsider with no axe to grind, added fuel to my growing anxieties about him. He had, I knew, suffered a great deal in the past year, for he was deeply attached to his sister. Family therapy, with its laying bare of conflicts and tensions, had frightened him as well as giving him insight. He needed now to enjoy himself, to benefit from the calmer waters in which we were sailing — to begin, like me, to spread his wings and develop all his interests.

The difficulty was that money had become desperately tight. There was absolutely no spare cash to help me open up Tom's life. I was so anxious about our finances that it was difficult to think clearly. The safety cushion of savings that I had put away in the early days after the court order was originally made was now fast melting away as I dipped into it constantly to supplement our day-to-day income. This frightened me. All too soon it would be gone, and then the cuts would begin indeed.

During the last six months, I had done all I could to speed matters towards returning to the court for an increase in our maintenance payments, but everything had been held up by an unexpected and unhappy stroke of bad fortune. When, in the summer, I had tried to contact John, my solicitor, I had been told he was in hospital. As time went by and he did not reappear, I pressed for more details, and his secretary reluctantly told me that he had cancer.

This was a grievous blow. Over the years, John had become a valued and trusted friend who many times had softened for me the freezing formulae of the legal world. He was younger and far fitter than I was, a keen rugby player, and always full of energy and enthusiasm. It was unbearable news. I grieved for his family. I felt I could guess what they must be going through. There was, however, still hope. John, I knew, loved nothing better than a good fight. I felt sure he would put up a valiant one.

In these circumstances, the urgency of our need paled into insignificance, and I could not possibly put anyone under pressure. But John did, indeed, put up a fight. Shortly after Christmas I had heard from him, as breezy and confident as ever, to say that he was back at work, and that the date for our hearing was fixed. He even apologized for the delays. I was more overjoyed to hear his voice again than I was to learn this news, and my relief was to sustain me throughout the ordeal of appearing before the registrar.

John had thought it best that I should appear in person at this hearing, to dispel any illusion that I might want the money to spend on fur coats and jewellery. I doubt if he really knew what it cost me physically and emotionally to do so, to sit quietly while the old wound was torn open once more, and our needs minutely discussed by strangers. His presence, and that of Joan who, sensing my longing for support, had taken time off work to come along, alone made it bearable.

To lawyers, such negotiations are very similar to a game of chess, with ritual moves. For those involved, it is like having an operation without an anaesthetic so that one can listen to the deliberations of the surgeon. John kept reassuring me during the long wait beforehand, emphasizing that it was all a game and should be treated as such, but I was not yet strong enough to achieve such objectivity, and sat there vulnerable to every scratch. What strength I had came from the knowledge that I was fighting once more for the children, and that I was not asking anything unfair or impossible. Happily, after a long hearing, the registrar agreed with me, and the maintenance was increased.

I felt faint and exhausted by the time we at last left the room, as well as angry at the humiliation of the whole wearisome process. I longed more than ever for financial independence. I questioned Joan about job prospects over a late lunch — as a personnel manager she was able to be more realistic than most — but she was far from optimistic. In any case, I knew all too well that the only job I really wanted to do was writing — and I still could not write. The block that had come into being before the onset of Joanna's illness was still there, apparently immovable, and I had begun to despair of ever getting rid of it.

It took some time, and no small amount of work from Ray, to discard the feeling of hopelessness which arose from the experience of going back to court. Ray insisted that I look upon it as an achievement, another fight won, rather than as yet another punishment. His constantly challenging approach to me was starting to have its effect. I was beginning, albeit timidly, to fire back at him, and even to derive an unexpected enjoyment from doing so. This very enjoyment gave me more confidence when it came to dealing with other people as well, so that in general I was finding more pleasure in everything I did. The difference in me was beginning to show, what is more — enough to arouse comment among my friends.

It became apparent even to me in the course of a somewhat painful talk with David. He, too, had been unlike his cheerful self ever since Christmas, almost as if he were reflecting Tom's mood. He was normally such a bright, bouncy person that I guessed that something important was troubling him. When I pressed him, he hung fire for a long time, then burst violently into tears — a rare occurrence for him. In the end he sobbed out that he needed a dad. All his friends at school had a dad, and he wanted one too.

All the old guilt raised itself up around me like a barbed-wire entanglement, waiting for me to impale myself. For the first time, however, instead of hurling myself onto it, I succeeded in putting into practice advice I had heard many times: I sat back and considered the matter from all possible sides. I remembered the talks we had had in family therapy about relationships with Paul. He might be my ex-husband, but he could never be the children's ex-father. I realized that the reasons I had had for vetoing the boys' trip to Canada the previous summer no longer applied. The crisis was now, I hoped, over. If Paul would have them this year, it would both give them an exciting and well-deserved holiday, and renew the contact with him that alone could lessen, however slightly, their feelings of deprivation.

Nor was there any need for me to play Cinderella. In all the years he had lived there, I had never been able to visit my brother Ian in Toronto. With only one fare to find, such a visit would now enter the realms of financial possibility. Joanna, I knew, would be going to her Swiss friends again, and Simon would be at Somerset Court. There was nothing to stop me. We could *all* have a fantastic holiday.

I put the idea to Tom and David, and watched their faces light up. Tom was given the responsibility of writing to his father, while I wrote to my brother. There were some initial difficulties over dates owing to the complicated commitments of the summer. In the end, providentially as it turned out, we fixed on the last week of August, and the first week of September, sandwiched neatly between the NYO course on the one hand, and the beginning of school on the other.

Joanna was most surprised when, during her half term week at home, we told her all about the project. It was still difficult to adjust to her arrivals and departures, and fatally easy to make her feel shut out of family affairs, so that I always tried to fill her in about everything, even my worries about Tom. She and he were very close, and she could play a useful part in helping him.

She had her own worries, however. Anorexia, in her case, as well as in that of all the sufferers I have met, does not seem to lift entirely away, even after such thorough treatment as she had had. It is not unlike a heavy fog which, even after it has been dis- persed by sunlight, tends to leave wisps and tendrils lingering in dark corners. My first reaction, when Joanna told me about these remaining traces of anxiety and guilt, was one of panic. Then, once again, I managed to stand back from it. I realized that above all she needed reassurance and encourage-ment, and did my best to give them to her. It was heart-warming to feel that she could once again accept them from me, but I felt that she needed some from outside, too, and suggested that she phone Ray, and talk it over with him. She did so, with the result that she went back to college in a much happier and more confident frame of mind, leaving me to cross my fingers and turn to the next challenge.

This was the imminent arrival of a strange French boy who was coming to stay for nine days as the first leg of a school exchange. Tom, in his turn, would go to France in May, during the summer half term. It did not occur to me at the time that, two years previously, I would never have dared to envisage such an extra burden as this.

There is an awesome element of luck in these school exchan-ges, and it was unfortunately ours this year to receive an only child who had never been away from home before, and who was struck dumb with homesickness the entire time. I knew from long experience with au pair girls that it takes at least three weeks to get the shy ones to defrost, so that the battle was lost before it was engaged. We all three did our best, but none of us could induce poor Didier to open his mouth either in English or in

French. All he wanted was to go home, and he left us feeling more than a little deflated by our failure. I also had some doubts as to the wisdom of Tom returning the visit in his present frame of mind, though Tom himself was very keen to go despite the conspicuous absence of even the smallest piece of common ground which he might share with 'his' French boy.

Still trying to attack his depression at what seemed its roots, I had been to see the maths teacher at his school, to put the problem to him. It turned out that there was very little he felt he could do about it. He told me that he had a timetable which allowed him no freedom of action, and certainly no chance to give extra individual attention. He tried to reassure me by telling me that depression is very common in boys of fourteen. He was possibly right — but I knew that not many boys of fourteen had Tom's personality and history.

Having drawn a blank at school, I tried to open another door for him by offering him organ lessons. He had pestered me for years to be allowed these, but I had always felt we simply could not afford them. Now I was too worried to care, and he began to learn from the organist at church, and to practise on the organ there. He enjoyed the lessons, but they did not lift his spirits for long. Tom's depression, as the music consultant had perceived, required far more drastic measures than these, but I was still too weary from the struggles of the previous year to make the necessary effort.

It was as if he were trying to prove something to me. He insisted on entering for the local Music Festival which we had, of course, completely missed the previous year. I tried hard to dissuade him, for it was obvious that he was in no state to do himself justice. Events proved me all too right, and tactless adjudicators added to his misery. June, to whom I had confided my worries, went with us to the last attempt, and I have rarely valued the support of a friend more as together we picked up the pieces of Tom's skin and tried to stick them together again.

It was a bad experience, and I longed for the support of family therapy — so much so that I phoned the long-suffering Ray, and asked him if I could take Tom to see him, outlining the situation which was fast becoming more than I could handle. Soon, I was doing the drive to Chiswick twice, instead of once, a week.

In the meantime, Tom's unhappiness over his viola had come to such a pass that I had been driven to take action. Ian, a well-known professional viola player who lives in our village, agreed to take him on as a pupil. We had known him, through Joanna, for some years, and I knew that he was used to teaching children with disturbed backgrounds. I felt certain he would do his best to relax Tom, and help him to enjoy his lessons again. Having made the decision, the transfer was quickly made. I had delayed acting for too long, so that we all now took off like Hunter jets, once again cutting through etiquette in a way that was becoming suspiciously familiar. Knowing what we had been through with Joanna, everyone was very kind and cooperative, so that no time was lost. Before long, Tom was coming home telling me what a marvellous time he had been having playing duets or learning some fantastic new piece of music — and I began, cautiously, to breathe again.

I also wrote a long letter to the National Association for Gifted Children to see if they could advise us on our difficulties at school. I was beginning to wonder, though not without deep pangs of guilt, whether a change might not be necessary there as well. Our local school had done so much for us, and shown us so much kindness, that I felt acutely disloyal — but Tom's wellbeing had, I knew, to come first.

The letters which came in reply, however, tended, like the maths teacher at school, to play the problem down. Once again, I was assured that boys of fourteen are prone to depression — clearly a widely-held view — and that it was unwise, if not impossible, to seek a change of school at this stage. I was only too willing to accept the reassurance, but the nagging doubt remained: with our family history, just how depressed was it safe to allow Tom to become? Boys can become anorexic, as well as girls. I felt I could not face the prospect of more upheavals, but all the same I put the idea of moving to a boarding school to Tom. I wanted to know if his feelings about it had changed at all since we had last discussed the subject, five years before. It seemed that they had. He was ready and willing to try it now. Having established that, however, I sat back and let things ride. I was really hoping that if I did not look, the problem would go away.

It was all too easy not to look. The summer half term had come. Tom went off to France with the school, for his return visit to our silent friend, while David had been invited to go camping in Wales. Joanna was back in Manchester after her break, while I — I grabbed my freedom with both hands this time and took off for Paris, to stay with an old friend of my student days, now married with grown-up sons, who lived in a large flat on the Left Bank.

I felt light-headed with the sense of release as Hélène walked me round my old haunts, and we picked up the threads of a friendship which had always been a strong one despite the separateness of our lives. We went to cinemas, art galleries, museums — and she watched with satisfaction my appalled reaction to the Centre Pompidou. I visited the old lycée where she worked as a reference librarian, and wished that similar jobs existed in English schools, for the work struck me as fascinating. I was coming back to life, and I loved every moment of it. Ray's incessant, quiet challenges were bearing fruit, and I walked with a new elasticity in my step.

Shortly before I left for France, there had been a session in his office when at last he had made me understand how much I punished myself, compulsively prolonging and exacerbating my own pain. He did it by actually catching me in the act, as I wept in front of him over miseries long past. Suddenly, as he asked me with an innocent expression what on earth I was crying about, the penny dropped. It was a moment of dazzling enlightenment, not unlike the day when Joanna, Tom, David and I had lunched together at the Bethlem hospital. Ever since the days of evacuation during the war, I had carried about with me my own private millstone — a crippling sense of inner worthlessness which had grown out of that childhood rejection. Able to venge my hurt and my misery neither on Hitler, the government nor my parents, I had turned on myself, using as weapons every criticism, every insult, every injustice, and every further rejection that came my way, hoarding them in a retentive memory for future use. Depression in middle life was the inevitable result.

As I thought it all through during the drive home, I felt like singing. Everything at last seemed to fit into place. I felt as Christian must have done when he dropped his burden, only in my case it was not because somebody else was forgiving me, but because at long last I saw how I could forgive myself. Now that I understood the reason for the depressions, I stood a chance of modifying them. The past could never be undone, and there would still come times when I needed to weep over it, but at least now I could simply acknowledge that — and live more comfortably with it.

Gaining that insight meant more to me than any academic achievement. I felt that I had just graduated from a far harder and far more important school of learning than any university. I only wished that I had been able to enter it earlier.

In view of all this, it was hardly surprising that I walked the streets of Paris with a spring in my step. I was ready at last to begin to enjoy life again. After long years lost in the fogs of depression, of feeling left behind and excluded, I was taking my place alongside everyone else, and it was a good feeling.

It turned out that all three of us had benefited from the break, which was just as well, in the light of what was to come. David had had his first experience of fine-weather camping — all his previous expeditions had been blighted by rain and cold. Now he had seen the Brecon Beacons in their summer beauty, and returned home full of stories about mountain walks, waterfalls, and the cosset lamb he had been allowed to feed. Tom had made the best of a difficult job in France, and his French was much improved — it was sheer bad luck that we had hit upon a family which could do nothing to help or interest him.

Within a week of the holiday, the storm broke. Tom plunged into a depression far worse than anything I had experienced with him before. He could barely speak. All the red lights flashed at once. I saw clearly, once and for all. There could be no more delay. And there was no such word as impossible.

It was fortunate that I had had a rest. If I was to obtain the help he needed it was necessary to embark on a concentrated stint of phoning and letter-writing. I began by contacting Margaret Branch, one of the founders of the National Association for Gifted Children, and who, though no longer working with them, I knew to be still deeply committed to the welfare of the gifted. Margaret had a reputation for a splendid disregard for mere practical obstacles. I was certain that if anyone could help us, she could. Nor was I wrong. Thanks to her I obtained an appointment for Tom to see an educational psychologist in London the following week. We needed the results of IQ tests as evidence that Tom was worth helping. Once they came through, I took to the phone once more.

Time was anything but on my side. The end of term was in sight, and all those who were in a position to advise us were showing an alarming tendency to disappear on holiday to distant places. In the end, after much deliberation, Margaret suggested that we apply to Highgate School, which had a very high reputation for music. Nervously, I contacted the headmaster, and could hardly believe it when he asked me to take Tom along for an interview.

We were both of us apprehensive when we entered his study. For once, I was too concerned over Tom to worry about the absence of support from a partner, and, during the friendly conversation which followed, I could only admire the skill with which Tom was put at his ease and drawn out to display greater animation than he had shown for months. When, as a result, he was offered a place in the school for the following term, I was overwhelmed — as I always seem to be when others recognize our struggles, and the reasons for them, and offer us kindness and support. The interview had left me with a strong feeling that Tom could be very happy at Highgate. There remained the problem of the fees — which I could not even begin to meet on our slender income — but here too the school came to our help. Bursary funds, to which many parents and former pupils generously subscribe, met the greater part of the boarding fees, while tuition was covered by the offer of a government-assisted place. Even our own County Education Authority gave a contribution.

Thanks to all these sources of help, the impossible had become possible. Tom was to start at his new school early in September, on the day after his return from Canada — I could only pray he would not be suffering too much from the effects of jet lag. It promised to be a lively autumn.

It was not a pleasant task, informing our local school of the impending move, after all that they had done for us. I was deeply grateful to them — but I could not let my gratitude blind me to the reality of Tom's needs. I felt as if I were swallowing every word I had ever uttered on the subject of education. Every time I opened my daily paper, I seemed to see articles extolling the virtues of the comprehensive system, and criticizing those who had the selfishness to opt out of it. So much, I thought ruefully, for generalizations. For when it comes to the particulars — namely, the deep unhappiness of a beloved child — few parents would cling to the theory once it had proved impracticable.

After all that had happened to us, there was no way I could leave Tom at risk. If, as I had come to believe, his depression arose both from the fact that he was almost totally deprived of the society of men, and from a feeling of isolation in the academic work which mattered so intensely to him, then no argument going would convince me that he ought to remain within a system in which he so clearly did not fit. In this all-out effort to rescue him, I was, for once, backing my own strong hunch that he would flourish only in an atmosphere where excellence was the norm rather than the exception, where he would not be nicknamed "Professor" by his fellows, but simply be accepted as one bright boy among many. If my hunch were to prove wrong, then I was strong enough now to accept it as one more mistake.

The continuous phoning and correspondence made it a somewhat chaotic background for Simon when he came home for his long July holiday, but this year he did not appear to mind. For one thing, his adored Joanna was at home, too, so that he could see for himself that she was "all well now". For another, he was showing signs of such considerable improvement in all aspects of his behaviour that he was much less dependent on me for amusement.

Over the years, in giving talks on autism, I had often told audiences how autistic young people, given the appropriate educational environment for their needs, continue to develop and improve until well into their twenties. I had read this, but I had never, of course, experienced it for myself. It was now as if Simon himself wanted to prove me right. He was asserting himself far more as an individual, stating his preferences and making decisions. He astonished us all one evening, for instance, by rising from his seat next to Tom, who was watching a performance of Mozart's *Idomeneo* on television, and switching off the set, remarking "terrible rubbish" with great conviction. It needed all my diplomacy to entice him into a different room, and settle him in another occupation, so that the opera buff could resume his viewing, though with a concentration frequently breaking into chuckles.

This July, Simon seemed, in fact, to me by far the most peaceful member of the family to be with. He had completely emerged from the silent, withdrawn years of his adolescence, and conversations with him, albeit incomprehensible to the average outsider, gave me great and increasing pleasure. Joanna was taking her driving test, an ordeal which severely taxed everybody's nerves, while both Tom and David were doing exams, and were very tense and prickly. By the time he returned to Somerset Court, I felt that Simon had actually made his own special contribution to the stability of the household during that busy month.

Immediately after his departure, routine vanished into the now familiar August chaos, as everyone disappeared in different directions on the same day. It was a relief finally to find myself heading down the motorway to Somerset, where I was to attend another painting course for a few days. I had been attending watercolour classes once a week during the past nine months, and was still finding great enjoyment and relaxation in the struggle to lessen the gap between vision and execution. I hoped to be able to visit Somerset Court while I was there, though I always found a one-day visit a great strain, as I suspect Simon did, too. This one, however, would coincide with the Summer Fair once more, which we both always enjoyed.

In contrast to the previous year, the course proved interesting and instructive. The main drawback was a vegetarian diet sprung on me without warning, and which I unfortunately cannot tolerate. Lowered as I was by increasing queasiness, it was hardly surprising that at the end of the week I picked up a severe gastric infection which made me really ill. The long drive home now became both difficult and dangerous, and my carefully made arrangements for collecting Tom on the way, at the end of his course, were shattered. At least it made me aware of our luck, that over the years my health had stood up to the severe tests imposed upon it by the complicated demands of the family. The experience, however, left me dissatisfied and resentful. My holidays were too rare and far too precious to be jeopardized by such a failure to give basic information. Living as I did under constant stress, I tended to have high expectations of my short breaks, so that I was more disappointed than average when they failed to come up to them. On the whole, I had been more than lucky with my brief excursions away from home, but the luck, it seemed, had run out when it came to art courses.

No sooner were we all safely home than Tom disappeared again, this time to the NYO, barely giving me time to deal with his laundry. Catastrophe had come very close when the dates of the NYO summer course had been put back from those originally given. It now officially ended on the very day we were due to fly to Canada. Fortunately, it was possible to retrieve him immediately after the last concert, held at the Barbican the day before our departure, though I could not for the life of me see how I was to do this myself.

The complications of the Canadian trip had become hair-raising. Paul had booked the boys' flights at his end without consulting me, while I, of course, booked mine locally — with the result that my plane took off first, in the middle of the morning, while theirs left in the evening, leaving them with the rest of the day to kill and the problem of reaching Heathrow by themselves.

Not for the first time, the family came to the rescue. Joan and Jane attended the Barbican concert, and brought home a tired Tom, while I waited with the washing machine at the ready, so that clean laundry would await our return from Canada and the rush to pack his trunk for school. One of our uncles, who had often helped me with the runs to fetch Simon from the coach bringing him to London from Somerset Court, had agreed to ferry the boys to the airport, and see them to the check-in. The tangle had unravelled, and the holiday became possible. . . . I was free to go to my brother, for the longest break I had known in nine years.

Joy was to travel with me. She had arranged to visit her niece, who lived just outside Toronto. Her presence beside me made the journey much more fun. She was completely recovered now, and was as ready to enjoy herself as I was. When the big jet at last roared into the air, we looked at each other and smiled. Neither of us had entirely believed the holiday would happen, but now, as we rose clear of the clouds, we could settle back. It was real.

Or was it? I felt, in fact, exactly as if I were moving through a dream sequence. I was travelling on a magic carpet which had lifted me clean out of all the never-ending demands of everyday life. They dropped further and further behind me as the plane sped west. For two whole weeks I was to stay with people who really cared about me, and who wanted to give me a holiday I would remember. Nor was there any need to feel guilty about the children, for they were having a holiday too. Joanna had gone off to Switzerland again, and I knew she would be happy there, amongst our Swiss friends. Tom and David would be able to phone me, if they felt they needed to, so that there was not the smallest anxiety to cloud the radiant blue of the sky outside the plane.

When lunch was finally served, the holiday spirit took us over completely. Rarely did an airline have two passengers bent more deliberately on enjoying every moment of the flight. No gadget was too small to interest us, nor did we feel critical of the meal.

We were no blasé travellers enduring a necessary period of transition from one country to another, but bright-eyed holiday-makers full of the joys of getting away.

The first face I saw as we advanced to meet the Canadian immigration official was that of my brother, looking like an excited schoolboy, with my sister-in-law, whom I had only met once for a few hours more than twenty-five years before, beside him. It was extraordinary, I reflected, as Joy and I awaited our turn, how this brother–sister relationship had blossomed out of such meagre beginnings so late in our respective lives. It had become very precious to me, and I rejoiced that now, at last, we seemed to be overcoming the barrier of distance.

The fortnight in Toronto was the happiest holiday I had ever had. I had been to more beautiful places, and basked in more hours of sunshine, but no-one had ever made me feel so welcome and cared for as Ian and Muriel — with whom, within hours, I felt as if I had been friends all my life. Not only had the burdens and pressures of single-parent existence been lifted off me for a while, but the loneliness, the sense of isolation, was banished too.

The feeling of coming back to life which had surprised me in Paris grew even stronger now, as together we visited the Canadian Exhibition, the lakeside, Niagara, Ottawa — where I made the acquaintance of my great-niece — and the lakes and forests of the Ontario countryside. We even went to a concert given by the Canadian National Youth Orchestra, about which I looked forward to teasing Tom. We met up with Joy and her family, and Joy and I swapped stories, each trying to outdo the other in new experiences. I was entranced by every aspect of life in this, for me, new continent — the birds, the flowers, the animals — even the recently killed skunk which we unmistakably met on the long drive to Ottawa — everything fascinated me. I was a child again, thrilled by everything.

Far too soon it was check-in time at the airport and I was having a fierce struggle to keep the tears at bay. I did not want to leave my family. The flight home had none of the glamour of the happy flight out. It was riven throughout the entire night by the howls of a battery of babies determined that no-one else should get a wink of sleep, since they could not. Magic vanished, to be replaced by reality which faced us once more with its usual offering of hard facts.

The first of these was that Tom and David, although their plane landed only a couple of hours after mine, took an hour and a half to be reunited with their luggage. Joy went on home whilst I fought sleep over many cups of airport coffee. We were a subdued trio by the time we finally reached our house, to be greeted by an ebullient Joanna who, ignorant of the ways of jet lag, had prepared a beautiful, elaborate meal for us which none of us, even David, could eat.

The second was that the central heating boiler had sprung a slight leak, and the resulting trickle had extinguished the pilot light in our absence — so that there was no hot water. With Tom due at his new school the next day, and the laundry piled around the washing machine, I had to contend with the always difficult and, in the event, impossible procedure of relighting it before I did anything else. On my stomach in front of its innards in the dark cupboard where it lives, prodding hopelessly around with a match, above a pool of water, too blind with sleep to locate the pilot, I knew I was home again.

I sank my pride and called the gas man.

He came with wondrous promptness. Civilization was restored, and the three of us fell into bed to snatch a few hours' sleep before I began work on Tom's half-filled trunk. Fortunately, as it turned out, there was no time, if I wanted this necessary sleep, to read the accumulated mail. When, somewhat restored, I eventually opened the pile of letters, I found one from my firm of solicitors, informing me that John had died peacefully in hospital.

This was reality inded, reality so harsh that I could not immediately take it in. It was several days before I could weep over this loss of a good and kind friend, who had done his best for me even when he was mortally ill. I knew I would never forget John. No small part of our survival was owing to his timely help. I mourned him, even as events swept me on.

I was still stupid with lack of sleep when, desperately nervous, I delivered Tom to his new school next day. I returned with yet another empty space in the car, and prayed for the success of the whole undertaking. If it failed, I felt we would all be at risk once more. I hoped that his happy and successful holiday with his father would tide him over the difficult first weeks.

We had all gained something during the summer which was to help us in the days to come. Each of us, Tom and David in their expeditions with Paul, Joanna in her Swiss mountains, and myself with my Canadian family, had added something very positive to our store of experience. We had all grown a little stronger.

Ray had encouraged me to attempt to meet up with Paul again, but neither he nor I had had any clear idea of the distances involved, and it had proved impossible. He felt that I was ready now to face this once so deeply dreaded encounter, and so convert distorted memories, anxieties and fear of pain into an ordinary, real event. I was privately determined, having failed to achieve it in Canada, to bring it off at the first possible opportunity. I knew it was time now to be free of Paul.

Tom's first weeks at his new school were hard on all of us. He found the transfer very difficult, and we shared his misery at weekends when he came home for his viola lesson. I was desperately sorry for him. Vividly remembering Joanna's unhappiness and its consequences, I came near to panicking several times. It was Ray, yet again, who kept us afloat. He told Tom to phone him during his weekends at home, so that they could talk through together all that was worrying him, and Tom duly did so. He encouraged the rest of us to support him, but not to sympathize with him. This was not easy in the face of his distress, but we did our best. So did the school staff at their end, and I was full of gratitude for the way they helped him during those first trying weeks, gradually winning his trust and respect.

We all, in fact, needed to do a great deal of readjusting once more. Having only just become accustomed to Joanna's comings and goings, the family structure was now undergoing yet more changes. After years of hectic activity, I now found myself with only one child left at home for most of the time. There were hardly any more runs. It all felt very strange — and empty.

David, however, who had begun by missing his brother acutely, began to blossom in the light of my undivided attention. His school work showed distinct signs of improvement, and he was more grown-up in all his ways — until, that is, Tom reappeared at the weekend, whereupon the said grown-up ways disappeared, and there began a savage jockeying for position. The resulting friction was extremely wearing. I always seemed to find myself in the exhausting role of piggy in the middle, only I never seemed to catch the ball.

The approach of the second NYO audition had been adding to Tom's tension. This year, I knew it mattered to him more than ever in his struggle to make himself accepted amongst his new companions, so that it was with great delight that I phoned his housemaster with the news that he had been successful, and was a member of the orchestra for another year. I knew very well that this was a trump card. His lifeline was secure, a continuity between the past and the present, and he could now begin to savour the realization that his first audition had not, after all, been just a happy fluke — he was valued.

Sure enough, from then on, Tom began to brighten and even, finally, to enjoy himself. Compulsory sport, of which I had once strongly disapproved, had broadened him out, and hardened his muscles. The pale youth was turning into a stalwart young man, alert and interested in all he was doing, and working hard to attain the high standards he felt were expected of him. He was already a different creature from the unhappy, drooping boy of the previous spring, and I rejoiced to see it, full of gratitude to all those who had helped us with the transfer.

It was thus a very propitious time for the arrival of a letter from Paul, announcing that he was coming over on business, and would like to see the boys. It was the chance I had been waiting for, and the success of the venture with Tom strengthened my decision. I arranged a weekend meeting, when Tom was at home.

I asked June to come over. Stronger though I was, I still did not want to face the encounter alone. Being outside the family, she had no tensions of her own concerning Paul to worry her, yet she was a good and close enough friend to give me the support I needed. Although determined, I was shaking with nerves, and I was more than glad of her quiet, kindly presence. Tom had arranged to met Paul down the road, but now I asked him instead to go and invite him in to coffee. I was more glad than ever of June's presence when I saw that he had the two-year-old daughter of his second marriage with him — he had not told us that he was bringing her to England as well — and I had not quite bargained for that.

It was a strange meeting. We had not seen each other for some six or seven years. Paul was as nervous as I was, and June played her part nobly by deftly filling in the inevitable tense pauses. Memories, dreams and fantasies — all could now give way to the ordinariness of reality. The only unreal element was the absence of pain. All that was left of those agonizing, unbearable emotions was compassion — for both, for all of us. We had, in marrying, brought such dire unhappiness upon ourselves and our children.

As he stood there in the old kitchen which had changed very little since his going nine years before, I suddenly realized that I no longer, in the least, wanted him to come back. I knew now that we could never help each other. We could be friends, in a somewhat superficial way, but no more. I could even admire the baby.

His coffee finished, he went off with the boys. I had arranged to spend the afternoon with a writer friend of mine, Kate Fordham, who is also a single parent. I was trying to guard against possible reactions. But we spent a pleasant afternoon shopping together — and there was no reaction whatsoever. I could not believe it. It was only when we were all reunited at home once more that I realized that Ray had been right: the meeting had at last proved to me what he already knew — I was free. Between them, Helen, the two therapists at the hospital, and Ray himself had given me back what had been missing ever since childhood: a sense of personal worth. I had looked on Paul, for the very first time, as an equal.

In fact I was more than free. Suddenly, I found myself with a job to do. For a long time, Ray had been prodding me to write about my experiences as a single parent, and I had stubbornly resisted, protesting that no-one would be interested in struggles that were, after all, very personal to me. But now a publisher to whom my agent had introduced me showed himself interested in the idea, and asked me for a specimen chapter. At exactly the same time, another publisher agreed to produce a paperback edition of my first book, and wanted an additional chapter to bring it up to date — as quickly as I could manage it.

The two-year-old writer's block vanished immediately. The watercolours were left to dry in their box. The year seemed to be gathering itself together into a grand finale. Mince pies, the puddings and the Christmas cake were all thrown together anyhow during brief excursions from the typewriter. I was writing again, and happy, and I did not mind how mad it all grew.

Joanna now added her pennyworth to the general excitement. She had received an invitation to give her first public perform-ance early in the New Year, in the concert hall of a nearby town. Home for the Christmas vacation, she put on the special dress that she had bought for it in Manchester. A great lump came in my throat. She looked so pretty, so full of health and wellbeing — and she had been through so much. More than anything else about my daughter, I admired her courage. Now I was delighting in seeing that courage rewarded in her happiness in her work and in college life. She, too, had seen Paul during his visit for the first time in years, and there had been no adverse reactions. She was even talking of going to visit him in Canada the following summer. The healing, it seemed, was general.

Joan was holding the family party this year. The Ford Escort, much worn by now, sank with a protesting groan as my four young people packed into it. When we made the sharp turn off the road up Joan's steep drive, the exhaust pipe scraped loudly and ominously on the gravel. It seemed to be emphasizing a point which I had only half grasped: I was not carrying round four children any longer. We could not go up slopes as awkward and as steep as this together any longer — the four young passengers would have to get out and walk.

There could hardly have been a more vivid illustration of the fact that, as a one-parent family, we had grown up.

CHAPTER THIRTEEN

Ten Years On

Joanna's concert was to take place in the middle of February, and, once Christmas was over, and a starry-eyed Tom returned from his NYO course, I had little thought for anything else. We had told the family about it at the Christmas party, and they had promised us solid support. Although this was no Wigmore Hall recital, it was nonetheless very important to her, for it was the first opportunity she had had of playing a concerto with a professional orchestra, and if it went off well I knew it would do much to restore the confidence that had been lost during her illness. I prayed that the hall would be full, which was asking a lot, since it is a large one for a small town. No doubt in the future she would often have to face empty seats, but for this first ordeal she needed to feel that people were with her.

My own weekend off at the music course came and went, as usual, far too fast. For once, however, my mind was only half on the lectures. Every other phrase sent it winging off to Manchester, to join my daughter. All the same, I was glad of the physical rest, for, having dispatched both pieces of writing to their destinations, and climbed over the happenings of Christmas, I was very tired, though not with the depressive tiredness of previous years. I enjoyed greeting again old acquaintances, for the course was a popular one and the same faces tended to reappear. We were all saddened this time to learn that the centre was soon to close, as part of the programme of cuts. I knew how much it had meant to me. I was always sorry when the course came to an end and it was time to go home.

Not so this year, however, for there was far too much to do. I was growing increasingly nervous, with a nervousness over which I had no control. It was not that I doubted Joanna's ability — I had heard her play too often for that — but I had not, in fact, heard her perform since before she fell ill with anorexia, and I was afraid that she might not be able to stand up to the stress of a solo performance in the town where she had been born, and where many people knew her. She was to play a Vivaldi concerto. The seeming simplicity of baroque concertos is deceptive — they are, in fact, in their purity, extremely difficult, and pitfalls abound. The orchestral cues for the soloist, for example, are all very similar, and even a small memory lapse can cause disaster, which I, of course, conjured up vividly in imagination. Such anxieties were, I suppose, inevitable after the terrible experience we had been through. Success would take her a big step forward, but failure — I could not bear to think what failure would do. It was as well we were living far apart.

We talked together on the phone just before she came home. We both felt that the twenty-four hours before the concert would be something of a test for the strength of our new relationship, and each wanted to prepare the other for possible eccentricities in behaviour. I was desperately afraid of turning overmaternal and smothering my daughter, whilst equally desperately wanting to make clear my support. Joanna, for her part, was chiefly worried about frightening me by being sick with nerves which, she confessed, happened every time she had an important performance. She tried to reassure me by telling me that this had always happened to Pablo Casals, but as I did not recall hearing that the great cellist had ever suffered from anorexia nervosa, the reassurance did not work very well. In the end, we laughed — and the laughter, somehow, restored everything to its true perspective.

The evening of the concert was one of the coldest of the entire winter, which cheered me in that at least no-one could be entirely certain why I was shivering. I could hardly believe my eyes when, with Simon, who was home for a long weekend, Tom and David, I finally took my seat in the concert hall. It was full. The larger part of the audience was composed, it seemed, of almost everyone we knew or had ever known: members of our church congregation, teachers, neighbours, friends, family — even our doctor who had brought her into the world — had turned out in the cold to attend the concert. Tears came to my eyes, and there was again a lump in my throat. Our survival as a family, and as individuals, had depended on several factors, but one of the most important ones had been that we lived in this unusually caring community. Now, wherever I looked, there were friendly, smiling faces, nodding encouragement.

I needed it. I was feeling sick, and my heart was beating a tattoo. My thoughts were with Joanna, in her dressing room, awaiting her call. I could not help her now. She was on her own.

When at last she came on stage, in her pretty blue dress, her long hair streaming down her back, I could see that she was rigid with fright. I huddled down in my seat shutting my eyes, willing her passionately to understand that it was all right, that everyone in the hall was with her.

As her opening bars sounded I could hear her tension and uncertainty in her tone, and my heart sank. My worst fears, it seemed, were to be realized. But then it was as if I could sense her gathering up the reins. That brave chin lifted in a way I knew well — and suddenly Joanna was a part of her music, and free of herself. The Vivaldi concerto, with its haunting slow movements and bright, busy, fast ones, seemed exactly the right work for this occasion, which was, in a sense, the real celebration of her recovery. Not that I could listen critically — not this time. I knew that it was going very well, and that was all the information that I could cope with — I was far too overcome with emotion. No doubt, as she advanced in her studies, she would come to play far better — even well enough to satisfy the perfectionist ear of Christa, who was sitting somewhere at the back of the hall. For now, for a student in her second year at college, she was doing outstandingly well.

When it was over, and the applause broke out, I saw her dazed look as she parted company with Vivaldi. Gradually, as she faced the enthusiastic audience, she became aware of them, and the colour returned to her cheeks. There was no sign of the awkward, adolescent platform manner of her pre-anorexia days. This was a mature young woman, able now to smile and move with grace.

I was drowning in wave after wave of thankfulness. This success had come at exactly the right time, the right moment in her recovery. Now she could build on it. If she indeed went ahead, as she hoped, to a performing career, there would be plenty of other terrifying moments, but she would probably never again stand on such a knife edge as this. There was a long and unpredictable hard road between the present and the achievement of her ambitions, but tonight she had proved something to herself and to others — that it was possible to emerge from nightmares, given an essential combination of courage, determination, loving support and professional help, and to take up one's place again in the light of day, amidst one's fellows.

Her happiness shone out through her exhaustion during the small party we held at home after the concert for the family and a few close friends. I was, of course, hostess, but tonight I was totally useless in this role — floating round several feet above the ground making inane if not insane remarks to whoever crossed my aerial path. It was Tom and David who actually looked after our guests, pouring drinks and passing the cheeseboard with an aplomb far beyond their years, whilst keeping a benevolent eye on my antics. They were both far taller than me now, and referred to me affectionately as "The Mother". They had suddenly become solid, and masculine, and protective — and I could see that, as with Joanna, a wholly different and very enjoyable style of relationship now lay ahead of us, in which I had to learn again to drop the maternal role, and acknowledge my sons as equals.

Simon, too, was glowing with pleasure at this unexpected party. We were all glad that his weekend at home had coincided with the concert so that he had been able to share our happiness. He had behaved beautifully during it, entranced at the sight of his adored sister playing her cello in front of so many people, and now, of course, he wanted to tell everyone about it. It had not been so very long, it occurred to me as I watched him moving from group to group, since he was shuffling round the cottage wringing his hands and moaning out his distress at her illness. It was reassuring that, after so much time at Somerset Court, he still obviously felt a part of the family.

My only regret that evening was the absence of Ray and his wife Vera, who had been intending to come, but who had been daunted at the last minute by the bitterness of the weather, which would have made a long drive from Northamptonshire a perilous affair on icy roads. It was nine years since I had first, in a state of hysteria, phoned him for help, and he had given it unstintingly ever since. In all that time, he had never once manifested impatience or irritation, and without him I knew that what had happened tonight could never have been. It was not only Joanna's performance that we were celebrating, I realized, but our survival and, thanks largely to Ray, there was no self-pity left around to mar our joy. We were a very happy, if weary, family that night when at last we stumbled off to bed.

The next day we were still floating high in the clouds. Simon returned to Somerset Court, and Tom and David to school, so that, fortunately, Joanna and I were alone together by the time the

reaction set in. It was severe — far more severe than either of us
had anticipated. Joanna, rather like me at the time of the
publication of my book, had somehow expected her life to be
permanently changed, but she was now discovering, as I had,
that life has a habit of continuing on its way like a river, leaving
only flood marks to prove that anything unusual has happened.

I envied her not a little when, at the end of her half term week,
she returned to college where I knew she would soon be caught
up again in the rush of activities, leaving me on my own at home
to feel flat and sorry for myself. It was a great relief when,
meeting one of the members of the orchestra in the street, she
reassured me that such post-concert blues were entirely to be
expected, and were only likely to stop occurring when Joanna
was playing in several concerts a week. It was just as well, I
reflected, for my own equilibrium, that the majority of her
performances were likely to take place away from home. Now
that at long last I seemed to be breaking free from depression, I
found myself growing alarmed and resentful if I thought it might
be setting in again.

In any case, I had work to get on with now, work, what is
more, that I loved, and gradually my low spirits cleared in the
face of the necessity for concentration. The publisher had given
the go-ahead for the new book, the contract had been signed, and
I, too, had something to which to commit myself. I had, in fact,
been working sporadically at it since Christmas in the hope that
nothing would go wrong with the negotiations, but only when
everything was signed did I feel secure enough to assume a real
routine.

Perhaps the word 'routine' is the wrong one to use. Women
with large families who live at home do not often enjoy the
privilege of regular working hours — especially if they have little
money so that there is no domestic help. I write, simply,
whenever I can, which means that the manuscript lives on top of
the fridge for easy accessibility and I work at the kitchen table for
the same reason. It is possible to concentrate, but it is necessary to
accept that getting angry at interruptions is a waste of the very
energy that is needed for concentration. As the book grows it
takes over the dresser as well as the fridge, absent-mindedness
becomes a domestic hazard, and the family begins to wear a
hunted, long-suffering look. Coexistence is possible with good
will on both sides, however, and this is what really matters. I

have even grown to like the sounds of the Elgar Cello Concerto, under practice in the sitting room, floating through to enrich my thought.

There was certainly no shortage of interruptions this year. The paperback publication of my first book, now retitled *Simple Simon*, was imminent, and this entailed a fresh round of publicity engagements. It had been planned to coincide as closely as possible with the launch of the National Autistic Society's twenty-first anniversary year, and as this in turn coincided with Simon's own twenty-first birthday I found myself once more carried high on a wave of celebration.

There was a difference this time, however. I was better equipped to be realistic about what the publicity could and could not do. I had no wild illusions that it could radically change attitudes to the plight of the autistic and their families — I knew by now that this was a long, slow process. Instead, I felt that if it could make even a small contribution to arousing interest and even the occasional action, I would be more than satisfied. Feeling this way, there seemed much more point to the whole operation, and I could enter into it wholeheartedly.

The day before Simon's birthday, Joan and I travelled down to Wells together. We planned to celebrate by staying overnight at a hotel, which gave us both a welcome break, and by taking Simon out to lunch next day. We had done this several times over the years, and I had always found it the most enjoyable way of visiting Somerset Court, since it cut out the fatigue of two long drives in the same day, whilst Joan's company eased the painful feelings of loss which recurred every time I hugged him goodbye and turned away to drive off home. I always felt she understood my pain, without the need for words.

This time, however, the visit was a very special one, for this was a definite occasion. Whilst Simon's twenty-first birthday might confer no privileges in the eyes of society, since he could never own property, vote, or even emigrate to many countries, it held a strange symbolism for me, his mother. At least his body was that of a man, even if his mind would always be that of a child.

The weather, naturally, did its worst. Joan and I had established what amounted to a tradition of driving down the M4 in force nine gales, but now we were in a holiday mood. We knew that warmth and good food awaited us at the other end, and we laughed with a fine display of carelessness as the juggernauts threatened to wash us off the road. Safely there, ensconced in comfortable armchairs, we lifted our glasses derisively at the British weather.

The gesture was not without effect, for the sun shone brilliantly as we drove the few miles to Somerset Court next day. It was, in fact, one of the happiest days I had ever spent with Simon. It was obvious, from the moment he walked into Mrs Elgar's office, that he was fully aware of the importance of the date. "It's my birthday!" he told me, with a delighted smile, as we hugged him.

We went with him to visit the workshops, and Joan made some cheerfully rash purchases, such as a large wooden bird table, which I saw was going to present some interesting transport problems, since it would not fit in her car. Then we took him off back to the hotel for lunch, having observed that roast chicken was on the menu — an absolute essential if one is hoping to please Simon.

In the restaurant, he opened the present from Joy which I had brought with me. It was a large musical box in the shape of a cottage — a stroke of genius on her part, as he adored musical boxes to the point of breaking one of hers simply by wearing it out. Now he had one of his own, and the other diners were highly intrigued as the strains of "The Floral Dance" tinkled out across the room. In fact, the dance wound its way through the rest of the meal, but smiles from the other tables showed understanding, and no-one objected. Clean plates and polished chicken bones left us in no doubt that he had enjoyed his meal. He even joined us in drinking his health with his first ever glass of wine — which had less effect on him that it did on me. He was to have a big party that evening at Somerset Court, with all his friends there, so that, although as always he looked puzzled and dejected when we kissed him goodbye, I knew it would not be for long. We hoped he would remember his twenty-first birthday — as we would.

I arrived home somewhat breathlessly to greet this year's French boy — David's exchange this time. As soon as I set eyes on Christophe, I knew that, this year at least, we had struck lucky. He responded to everything and even won approval at judo with his swift reactions — it turned out that his brother was a judo instructor. By the time he left us, I had become very attached to him, while he had entirely lost his sentimental French heart to

Joanna. He, who claimed only to appreciate pop music, and was incredulous at our ignorance of pop singers and groups, sat entranced by the piano, listening to her playing pages of Chopin, Debussy and Beethoven, adoration in his eyes. I could see that I need have no worries over David when he made the return visit.

Our visitors — Tom had had a school friend to stay as well — had barely departed when angry feelings which had been simmering for a long time between David and Joanna suddenly erupted with a violence which startled and alarmed us all. All three young people found it extremely hard to cope with the process of gradual separation from home. Joanna and Tom both needed to find their old places waiting for them — their beds, their rooms, even their places at table unchanged — so that they could, immediately upon their return, find themselves part of the family once more. David and I, who had to cope with our feelings of loss each time they went, tended to cling to the routine we had constructed in their absence to make the emptiness of the house bearable — a routine, naturally, which excluded them. None of us had quite been able yet to accept this fluctuating state of the family as normal, and David, in particular, who was assuming far more responsibility, resented being treated as a little brother by his elders when they returned, and he was now making this resentment bitterly vocal.

The trial flights of the fledgelings are nerve-racking for all families, but our experiences had made us particularly vulnerable. It took Ray to sort all the anger out. Patiently, he talked to each of us, and then sat us all round together to work out what was going wrong. We had visited him at his home, and Vera had laid on a delicious meal for us, which inevitably turned the occasion into something of a celebration. We did not often need help now, but at times like this I was still deeply glad of Ray's skill. It was still fatally easy to misunderstand — to be blind to the needs and fears of the two who were making their first steps in the world outside, as well as to reassure the one who was still at home that he was still equally loved at weekends and holidays. The old feeling that there was just not enough of me to go round was threatening to return — until, as we drove home, I realized that this time Joanna, Tom and David had understood. They were sufficiently adult now, and had received enough help, to be able to absorb Ray's words and to apply them. Although I was still nominally at the helm, the running of the ship was becoming more and more democratic, and the onus was no longer so heavily on me. It was a very comforting thought.

As if to make quite sure that I understood that this year, to whatever dizzy heights it might occasionally rise, was as full of the harsh stuff of reality as any other, I now had to turn my attention to an impending battle with the DHSS — over Simon.

It had all started the previous year with a minor skirmish. Two formidable ladies from our local office had suddenly descended on me to investigate my application on Simon's behalf for supplementary benefit, an application I had in fact never made. He received invalidity benefit. They asked to see my court order for maintenance, made a few notes, and departed. A few days later, a letter informed me that the application I had never made had been turned down. Any threat to Simon's wellbeing always makes me intensely anxious — but I was completely mystified. No explanation was ever forthcoming. It was only when I phoned the National Autistic Society that I learned that all the residents of Somerset Court were supposed to be in receipt of supplementary benefit — a fact which had contrived to escape me. As we had just been turned down, here was a fresh anxiety.

The reason given for refusing the benefit was that, according to the court order, Simon had an "income". The order had been carefully worded that way, it may be remembered, so that I should not have to pay income tax on maintenance payments.

This had all happened just before going back to court for the increase of maintenance, and I had told John, my solicitor, of the problem, and asked him to reword the new order so that Simon's money should be payable to me, even though this now put me back once more in the tax bracket. He duly did this. According to Inland Revenue law, Simon no longer had an income.

So that when, in the autumn, I had applied once more for supplementary benefit on his behalf, it was with complete confidence that the application would go through. When it was rejected, on precisely the same grounds as before, I could not believe it. What John had not realized, and I had not even remotely suspected, was that Inland Revenue law, and Welfare law, though they share a common language, do not interpret it in the same way. According to Welfare law, the wording of my new court order still meant that Simon had an income — even though I was now paying tax on it.

I was not only in a panic, I was furious. I felt as if I was caught up in some childish game of words, in which Simon and I were the inevitable losers. I went back to my lawyers, but they were unhelpful. Since John's death, I had found it very painful to deal with the other partners in his firm, simply because they were strangers. Formal letters were anathema to me after his humorous missives. It seemed the right time to make another change, and Ray, when I consulted him about it, encouraged me, recommending to me a solicitor whom he knew to take a special interest in the handicapped. Since I would have the responsibility of Simon for the rest of my days, I needed a legal adviser who would be a friend, and a friend prepared — as my present difficulties showed — to fight, and fight hard. There was no panic this time over making the change, and it was effected smoothly.

Meanwhile, I had appealed against the decision to reject my application. The case was to go before a tribunal — and this was what was facing me now.

I knew I could not win against so weighty an adversary, but I was so angry that I wanted some better explanations. I felt that my handicapped son was being discriminated against because his parents were divorced. If Paul and I had still been married, there would have been no court order, no maintenance payments, and no possible existence of an "income". Even as things were, Simon's "income" did not go individually to him, but, pooled with that of the other children and my own, paid for the upkeep of the home that was so important to all of us. When one DHSS officer told me that Simon was lucky to have a home to go to, and that such reasoning could not affect the assessment, I nearly exploded. It seemed to me that while I was talking about the realities of living, all the DHSS could do was to recite a list of rules which bore very little relevance to them. This feeling was reinforced when, shortly before the tribunal, I received an official letter supposedly setting forth, for my benefit, both sides of the case. When I had read it, I decided it had to be a joke. While I could, of course, understand my own case, since I had taken some trouble to set it forth lucidly, I could no more understand that of the DHSS than if it had been written in Sanskrit. It was pure gobbledegook. No lay person could possibly have understood it — which completely negated the point of sending me the letter.

Perhaps what was the most saddening as well as the most infuriating aspect of the whole affair was that it gradually became obvious, in all the many conversations I had with them, that the

DHSS officers themselves both agreed and sympathized with me
— but they were hamstrung by their own regulations which they
could not break without actually breaking the law. I cannot
believe, as a fervent supporter of the Welfare State, that those
whose vision it was ever dreamed that its rules could acquire such
divine status that they could not be changed, even when, through
their rigidity in the face of a fast-changing society, they actually
harm the weak and the vulnerable that they are supposed to
protect. Nor could I accept that these rules should be set out in a
terminology so obscure that they were unfathomable by the
ordinary man or woman.

At the tribunal, I did my very best to explain this point of view
to the three lay adjudicators — which was, I suppose, a waste of
time since they had no more power to change the law than I did.
At least I had the ironic satisfaction of seeing that they understood
me, whereas the poor DHSS official had a far tougher time,
repeating his case again and again before they appreciated the
finer nuances of the jargon. I began to feel sorry for him, for he
was clearly not relishing his job. In fact, after the hearing, he
came up to me outside and apologized for being obliged to cross
swords with me. He was so kind, and so clearly distressed, that
my anger vanished.

He explained that if the DHSS had had power of discretion
Simon would have received his benefit, but that this power had
been rescinded a few years before in an attempt to tighten up on
the distribution of benefits. He advised me to admit defeat, and to
return once more to the court to have Simon's name left
completely off the court order, so that Paul's payments for him
would become voluntary.

I was caught, and I knew it. I would have liked to take the
matter much further — to force it out into the open and show it
up for the charade it really was — but for all our sakes I knew I
must, then at least, forego the pleasure. We had had enough
anxiety. What we needed now was to have Simon's position
clarified and made as secure as possible, so that we could all
relax. Nonetheless, it was very galling. It was even more so
when, a few weeks later, my accountant advised me on my new
tax position. The increase of maintenance, coupled with the
rewording of the order, had moved me into the tax bracket to the
point where I had actually lost half the increase — and I still had to
pay part of the costs in obtaining it, not to mention the additional

bill which would now be forthcoming after changing the wording yet again.

"You really are unlucky!" exclaimed my new solicitor, when he had studied my position. "You fall between every stool there is."

I smiled bitterly. After nearly ten years of struggling and juggling with a small income, after stretching every pound like an overwound cello string, and appealing to others when it would stretch no further — simply to give the children not luxuries but their basic needs — I had no illusions left concerning my financial position. It was a trap from which there was no visible escape. If I worked to better it, I would, in fact, lose, since Inland Revenue and contributions to Joanna's grant and Tom's assisted place between them would make mincemeat of anything I earned. The only consolation was that at least I was doing work that I loved and which satisfied me. Paying the bills was a separate issue.

The solicitor promised to be as speedy as possible in obtaining the revision of the court order. He was as good as his word, and it was within my hands within weeks. I had liked him at once, and knew that I had found another firm support as we shook hands at the end of our meeting. Joanna then took me off for a much needed cup of tea. The fact that she was there, instead of Joan, marked the development of our relationship. I was acknowledging the fact that there was no longer any need for me to protect her, so that she could feel herself fully my friend, well able now to support me when the need arose. Thanks to family therapy and to Ray, we were negotiating this difficult transition in our relationship with more success than I had dared hope for, and each time that Joanna came home, we seemed to enjoy each other's company more — though we still hated separating. Now we lingered long over our tea, and gossiped cheerfully until it was time for the train home.

At the end of May, we were all invited to a wedding — that of the youngest of the large network of second cousins. It was the first wedding I had attended since Paul went, though Joanna, Tom and David had been to many when they sang in the church choir. Before the ceremony, I had been somewhat apprehensive — I was not sure whether or not it was going to hurt. It turned out, on the contrary, to be one more proof of the extent of my recovery. Far from feeling any renewal of the old pain, I enjoyed the service, and admired the sweet-faced bride and her three serious little bridesmaids. I was proud of my family as they stood beside me — good-looking and clear-eyed, a family any woman might be proud of. There was no sense of failure to mar the day, only one of elation that we had come this far.

Nor did the feeling soon die away, for Ian and Muriel were about to arrive from Toronto for a two-week stay. I had been hoping to visit them in Canada again during the summer, but the hope was beginning to fade. Not only was money very short once more owing to the large legal bills, but, as Joanna now definitely intended to visit Paul in July, he could not afford to invite Tom and David as well. This meant that they would be at home, and I, in consequence, was not free to go. This was hard, but there was nothing for it. At fifteen and fourteen they were too young to leave, and I had not the money to take them with me. I cheered myself with the thought that, with a book half written, I did not really have the spare time, in any case, and began to cast around, none too successfully, for more modest holiday ideas.

In the meantime, I made the most of my brother and sister-in-law's company in my own home. The May rains had given way to clear, sunny weather, and they were able to reap the full benefit of the garden — a luxury, I now realized, for high-rise apartment dwellers. Every blackbird in the neighbourhood came to serenade them, as if to convince these visitors from the New World that England in June is by far the most beautiful place to be. They went home fully concurring in this, with memories to cherish of meetings with old friends and relatives. They visited our mother, still flickering on in the nursing home, and were rewarded by a smile which spoke more eloquently than she now could of her joy at seeing them.

During their stay, I had received a phone call from the TV producer of the "Light of Experience" programme which I had made after the initial publication of *Simple Simon*. She was hoping to make a "Light of Experience Revisited" series, and wondered if I again would like to take part.

The invitation seemed to present me with something of a problem. When I had made the first programme, in 1978, I had been very clear and certain about my religious faith, and had spoken about it with great confidence and gratitude — a confidence I was far from feeling now, though the gratitude remained unchanged. The departure of Peter and Marilyn, the subsequent depression and near breakdown, Joanna's anorexia and all the therapy it had brought us, between them had changed the face of my world. I was no longer at all certain where I stood in terms of a spiritual life — or, indeed, if I even had one. I had grown to mistrust words, especially when they were used in lieu of acts. An arm round my shoulder, an offer to drive us to the hospital, meant more to me than a prayer for they represented an acknowledgement of the concrete nature of our needs, an enactment of Christ's teachings which I still venerated deeply, whilst disliking dogmatic utterances.

I had grown critical too, as we emerged from our ordeals, of a church which does not appear to be able to come to terms with the realities of the society in which it has its being — with divorce, remarriage, or the needs of the one-parent families, the debris of all the changes. After ten years as the head of our family, I could not accept its attitude to women, and its failure to recognize their problems.

Yet I still loved it deeply, and that was the rub. I could not cope with all the contradictions in myself. After hours of thought, I decided that this was not the sort of problem that could be quickly resolved for the benefit of a television programme. The only honest contribution that I could possibly offer was to describe it. I put this to the producer, and she accepted it — which was a relief, chiefly because she seemed to feel that many others would identify with my difficulties, whereas I had been feeling very isolated by them.

Joanna, who had experienced very similar problems, had, after considerable thought and reading, found her own solution by becoming a Quaker. I attended a meeting with her, and was moved by the profound peacefulness of the silence I found there, just as she had described it to me. I could well understand how it appealed to her in the hustle of college life, and the never-ending roar of a great city like Manchester. Moved though I was, however, I still did not want to break from my own church which by now felt like an extension of my family. I knew that, like any loving family, it could tolerate the growing pains of one of its members. It had played too important a part in our survival for me to take my relationship with it lightly. I preferred, as in so many other things now, to stand back, and to wait — unlike my impetuous daughter.

The time had come for her departure to Canada. She was hoping to visit Ian and Muriel, and Joy's niece, as well as Paul. Although I had supported and encouraged the project from the start, it was far from easy to see her go. It proved, in fact, to be the hardest challenge I had faced since the end of family therapy. I was desperately anxious for her. I knew that a stay of several weeks in Paul's home, with his wife and a small half-sister, would be an emotional strain, and I was still not sure that she could cope with it. The whole month that she was away I was wrestling with my feelings, trying to stifle my anxiety, frightened that the whole episode still seemed to be causing me so much pain.

There was no way this year that I could expand my own life and find exciting things to do. On the contrary, I was on my own at home with Simon to care for. David was still at school all day, and Tom, who had broken up early, had gone off to Paris to stay with friends of Hélène with whom he stood a better chance of learning about French life and culture than he had the previous year. Cinderella had returned, for the time being at least, to the cinders. It was very difficult to remain cheerful when I was alone all day with an autistic young man, however much I loved him. I could neither do my own work nor communicate sufficiently with him to rid myself of the dreaded feeling of isolation which threatened me once more.

Worse was to come. June had gone into a nearby hospital to have an innocent-looking lump removed from under her arm. Its innocence, however, was only skin–deep, for it proved, after tests, to be malignant. At first we both buckled under the shock, June at this sudden face-to-face encounter with the hardest of realities, and myself at this threat to someone who had in a few years become one of my dearest friends. Then we rallied, and began very determinedly to study the odds. As we realized that they were more favourable than in the case of many cancers, the stronger grew our determination to fight, to fight with every weapon ever discovered. As soon as she was out of hospital, she wrote off to the Bristol Cancer Help Centre, to learn how best to help herself in this most primitive of battles, and, after discussion with the surgeon, began a course of chemotherapy. She often came to stay with us during these nerve-racking early weeks — and here it was that David came into his own.

I had often thought, watching his patience and perceptive practical support of Simon, who shared a room with him when he came home, that David had special gifts when it came to dealing with anyone who was in any way handicapped or under stress. He had often helped Joy when she was ill, and she had a very special corner for him in her affections. He did not swamp anyone with demoralizing sympathy, but saw what needed doing and did it, while his infectious grin and gentle teasing worked wonders on a drooping morale. He had learned a lot about other people's needs in family therapy, and, as he grew older, was becoming ever more adept at applying the knowledge. Now he took June under his wing, to such good effect that I think he did more than any of her adult friends to steady her, and set her walking firmly in a positive direction.

At last, it was time for Joanna to come home. We went, Simon, David and I, to Heathrow to meet her. At the sight of her, in radiant health, delighted to be back with us again, and clearly in no way disturbed, my spirits soared, and the last painful weeks seemed to fall away as if they had never happened. Ray came to see us the next day, so that we could both talk over our reactions. He made me realize how much of my pain had stemmed from the sheer difficulty of letting go of my daughter, of accepting the separateness of her life, her adulthood, and he cheered me by pointing out that this type of separation was never likely to be as difficult again.

Joanna had had a wonderful holiday. As she gradually told us about it over the next few days, I could see how much the experience had added to her maturity and self-confidence. The old ghosts, it seemed, were laid at last for both of us now. Her Canadian trip had been a bad ordeal for me, but now I felt that it was worth it. She had proved beyond doubt how well she could handle herself in difficult situations. It seemed as if my anxieties were at last being laid firmly to rest.

Tom came home in his turn full of enthusiasm and affection for the extremely kind family he had stayed with, for their cooking in particular, and in general for all things French. He had been shown the sights of Paris, but more than anything else he had enjoyed the experience of living in a large, interesting and happy French family, who had clearly taken him to their hearts and treated him as one of themselves. He was most pleased to watch me turn green with envy when he told me that he had even been to a concert in the Sainte-Chapelle — something I have always wanted to do and never managed. I was, of course, more than glad that the mistake of the previous year had been rectified, and that he now had some rather more favourable ideas concerning

France. I loved it too much myself to want my children to have unnecessary prejudices.

The beginning of August saw our usual dispersal. I had decided to give art courses one last try, taking care this time to select one that was run by a county authority and so would be likely to offer a minimum standard of comfort. Which was precisely what it turned out to do. As I looked at the stained and peeling walls of my room, and gazed at a view of open dustbins, I was tempted to return home. It did not help that I was dead tired — more tired than I could remember being for years. The July difficulties had taken more of a toll of my physical strength than I had realized. Nor did I feel the least desire to paint, despite the very good tuition — all my creative urge was now going into my writing. Painting, it seemed, had served its purpose, just as recorder playing had once done, in giving me a pleasant and stimulating occupation, to which I could turn when the writing was in abeyance, but neither of them could flourish when the writing filled the foreground. All I really wanted to do during this five-day break was to go out into the beautiful grounds and sleep in the sun.

I did learn a little more about technique, however, so that the course was not a total loss. On the other hand, it had not refreshed me in the way that I needed, and I resented its discomforts too much to contemplate ever making it again one of my too-precious breaks. Three failures had to prove something.

It was a relief to be at home once more, and to plunge again into the writing which by now was drawing me like a magnet. One part of me, all the same, protested at such continuously demanding treatment.

Since first going to acupuncture, I had had no further trouble from my lower back. Suddenly, now, as I sat each day at my table, it flared up again, and I found myself once more in severe pain, as severe as ever it had been before I found my acupuncturist. I phoned him in some panic, only to find that he was away on holiday. It took me some time to locate a substitute — in London. It was a very strange feeling when, on arrival at his door, I discovered that he practised in the same block of flats where, five years before, I had attended the osteopath. I took the lift with a strong feeling that my life was moving round in cycles.

Yet, as I sat carefully in the waiting room, I reflected that the situation felt very different this time round. Although it was true that I was once again in bad pain, I was no longer terrified that I would be unable to continue struggling beneath the enormous burden that I had taken on. Even if I should be unlucky enough to be put out of action, the children would be able to carry on without me. Our lives would not fall apart. The back pain was back pain — and nothing more. Experience had, in any case, given me great confidence in the efficacy of the treatment. This proved not to be misplaced. After a couple of visits the back grew much better, and I could contemplate the rest of the summer's activities with somewhat more assurance.

Joanna went off again, this time to attend master classes which were part of the Lucerne Music Festival. When they were over, she hoped to spend a week's holiday with Christina, Werner and the children before making her way to the International Cello Festival at Nemours, in France, where she was to meet up with three other cellists from her college for yet more master classes. She was having a very busy summer indeed — in fact, she would only be home for a couple of days before leaving once more, this time for Manchester and the beginning of term.

I missed her very much, but now I was no longer worrying about her. Joanna was a separate, adult person now, and could very well take care of herself. Anorexia had faded into a dark episode in the past.

It was Tom who spotted a solution to our holiday problem — in the pages of our daily paper. Originally, June, now convalescent, and I had intended to go off for a week in a hotel together, leaving the boys to devise a camping holiday for themselves. Tom, however, showed me an advert for a hotel offering four holidays for the price of two. It was in such a beautiful situation, by a river in the Welsh mountains, that we could not resist it. We reasoned that the two boys could still do their own thing in the form of daylong hikes in the mountains, leaving June and me to go at our own pace loafing around the shady valleys. The weather had been sunny and hot for weeks, and showed no sign of changing, so that we were delighted when our booking was accepted.

We should, of course, have known better. The hotel was comfortable, the food reasonable, and the location a delight. The heat wave, however, true to our long-established form, broke within two days of our arrival, giving way to storms and gales which lashed the trees by the river until we thought they must fall beneath the onslaught, and turned our gently splashing, peaceful stream into a muddy, yellow torrent. The hikers, nothing daunted, set off for the heights regardless, returning in the evenings soaked and dishevelled, absurdly pleased with themselves, and with raging appetites.

I had taken my work with me — I knew better now than to try and leave it. A few hours spent with it in the morning would leave me good-tempered for the rest of the day, so that June was happy to leave me to it. For me it was a complete luxury to be able to write whilst free from household cares, and I made the most of it.

By the end of the week we all felt better, if windswept. June, in particular, seemed to have made excellent progress. The week's rest had built up a solid determination to go on with normal life as much as possible, and to beat her illness in the process. She hoped to return to work within a few days. The chemotherapy, which was in modified form, made her very tired, but had no other ill effects, so that she hoped to be able to cope with office routine, despite the daily journey that this necessitated. We both knew that a long battle lay ahead of her, but the knowledge that she had a good chance of winning it gave us both heart. At least we could all make certain that she never felt too alone with it.

Joanna reappeared from her wanderings on the Continent, weary and rumpled from a night crossing of the Channel, but full of enthusiasm and new resolutions. She told me that she had learned an enormous amount from the master classes. I blenched slightly when she spoke of putting in more hours of practice each day, as she was trying to change her style — some painful memories surfaced like bubbles from the past — but I could see that this was no hysterical flight into obsession. It was, rather, the seriousness of the dedicated professional. She seemed now to know exactly what she wanted to do, and her feet were firmly on the ground. She had grown up as a musician, as well as in herself. As she set off to begin her third year at college, I felt it could well bring some interesting developments.

Tom and David returned to school. Tom had done well in the two O-levels he had taken early, and seemed entirely happy to be going back to boarding once more. He was looking forward to sharing a den this term, for he had now moved into the senior school. He had a hard year's work ahead of him, but I could see that he was enjoying Highgate life more than ever. I thanked my stars that this time I had listened to the voice of my own judgement, and not heeded those who had tried to reassure me. Tom, now, was thriving. The life of a caring boarding school, with high academic and musical standards, had been for him the only solution to his feelings of intellectual isolation, with no father to support him.

David was different. I still checked with him from time to time, but he remained unshaken in his desire to remain at home. He needed above all to feel needed, and since, of course, there was no disguising the fact that he was, we could both feel comfortable. He cherished a long-standing ambition to go into the Police Force, a job I felt would suit him well, and if when the time came his application was successful I was hoping that a spell at the Cadet College would make the inevitably difficult separation easier. For the present, he, too, was flourishing and maturing, whilst life in a comprehensive school seemed to present him with no especial problems.

For a few short weeks I was free to get on with my own work. Then began the long string of mid-term holidays, only two of which coincided.

Simon's ten-day autumn break was the first. As soon as we reached home, I realized that it was going to be no easy one this time. For no reason that I could fathom, this was not the peaceful, cheerful Simon of the summer. We were back to long faces, go-slows at meal times, and complete emotional withdrawal. It was a forceful reminder of the unpredictability of the autistic personality. For the last two years, we had seen very considerable progress, but now we seemed to have lost all the ground that had been gained. There was nothing for it but to accept it, and wait for better times. Half way through his stay he began to cheer up a little, and I wondered if he had been worrying that he was only home for a long weekend, but there was no way I could verify this, since he could not tell me.

Simon was no fairy-tale prince, to be released from enchantment at the end of the story. The hard facts of his autism would be part of my, and of his siblings', reality all our days, and it behoved us all to thank God for the existence of Somerset Court, which allowed us most of the time to go on with our own lives, whilst giving him a full and worthwhile one of his own. The agonizing decision to send him there had been, I was sure, the right one. If I had been left alone with him at home, I would not have stood a chance of coming out of my depression, deeply though I loved him. It was hard enough, even for this limited period, when there was no break — our local social services department was too hard-pressed to offer relief now.

It did not help when I discovered that the Somerset DHSS, who held Simon's particulars, had cut the supplementary benefit, which it had taken me so much time and money to obtain, for the period that he was at home. This was money that I badly needed to pay for necessary clothes and accessories. The more I thought about it, the angrier I grew. When I talked with other Somerset Court parents, I found that many were suffering — though it was when I found that some were not, depending on which office held their papers, that I saw red. I wrote off a long letter to my MP. If he had not taken action, I was ready to write to the Queen herself, but in fact he sorted it all out with great speed and efficiency, and within a couple of weeks I received a cheque for the missing money and another incomprehensible form. The letter of apology only went to the MP.

The incident made me realize that part of the realities of my son's autism were these never ending battles. They would never cease until the day that our society awoke to the fact that they cost more than preventing them by forethought and realistic compassion, and that day, I feared, was unlikely to dawn in my lifetime.

It was, altogether, a depressing ten days, and I realized that, before too many years passed, we would have to find a solution to the problems they raised when they came round each year, though I was none too sure what form it would take.

A week later, Tom and David broke up. At least it was possible, though not easy, to work when they were around, and they understood my needs enough to make sure that I had some time to myself each day. They returned to school, and a few days later Joanna appeared, so that I was typing once more to the strains of Elgar. The sole difficulty of this was that the sounds she was making were so beautiful that I kept finding I had stopped to listen, which hardly helped concentration. Although she practised for much of the day, this no longer upset me as it once had. I knew that she was in control of her music, not the other way round. In the master classes she had learned, as she had recounted to me ruefully, that it was possible to have your style of playing taken to pieces, before strangers, and to survive, even to gain from the experience. The result was that everything now seemed to be moving forward together. We coexisted, although we were both working extremely hard, very happily.

There was, I thought, just one more ghost left for us to lay, and it was that of Guy Fawkes. In all the years since Paul had left us, we had never again been together to a Bonfire Night celebration. There are always several of these in the villages around where we live, and once we had actually set out for one — only to have me return home in tears, unable to face it. Guy Fawkes night held a symbolism for me that it did not hold for others. It had been the last thing we had done as a complete family. Although I hated depriving the children of the fun and the excitement, I could not meet the pain which the sight of the fire and the fireworks would surely reawaken, and each November the Fifth I stayed firmly indoors. Perhaps if friends had invited us it might have been different, but this was a need no-one knew of.

It was time now, I decided, to confront that old fear and reduce it to ordinary proportions, as we had all the others. There was to be a bonfire and firework display at David's cricket club, and I suggested to Joanna, Tom and David that we should go, telling them why. They welcomed the idea, though only Joanna fully understood what it meant to me — she was the only one old enough to have vivid, detailed memories of that terrible night before Paul went.

As we parked the car, I was more than grateful for her understanding, as she slipped her arm through mine. I had not been prepared to find it so difficult. It was such a strain that I began to wonder if, after all, this was not just another example of wearing a hair shirt. But all three reassured me. We were simply clearing away some old, dead debris, and it was hard work. It would never be so hard again. This Bonfire Night was something the four of us had done together, as we had so many other difficult things.

As the flames died down, and the big box of fireworks became nothing more than a scattering of empty shells on the damp ground, we walked slowly away across the field in the dark to the car, each busy with his or her own thoughts. There was something of a sense of anticlimax, for the big crowd which milled between us and the promised hot soup was too dense to negotiate with any comfort.

It was David, the perceptive, the ever-practical, who suddenly suggested that we should take ourselves to the pub. Joanna backed him instantly, for he was somewhat unnerved by his own temerity. I had begun to protest that he was not old enough, when I realized that he was. As so often happened, he had sounded exactly the right note. The pub was just across the lane. It was a typical old country one, and I knew it would have an open fire.

Gathered together round it, crunching crisps, warming our toes before the friendly glow of the logs, we toasted each other. Although nowadays we spent so much time apart, we knew tonight that we were still very close. The traumas and anxieties of the last ten years had only served, in the end, to forge bonds between us of which each one was now sure. We could feel them as we raised our glasses.

No, this had not been an evening of self-punishment. This was a Fifth of November which it would in the future help, not hurt, us to remember. We were not drinking to gunpowder, treason and plot, but to something far more positive. We were drinking to our continuing love for each other. Whatever difficulties our lives might bring us, whatever losses, this was a fact — one to which each could always turn for support.

We were warm again, and relaxed, by the time we finally reached home.

CHAPTER FOURTEEN

The River Goes on Leaping

This, of course, is not the end of the story, for it is a living one, and not an artistically shaped piece of fiction. Each day that passes takes it on a little further. I am merely breaking off at a convenient milestone — the end of a decade — from which I can turn and look back over the road we have travelled.

The ten years began with what seemed at the time like an irremediable disaster. The trauma of it was so great, in the four children, and in myself, that it did not seem possible that we could ever recover.

They end with the children almost full grown. The three normal ones are healthy, fun–loving, caring young people, while the autistic one lives as full and varied a life as it is possible to have with such a handicap. The trauma is behind them. The only outward mark of it is an occasional quietness, a turning away when they see another boy or girl enjoying a laugh with their father, or an ordinary, two-parent family having a good time together. On the whole, they have learned to live with their sense of loss, and have come to terms with it. I, too, am beginning to enjoy life again, and to seize all opportunities of widening and enriching it. I, too, still have my moments of nostalgia, a sadness for what might have been — but in all of us this is no more now than an acknowledgement that we have all been through great pain, and that, because of it, we sometimes need comfort. It is not depression. Having found the needed support, either from each other or, as the case might be, from friends, we are ready to move on again.

We have travelled, during those ten years, an even harder way than was once forecast for Paul and me by the paediatrician who diagnosed Simon as autistic. I thought then that I had reached the uttermost depths of pain when I learned that my beloved eldest child was mentally handicapped. It was as well that I could not foresee the still darker ones which lay ahead when, alone, I had to watch the sufferings of all my children, adding to my pain by constantly blaming myself until in the end I broke beneath the agony of it and howled aloud for the help no-one had realized that we needed. Joanna, too, in her separate anguish, took the same negative path, though her scream for help took on an even more self-destructive shape. Yet it was her slow, fascinated dance of death which saved us all. It was the appalling, unthinkable approach of that dread spectre which summoned up in me the last surge of maternal strength which finally broke the barriers of anxiety and distance to sweep us all to the safe care of the Maudsley Hospital.

I often wonder now at that strength which, even after the years of grappling with autism, I did not know I had. It is completely primitive, and is subject to no law. It must, I think, be one of the strongest forces in the natural world. Without it, I could never have lived through those terrible early years after Paul's departure, when, in my ignorance, confusion and grief, I knocked on door after door only to find, far too often, the indifferent face of officialdom.

Today I know that those early years need not have been so hard. If society had been geared to deal with the havoc it was so busily creating in the rush to the divorce courts, if the effects of marital breakdown on children had been even remotely understood, I would at least have had some established and accepted centre to which to turn for the information, support and practical help I so desperately and obviously needed. It is, to me, glaringly obvious that any human being, male or female, left alone with the care of small children is going to need these things. For all my academic background and professional training, I was as vulnerable as any teenage mother: grief and stress make no distinctions. If anything, they made it harder for me — in order to ask for help, I had to fight the feeling that I was losing face. My blind, uninformed search led to some costly mistakes, which added greatly to the tension and anxiety of our situation — and, of course, affected the children.

This unconscious strength kept us afloat throughout all those early difficulties. It enabled me to turn to music and use its healing powers to help my family. I turned to it against all common sense, shutting my eyes to the heavy financial cost, despite the acute shortage of cash. Signing Tom up for cello lessons when we had no financial settlement and no regular income was against reason, an act of pure obstinacy and determination to find the money. If I had not done it, he would not now be a member of the National Youth Orchestra, and beginning the composition of his first symphony. I had seen the therapeutic effects of music on Simon when he was at his most disturbed, and I believed it could help the others in their distress. It was this belief which took me past all the obstacles, to the discovery of a lifeline which was to play a major part in the recovery of all the children.

This same strength also enabled me to perform financial juggling acts of which, at one time, I would never have thought myself capable. Shortage of money has, inevitably, been one of the threads which run the length of this story. It has caused tension and bitterness throughout the entire ten years. If I had been left on my own, there would have been no problem — I could have gone back to my old, well-paid job, and enjoyed living up to the current ideals of self-reliance. I had liked this job, and it had suited me, but there was no way I could have done it properly on top of caring for four disturbed and unhappy children, one of them mentally handicapped. Indeed, as time passed, and their needs became ever more complicated, I had to face the realization that, with no adult to give me support at the home end, there simply was no outside job I could cope with in addition to all I was doing for them.

For their sake, I have had to accept my hated dependency on the man who left me, and, indeed, count myself lucky — as I certainly do — that Paul has continued to pay, and pay regularly, enough to keep the five of us clothed, housed, warm and fed. I am devoutly grateful that I have never had to submit to the humiliations of depending completely on social security, and that we have never had to move from our lovely old house and the neighbourhood where we have known such kindness. I am glad and grateful for all these advantages, yet at the same time they have exacted a heavy emotional toll, for I have never been able to feel sure that they would continue. This insecurity led to heights of anxiety and apprehension which few have suspected, whilst the longed for independence, which alone could have reduced them, remained always tantalizingly out of reach. Only that same, blind, maternal obstinacy enabled me to live with such pressures.

It was too blind, however, of itself to bring us through. I could see and feel and suffer with the children's pain, but I could not always understand it, and all too often I allowed it to increase my own deep sense of guilt and failure. This would, in the end, have been our undoing — and it came very near to being so.

Family therapy gave us a precious chance to understand each

other and our reactions to what had happened to us. Without it, I, who had worked so hard for them, would never have been able to let go of the children when they became adult, despite all my good intentions in that respect — and they would not have been able to let go of me without incurring even more pain and guilt, enough to mar all their future relationships. It was the turning point in the development of the family. By the time we said goodbye to our therapists we had, despite the terrifying experience through which we had just lived, gained a new belief in ourselves. We were no longer failures. We had learned far better how to support each other, and to use positively the close bonds which the years had forged between us.

I am convinced that, despite their inherent dangers, those bonds enabled us to survive emotionally — all of us. I also think that they could never have been so strongly formed if Paul had remained in this country. I believe that in going to Canada, he did the best possible thing both for his second family and for us. The children were too disturbed to continue to cope with what they described as "feeling torn apart". They needed continuity of loving care, and, especially, they needed therapy. Paul has never lost touch — there has been a constant supply of postcards, letters and gifts, and there has been the occasional visit. But by making these infrequent, he gave us a chance to rebuild as a family, and for the children to find emotional security once more, in each other and in me. Now, supported and reassured by the therapy, and by the feeling of having deep roots, they are ready to enjoy a relationship with their father, and to benefit from their visits and excursions with him. Even then, we have always been glad of having Ray to turn to when feelings have become unexpectedly difficult or alarming.

They are almost ready now, the children, to lead their own lives. They are no longer wholly dependent. Somerset Court, college, boarding school and the playing fields claim them for much of the time. When they reappear they are inevitably, it seems, hungry and tired, and in strong need of the reassurance that home is still there, and that they still belong to it. It always makes me happy that they are so glad to come back — but now I am equally glad that they do not stay too long. It reassures me to see them go off cheerfully, though the parting itself still hurts. It makes me feel that the job is, indeed, well done.

A friend once surprised, and shocked, me by referring to the time and energy I had given to the care of my children as an enormous sacrifice of myself, my career and my independence. When I look back over the struggles, the loneliness and the heartaches of the last ten years, I can see how she came to that conclusion, but I have to smile at the way she saw only the shadows in the picture — which perhaps were darkened too by some of her own fears.

For what she failed to see was that the children — Simon included — have given me as much as I have given them, and have taught me more than I have ever taught them. To them, to these years of learning to support, care for and understand them, I owe my maturity as a human being. To Simon, Joanna, Tom and David I owe what to me are of greater price than any personal success in a career, any sum of money in the bank, any illusion of freedom: moments of such immeasurable intensity and profundity of feeling that they have made of my experience a treasure house. Now, if I want to drive away dull care, I have only to remember Tom's bright face as he sang Amahl, the pride in David's eyes when he took me out to dinner in a London hotel when he was barely seven, Joanna's Vivaldi concerto in which she proclaimed her return to health and strength, the affection in my autistic Simon's eyes, as he drops a kiss in my hair — and hundreds of other moments like them. The list could go on indefinitely — a catalogue of my incredible wealth.

I do not know what further struggles and difficulties lie ahead of us. I am sure that there will be plenty, for, as Tom once saw very clearly, the river goes on flowing, and there is no shortage of stones. Yet whatever they may be, we can go forward now knowing that it is possible to meet them without panic, in knowledge of our strengths and our weaknesses, and with a trust founded on experience in those great resources from which it has been given to us to draw.

"Though it cost all you have, get understanding," says the *Book of Proverbs*. For many of us who try to follow that ancient advice, it does cost just that — and it may well take the whole of our lives. But then, it was not advice that was lightly given. Confronted by pain and loss, it may well seem impossible even to attempt, and few of us can do it without help. The effort, however, carries its own reward — and that, perhaps, is the secret.